BRYAN J. CA

COMMUNICATING
ACROSS THE DISCIPLINES

Kendall Hunt
publishing company

Cover image © Shutterstock.com

Kendall Hunt
publishing company

www.kendallhunt.com
Send all inquiries to:
4050 Westmark Drive
Dubuque, IA 52004-1840

Copyright © 2016 by Bryan J. Carr

ISBN 978-1-4652-7195-2

Printed in the United States of America

CONTENTS

CONTRIBUTORS

Bryan J. Carr is an Assistant Professor in the Communication and Information Science departments at the University of Wisconsin—Green Bay. His areas of expertise include the study of race and gender representation in popular culture, particularly superhero comics and video games. He earned his Ph.D. in Media Arts from the University of Oklahoma's Gaylord College of Journalism and Mass Communication, where his dissertation critically analyzed the cultural and paradigmatic implications of some of the most popular video games on the market. In his professional career, Bryan worked for several different television and radio outlets, doing everything from news announcing to commercial production. His work on popular culture and identity has appeared in publications such as the *Journal of Entertainment and Media Studies*, the *Journal of Graphic Novels and Comics,* the *Southwest Mass Communication Journal,* and edited volumes such as *From Jack Johnson to Lebron James, Parasocial Politics* and *Re-Framing Identifications.* He is also a regular contributor to the technology and video game news site Shacknews.

Meta G. Carstarphen Ph.D., APR, is a Professor at the University of Oklahoma in the Gaylord College of Journalism and Communication. Her research interests include rhetoric and writing, historiography, race/gender/class identities, and tourism media and diversity. An award-winning magazine author, her books include *Sexual Rhetoric: Media Perspectives on Sexuality, Gender and Identity, Writing PR: A Multimedia Approach, American Indians and the Mass Media,* and *Race, Gender Class and the Media.* She teaches undergraduate and graduate classes in race/gender/class and the media, strategic communications and rhetoric.

Phillip G. Clampitt (PhD, University of Kansas) is the Blair Endowed Chair of Communication at the University of Wisconsin–Green Bay. He was previously designated the Hendrickson Named Chair of Business. His most recent book, *Communicating for Managerial Effectiveness* (Fifth edition), is a Sage Publications best seller. In addition, he coauthored *Transforming Leaders into Progress Makers: Leadership for the 21st Century* and *Embracing Uncertainty: The Essence of Leadership.* Along with being on the editorial boards of numerous professional journals, his work has been published in a variety of journals, including the *MIT Sloan Management Review, Academy of Management Executive, Management Communication Quarterly, Journal of Business Communication, Communication World, Journal of Broadcasting, Journal of Communication Management, Ivey Business Journal,* and *Journal of Change Management.* As a principal in his firm, Metacomm, he consults on communication issues with a variety of organizations, such as PepsiCo, Manpower, Schneider National, American Medical Security, Dean Foods, The Boldt Company, Thilmany Papers, Dental City, Prevea, The U.S. Army War College, Appleton, and Nokia.

Dr. Ioana Coman is an Assistant Professor in the Department of Communication at the University of Wisconsin—Green Bay. She earned her MA and Ph.D. degrees at the University of Tennessee and she has two Bachelor Degrees (Public Relations and Political Sciences/International Relations) from The University of Bucharest University and National School of Political Science and Public Administration, in Romania. Dr. Coman's background involves European and American professional experiences (including her work for the National Romanian Television, Cultural Channel and the Scripps Network, Press Department, DIY Network). As a Graduate Teaching Assistant at the University of Tennessee she won the *1st Place at Teaching News Terrifically in the 21st Century competition* (AEJMC, 2013) for one of the innovative assignments, obtaining the "highest score recorded by a graduate student in the competition's four years, equaling that earned by the top full-time faculty submission." Focused on interdisciplinary approaches, Dr. Coman loves both teaching and doing research in the journalism and public relations fields. She currently teaches various journalism and public relations classes, including Media Workshop I & II; Advanced Reporting; Digital Journalism; Cases in Communication and Media Management; Public Relations Writing. Dr. Coman's research concentrates on crisis communication, mainly the analysis of media, PR and publics' discourses, within the new and social media context, at both national and international levels.

Dr. Adolfo Garcia has a master's in communication from the University of Wisconsin—Milwaukee, and a doctorate in communication and conflict resolution from the University of New Mexico. Professor Garcia began at UW-Green Bay in 2007 and taught in the Communication department, specializing in Conflict Resolution. Before leaving the University of Wisconsin—Green Bay, Dr. Garcia had the pleasure to hold the position of UW-Green Bay Teaching Scholar twice, and during the 2014–15 was a UW-System Teaching Scholar. Dr. Garcia created a new major and certificate program in conflict resolution. Courses in this area included mediation and conflict resolution, service learning in conflict resolution, small group communication, and human communication theory. He has also worked extensively with the teaching and learning center at UW-Green Bay and has published research in the scholarship of teaching and learning. Since starting at State University of New York—New Paltz in the Fall of 2015, he has taught introduction to communication, argumentation, and conflict management.

Christa Tess Kalk, Ph.D. is a Professor of Communication Studies at Minneapolis Community & Technical College in Minneapolis, Minnesota. She has been teaching in the Communication Studies field for over 13 years at both the undergraduate and graduate levels. She has published a variety of teaching materials and frequently presents her research at conferences. She has also been a featured speaker in numerous forums including a Congressional Hearing in 1998 and was the Keynote Speaker for the Northwest Communication Association Conference in 2014.

Amanda Kate Kehrberg is a doctoral student in the Gaylord College of Journalism and Mass Communication at the University of Oklahoma. She earned her master's in American media and popular culture from Arizona State University. Her research focuses on technology, diversity, and public relations, and she has published work on PR, fandom, and rhetoric. She currently teaches classes for Oklahoma and Arizona State on new media and public relations writing.

Jared Schroeder is an assistant professor in the Division of Journalism at Southern Methodist University in Dallas. His research focuses on the future of the press clause of the First Amendment and how the Supreme Court understands and interprets freedom of expression during the network-society era. He most recently published "Focusing on How Rather than on Whom: Constructing a Process-Based Framework for Interpreting the Press Clause in the Network-Society Era" in *Communication Law & Policy*. Jared primarily teaches communication law and journalism history courses at SMU.

Dr. Danny Shipka is an assistant professor at Oklahoma St. University and received his Ph.D. at the University of Florida. He has taught public relations and strategic communications for over 10 years. He is passionate about both strategic communication and popular culture. His previous book *Perverse Titillation: European Exploitation Films 1960–1980* (2011) looked closely at film industries of Italy, French, and Spain as they produced a stunning amount of horror and sexually explicit films that influenced modern filmmakers. a second book due in Aug. 2016, *Global Fear: International Horror Film Directors* written with Dr. Ralph Beliveau from Univ. of Oklahoma continues the examination of this phenomenon.

CHAPTER 1

Introducing Communication across the Disciplines

This is going to sound strange, because you're reading this request in a textbook (and one you have only just met at that) but I want to ask you to ask yourself a question. The question is: how many times have you communicated today? Have you talked to a friend or a loved one? Sent out a Tweet or a Facebook message? Called an office on campus? Gestured at someone who cut you off in the parking lot? Feel free to think about this seriously for a moment. Put a number on it if you can. You can even write that number in the margins of this page, I won't be offended.

I don't know you personally but I am willing to bet the number you came up with was pretty high. The reason for that is simple: as human beings, we are communicators. We communicate constantly, and whether we are talking with our friends or strangers halfway around the world, we have an innate need to express ourselves and convey ideas through multiple forms of communication. These forms of communication may be verbal or nonverbal. They may be face to face or mediated by computers, cell phones, and the virtual worlds of video games. In fact, you are probably communicating all sorts of things about yourself to the world around you as you read this introduction—passers-by may notice the way you dress, the way you sit, and if you look

1

intently enough at the book, they will probably also leave you alone because you are sending a clear nonverbal signal you are not to be bothered. We communicate ourselves into the world often without intending to do so.

Communication comes naturally to us, even as the way we communicate changes and differs from individual to individual and culture to culture. Even before codified systems of language, we developed ways of conveying intent and meaning. These shared sets of meaning created communities and cultures with their own unique experiences. We passed on our traditions and history to future generations through storytelling before writing ever existed. Our entire ideas of culture, society, and democracy are by and large systems that have been created through the process of communication and assigning specific values, beliefs, and meaning to objects, terms, and concepts. When these systems took root, we developed specific procedures, jargon, and systems of etiquette aimed at ensuring that they operated efficiently and smoothly through communication and consensus. As we developed media that conveyed our ideas, thoughts, and experiences, we developed separate languages that dictate how ideas can be conveyed without even saying a word. These new media languages in turn help to make the world smaller and more connected, bringing us into contact with people and cultures that no longer seem foreign and distant.

Sometimes we're afraid of communicating—of saying the wrong thing or speaking in public. Still, we communicate anyway. We communicate both in our personal lives and especially in our professional ones. In fact, communication is a fundamental part of most professional disciplines. Research has shown that above all else, employers are looking for communicators. Every year, the National Association of Colleges and Employers sends out a survey to its employer members asking about the qualities they are looking for in a new hire. Communication skills consistently make up the top rankings. Employers are looking for prospective employees who can communicate with internal and external audiences, make decisions and solve problems, and sell or influence others—and that's just a sample of the communication-related characteristics they seek (NACE, 2014). The area of communication study is vast and multifaceted and highly in demand.

It is for that reason this book exists. Many introductory communication textbooks will spend a great deal of time on theoretical approaches to communication, on models, and on the elements of human emotion that drive communication. This is inherently valuable and there is discussion of these topics in this book, but my goal in writing this textbook is different and also admittedly simple. I do not only wish to provide you not only with a thorough grounding in the guiding principles of communication and the foundational theory and concepts from which our understanding of communication in the 21st century derive. Nor do I intend only to offer an overview and understanding with how communication is used professionally and the new and interesting ways in which human beings communicate. I do not solely wish to highlight those fields in which communication is a vital component, an integral and necessary skill to be practiced and executed daily. My goal with this textbook is to do all of the above and to do so in a manner that helps you understand and apply the core concepts of communication across a variety of different disciplines. Simply put, I want this textbook to give you the foundation you need to start a career in communication or learn how communication principles can help you in any career.

The core principle of this textbook is one that I have developed during my academic and professional career and used throughout my classes. Some of my colleagues adore it for its simplicity, others dislike it for the same reason. You are welcome to your own perspective after reading this text, but I find that the more courses I teach and the more students I work with, the more it remains true. I call it Carr's Primary Principle of Communication.

Carr's Primary Principle of Communication: Regardless of the communication field, we all use the same basic skills!

Note that this principle, though universally applied, requires a few caveats. First, it should be noted that I am not saying all communication jobs are the same. This is obviously not the case—a public relations practitioner is not the same as a journalist, for example, as they each have different goals and means of attainment. Nor am I saying that one set of skills is necessary for success in all careers—certainly, training in radio broadcasting would not inherently prepare you for a career in human resources! Yet at the foundational level, there are similarities even among the differences.

1. Communication is built around finding the proper means to convey ideas, concepts, and feelings. Whether you're trying to find the right words to say what you mean in a conflict or the right visuals to catch the eyes of a customer while making a television ad, communicators craft their messages for maximum impact.
2. Communication is built around making persuasive cases, regardless of the medium. A PR practitioner trying to repair relationships with a public by demonstrating how their firm is correcting a previous problem is making a persuasive case just as a conflict mediator trying to encourage both parties to focus on common ground is making a persuasive case.
3. Communication is built around understanding your audience and tailoring messages to them. Advertisers and broadcasters do this all the time through the creation of advertisements and programs specifically targeted at given demographic and psychographic groups, but it is at the heart of organizational communication as well as those working inside organizations figure out the optimum means and times to reach employees.

Moreover, even if you are reading this text and not preparing for a career in communication, you are still going to have to know how to do these things. Imagine a nursing student who does not know how to interact with patients and convince them of the importance of particular health-care regimens or a research scientist who struggles with presenting their findings to laypersons and the general public. The lack of communication skills makes each of these jobs just that much more challenging. Communication is vitally important regardless of your chosen field, and this book aims to demonstrate how the fundamental elements of communication are consistent even when the career and its responsibilities may not be.

Book Overview

In order to give you the best possible introduction to communication across the disciplines I can, I enlisted the help of some of the best writers and scholars in the field to help chart a course from the foundations of communication to the ultimate outcomes thereof. Our journey will begin in Chapter 2 with a discussion of rhetoric and persuasion, as well as the rhetorical criticism skills necessary to critically analyze and construct communication. Chapter 3 focuses on understanding communication as a sum of its component parts, starting with basic communication models and theories and expanding them out to explore how we construct meaning in both verbal and nonverbal communication. Chapter 4 is all about the importance of relationships and cultural connections in communication, as well as how communication and interdependence create conflict, which must be managed. Chapter 5 focuses on theoretical and critical approaches to communication, building on the rhetorical foundation laid out in Chapter 2 to offer different theories and approaches that can be used to analyze and understand different forms of communication. Finally, Chapter 6 tackles the subject of identity and how our communication choices and activities allow us to perform certain identities to ourselves and others around us.

From here, we start to take some more applied looks at communication. Chapter 7 starts by looking at traditional broadcast media and how radio and television have evolved and changed today. Chapter 8 focuses on digital and online media, with specific attention on how the Internet affects the way we communicate and construct identity as well as how interactive media such as video games and social networks affect our communicative efforts. Journalism is perhaps the communication discipline that is undergoing the most significant change in the contemporary climate; to that end, Chapter 9 focuses on how journalism has developed over time and the challenges the discipline faces, given its inherent responsibility of acting as a government watchdog. Chapter 10 offers insight on the unique style of writing that journalists use, from story structure to sourcing and fact checking, as well as the ethics of journalism to help navigate the gray areas that can so often form in an era of immediate reporting and social media.

Public relations is perhaps the fastest growing of all the communication disciplines but is also one of the most misunderstood. Chapter 11 seeks to offer a solid definition and explanation of the field. Chapter 12 looks at how the fundamental theoretical approaches to public relations have developed over the years and how practitioners view their responsibility to their clients and the publics they serve both in times of quiet and in times of crisis. Finally, we conclude with discussion of communication in organizations and groups in Chapter 13, from how communication structures organizations to the development of important leadership strategies.

I hope you find this book useful and informative regardless of how you end up using the information inside it. We have worked to provide an experience that is both comprehensive and unique to many introductory communication texts that will help provide you with the knowledge and skills you need to start your career and identify potential areas of interest. This text is only the beginning—expand upon it by applying what you learn to your class lectures and your everyday life, ask questions, and challenge the world around you. Learning is not just reading and repeating facts, it is about illuminating the connections between facts and concepts. To that end, let's get to work.

References

National Association of Colleges and Employers (2014). *Job outlook 2014 spring update.* Retrieved February 5, 2015, from http://career.sa.ucsb.edu/files/docs/handouts/job-outlook-2014-spring-update.pdf.

Rhetoric and the Foundations of Communication

If you are still reading this textbook, then congratulations! You are engaging in an act of communication, albeit a relatively limited and one-sided one. You cannot talk back to the textbook directly, after all, and if you did people might start to look at you strangely. Yet this book is still conveying ideas and information to you via words, sentences, and paragraphs. Later, you can tell people what you learned, they can tell others, and so on. We live in a constant, ongoing world of communication, one so integral to who we are that we do not always actually think about it. What is communication, anyway, and how do we do it? The latter question is one we will answer throughout this text, but let us turn our attention now to the former. Perhaps the best way to do so is to start at the beginning of our contemporary understanding of communication. To do so, we need to start talking about rhetoric.

What is Rhetoric?

No doubt you have heard the word "rhetoric" before, though perhaps not always in the best of connotations. For example, perhaps you've heard of a politician's "fiery" or "violent" rhetoric. Maybe you've heard someone ask a patently obvious question, then wave it away by saying it was simply a "rhetorical question." You may have also heard someone dismiss a speech or a conversation by calling it "nothing more than empty rhetoric." We often view rhetoric in a negative light. Yet, it is fundamentally important to communication and the professional fields within it and useful across the disciplines.

Any discussion of rhetoric must begin with its originator and most famous practitioner, the Greek philosopher and teacher **Aristotle**. Aristotle, who lived from roughly 384–322 B.C., was part of a long line of famous Greek scholars, learning under the tutelage of the philosopher Plato at his academy in Athens; Plato had been the student of the equally famous Socrates, whose Method your teachers may have or still currently use in the classroom (Adler, 1978). A gifted student, Aristotle turned teacher himself later, opening his own school, the Lyceum, in 335 B.C. Here, he taught many who would become influential leaders and members of Greek society. Among that number was no less than Alexander the Great (who was himself the grandson of the king for whom Aristotle's father had served as physician). Aristotle grew his school until Alexander died in 323 B.C., at which point he exiled himself to an Aegean island and passed away shortly thereafter (Adler, 1978). During his life, Aristotle was involved in many of the great debates and arguments of the day, none more important to our current discussion than the argument over how to communicate ethically and effectively.

Aristotle was particularly invested in the idea of how we come to understand the world around us and drew a significant amount of influence from those who came before him on this point. As Plato (360 B.C.E.) suggested in his allegory of "the cave," humanity is largely constrained by their perspective and will accept as reality that they can see even if it is an inaccurate representation of the truth. In a similar manner, Aristotle suggested the way we communicate and speak can have a significant impact on our perspective and the way society operates as a result, believing very strongly in the power of logic, philosophy, and rhetoric to advance understanding.

Much of Aristotle's life was devoted to these questions, and he addressed them in *The Rhetoric*, a work that was less a published narrative and more a collection of notes from his students (not unlike the notes you take in class). In fact, Aristotle likely never intended for his work to be published, so one could argue that we are lucky students showed up to class that day! Rhetoric, as Aristotle suggests, is the "counterpart of dialectic" (Cooper, 1960/1932, p. 1). This is an important point, as it demonstrates how Aristotle saw rhetoric and the way in which it should be used. **Dialectic** is essentially the process of using arguments and discussions to resolve problems or inform others, as suggested by Plato (360 B.C.E.). In Plato's view, we use dialectic to arrive at a common truth or reality. Plato, while an advocate for dialectic, took a negative view of rhetoric in much the same way many of us do today—he saw it as a waste of time, concerned less with the development of intellect or serious conversation than it was deception and self-aggrandizement (Losh et al., 2014). In Plato's view, the focus of teaching and philosophy should be about morality and human advancement.

Aristotle too valued dialectic but had a difference of opinion with his teacher. In Aristotle's view, rhetoric is what we use to engage in the dialectical processes that make up everyday life—how we choose certain words, make certain cases, or elaborate on our ideas in such a way that we may persuade others or encourage them to think a certain way. In short, **rhetoric** consists of the strategies and tactics we use when we use communication to persuade others or prove a point. Rejecting Plato's view of rhetoric, Aristotle saw it as fundamental to advancing discussion and argumentation for the betterment of society—particularly important in the early days of ancient Greek democracy (Losh et al., 2014). Aristotle suggested that society benefits from the expression of differing viewpoints and that rhetoric could be used by those who had truth on their side to persuade others of that truth effectively, leading to a better outcome for all.

The Branches of Rhetoric

To understand why Aristotle thought this way, it is probably helpful to understand the ways in which he felt rhetoric should be used. Aristotle viewed three main "branches" or uses of rhetoric. The first, **deliberative**, is focused on how rhetoric was used in dialogue and discussion about matters of state or policy (Cooper, 1960/1932). To see this in action, one needs only to turn on C-SPAN to watch our representatives in Congress argue and debate over issues of domestic and foreign policy using fiery language, gestures, or even signs and props. While Aristotle was concerned primarily with how rhetoric would be used in political matters, we use deliberative rhetoric in many different ways as well—have you ever been in a situation where you were a part of a group deciding what to get for dinner? One member of the group likely laid out a specific case as to why pizza would better meet the needs of the group than hamburgers or Chinese food and convinced the others to go along with it. That individual was practicing a form of deliberative rhetoric, albeit a less formal one Aristotle had likely not considered in his teaching.

The second branch, **epideictic** rhetoric, is concerned less with dialogue and more with the assignment of praise or blame for an individual's actions. To Aristotle, this form of rhetoric was built around determining the honor and credibility of an individual or a speaker (Cooper, 1960/1932). To Aristotle, identifying one's virtue and making it clear to the audience was a vital part of any speaker's rhetoric. Think about it this way—are you more likely to trust and listen to someone who is able to prove themselves trustworthy? Generally, we prefer to interact with those who have these characteristics.

You may be most familiar with the third branch of rhetoric, **forensic** rhetoric. Forensic rhetoric, in Aristotle's view, is when rhetoric is used to prove an individual's innocence or guilt (Cooper, 1960/1932). Forensic rhetoric is most often used in courtrooms, where the prosecutor attempts to present evidence proving an individual's culpability in a crime and the defense attorney presents evidence that is meant to exonerate or lessen their culpability. We may also use **forensic** rhetoric to construct a different kind of case as we try to debate and persuade others of the best course of action—in many ways, deliberative and forensic rhetoric can be very closely related.

Based on these three branches of rhetoric, you can probably start to see a clear picture of how Aristotle looked at communication. To Aristotle, rhetoric was a tool to be used in many different situations—to advise, to condemn, to praise, to set free, or to imprison. However, no matter the ultimate use, rhetoric allows us to persuade and communicate with others strategically using logic and proof rather than simply discussing in an open-ended manner. Aristotle took a noble view of rhetoric, suggesting its importance to conveying truth and virtue, but admitted at the same time that it could be used for bad reasons as well as good ones. No matter the purpose, Aristotle argued that for rhetoric to be effective, a speaker had to be able to use all the tools available to them. Let's take a look at some of those tools now.

The Rhetorical Appeals

In *The Rhetoric,* Aristotle identifies several means through which a speaker can appeal to their audience and communicate with them effectively. These means, also called appeals, derive from his view of the different branches of rhetoric and their purpose, and each appeal has certain rhetorical situations where it is more effective than others. Aristotle identified three main appeals that contemporary rhetorical scholars (and communication practitioners in general) recognize and use every day—ethos, pathos, and logos.

Ethos is marked by Aristotle as an appeal in which the speaker utilizes their innate character and credibility to make their case (Cooper, 1960/1932). Aristotle argued that this may perhaps be the most powerful appeal of all—again, he viewed virtue and truth as the most important parts of communication and a fundamental goal of using rhetoric. For evidence of the power of an ethos appeal, you need only look as far as commercials. Many companies hire established individuals with a great deal of credibility to act as **spokespeople** for their products. For example, in 2010, the luxury car company Mercedes-Benz hired Jon Hamm, an actor from the popular television drama *Mad Men,* as the new spokesman for their company's television advertisements (Stuart, 2010). Hamm, as an award-winning actor with multitudes of fans, was selected not only for his pleasant voice but also specifically for his credentials. The idea behind this advertising campaign—and any advertising campaign using a spokesperson—was to use the credibility of the actor or individual acting as a spokesperson to lend greater legitimacy to the product, and in so doing convince the viewer to invest in purchasing one. Ethos goes beyond advertising, however—journalism is built around the notion of credibility, as we will discuss later in this text. News stories also often use government officials, representatives of the police, and health experts to add legitimacy to their stories. Moreover, those in a position of authority tend to use that authority as an ethos appeal—your college professors have devoted their lives to studying the subjects they teach, building credibility they can then use to persuade you of the importance of learning material in the classroom.

Throughout *The Rhetoric,* Aristotle is careful to point out that proper rhetoric and virtuous discussion are built around rational logic and proof, rather than irrational emotional appeals. Yet even Aristotle acknowledges that the emotional impact rhetoric has on the audience can be significant in determining how they respond to it. **Pathos**, the second of Aristotle's appeals, is concerned with using rhetoric to touch on certain emotions. As Aristotle suggests, we tend to make "very different decisions under the sway of pain or joy, and liking or hatred" (Cooper, 1960/1932, p. 9). Using an individual's emotions—appealing to a sense of patriotism, drawing upon fears and doubts, or engendering pity and sadness—can be a very potent form of rhetorical appeal. You do not need to be a historian to be familiar with the various forms of **propaganda** aimed at encouraging individuals to enlist or take on other responsibilities during the World Wars and other conflicts. Think of "Rosie the Riveter" during World War II, a propaganda icon aimed at promoting a united war effort and encouraging women to participate in the factories back home while American men fought overseas. Rosie was just one of many different propaganda messages during the war. Posters promoting the purchase of war bonds and the recycling of scrap metal promoted a sense of patriotic unity while other propaganda served to paint America's enemies as an insidious invading force—even children's comic books got in on the act, with heroes like Superman and Captain America fighting Hitler and other Axis leaders. Through a contemporary lens, much of these propaganda pieces feel antiquated or even regressive, but they are clear examples of pathos appeals.

Because Aristotle viewed logic and truth so highly, it is no surprise he also viewed the use of logic and evidence as a powerful means of persuasion. Rhetors who use **logos** attempt to construct arguments through the use of persuasive proof and evidence rather than simply credibility or emotion (Cooper, 1960/1932). Think back to our discussion of forensic rhetoric. Say you are a prosecutor attempting to prove that a criminal robbed a bank. Simply providing an accusation is not enough to get a conviction, in order to do so you must be able to prove that your accusation is true and accurate and worthy of punishment. Your argument will be based on evidence—a security camera that caught the criminal leaving with money, fingerprints found at the scene, a mask and gun that were thrown away in a dumpster nearby, witness testimony. All of these elements together act as logical proof and evidence that your accusation is true and accurate. Without them, your case falls apart, but if you have indisputable evidence your case becomes very persuasive.

At this point, you may be wondering which of the three appeals is most effective. Aristotle does not give any such obvious answer. Instead, he suggested that using all three is vital to using rhetoric effectively and being a powerful communicator. You may find that combining multiple appeals together is the best way to make a persuasive argument—think of a public service announcement that uses traffic fatality statistics as well as pictures of children killed in car accidents to advocate against drunk driving. The pathos appeal is clear, but the logos appeal (the statistics) underscores the emotion and suggests that it happens on a grander scale than just one case. You could even implement an element of ethos and have the message delivered by a parent of one such child or a police officer who has been tasked with working some of the accident scenes. Taken together, the persuasive argument of "don't drink and drive" is much more powerful than if only one of the different appeals had been used.

There is one more element of rhetoric we have not discussed and it is one of the most powerful of all. That concept is **kairos**, or the proper time and place for speaking (Losh et al., 2014). In communication, just as in comedy, timing is everything. The idea behind kairos is that for rhetoric to be effective, it must come at the right time and place. Think of communication as having an expiration date, just like a carton of milk. If you make your case too late, it doesn't matter how good it was, it has spoiled now and nobody wants it. However, being too early can also dilute the impact of communication—your audience may not be prepared or interested to hear what you have to say or the point of decision may be too far off into the distance for them to consider it at the moment.

Even when something needs to be said, sometimes it is advantageous not to say it. Let's say one day at your office tempers are running high over layoff concerns. In order to finish your project, you need your fellow employees to submit the figures and designs they have worked on so you can compile them. However, if your fellow workers are agitated and angry, that request may fall on deaf ears and they may simply ignore you. Learning how to say the right thing at the right time is tricky—for every "great last words" story, there's a dozen more examples of people who didn't say the right thing at that moment—but it is an important part of communication. Learning how to "read the room" and understand what people are thinking and feeling is a subject we will discuss in the next chapter.

The Canons of Rhetoric and the Structure of Speech

So far we have discussed what rhetoric is, the different forms it can take, and the appeals we can use from a strategic standpoint. But how do we actually begin to communicate? What are the best practices for communication, and how can we start to think about it from a mechanical standpoint? Aristotle touches on these ideas as well and provides a foundation on which we will expand in the coming chapters.

There are five **canons** or parts of rhetoric identified in the Aristotelian view of the subject. According to most translations of *The Rhetoric*, they are invention, arrangement, style, memory, and delivery (Welch, 1987). The first, **invention**, is essentially the content of the speaker's rhetoric and what they will say—essentially, generating the content for the communication (Burton, 2007). To demonstrate, let us assume that you were to write a paper on the subject of rhetoric for a communication class. Your invention step would involve your initial brainstorming of what specifically you want to talk about and your gathering of scholarly books and sources to conduct initial research to prepare.

The next step, **arrangement**, is concerned with how a speaker arranges and organizes the invented elements in a way that makes sense or more effectively makes the speaker's point (Burton, 2007). In your essay paper, you likely follow a straightforward format—an introduction, a thesis, a body of a few main points, and then a summary and conclusion. This is a form of arrangement. Filmmakers also engage in this step when they edit their films together—in some cases, they may even eschew a "linear" approach of a beginning, middle, and end in favor of an approach that jumps around in time as Quentin Tarantino does with his films *Pulp Fiction* and *Kill Bill*. Regardless of your arrangement, it needs to make sense to the end audience and serve your overall point.

Style is a canon of rhetoric concerned with how the speech or communication is delivered or conveyed rather than its content (Burton, 2007). In written form, this might refer to the way in which you write or the specific language you use. In spoken form, style refers to the accoutrements a speaker uses to accentuate their spoken words. So if you were to present the paper you had written for communication class as a speech, you might have a moment where you pause for dramatic effect or slap the podium with your palm. How you use style to engender specific reactions is the canon of rhetoric known as **delivery** (Burton, 2007). We often say a speech is "all in the delivery." If you are trying to use particular rhetorical appeals, the style with which you deliver a speech can facilitate them—a boisterous, aggressive speech will initiate a different kind of pathos appeal than would a quieter, more somber approach. Similarly, if you are delivering a spoken speech, you should also be able to recall details extemporaneously from **memory** without having to look at notes—this too makes your speech more powerful, which is why it is the final canon of rhetoric.

These five canons of rhetoric influence the message you will deliver and how you will deliver it, and how much time or energy you put in any one step can have an influence on the outcome, though arguably some are more important than others—if you do not have anything to say because you did not do much Invention, you may not have much of a message with which to influence anyone. Regardless of how you get to your communicative message, all communication has some basic elements in common. Aristotle identifies these in *The Rhetoric* as the **parts of speech**, which serve as a sort of prototypical model of communication—and one we will be building upon as we go through this book. The model is simple—Aristotle identifies a speaker, a subject, and a person addressed.

The **speaker**, as you might imagine, is the individual or organization from which communication originates (Cooper, 1960/1932). Because much of Ancient Greece's communication was built around discussion in public forums, Aristotle envisioned the speaker as an individual orator speaking to a group. Today, we get communicative messages from many different people, organizations, and sources, but we can still identify the source of a message in this way. Most contemporary communication models expand on the "speaker" concept for this reason. The **subject** is the topic being discussed—for example, your discussion of rhetoric in the speech for your communication class. Finally, the **person addressed** is the recipient (or recipients) of the message. Again, Aristotle viewed the person addressed as an individual or gathered throng of people at a public speech, though our contemporary view of communication is more multifaceted and complex. Throughout this text, we will discuss other communication models that build upon Aristotle's original work and adapt it to more complex and mediated forms of communication.

Other Views of Rhetoric

Aristotle is considered the progenitor of modern rhetoric and his work is foundational to our contemporary understanding of communication. However, he was far from the only individual in the ancient world concerned with issues of communication and rhetoric, and too often we may fall into a Western-centric bias that marginalizes the importance of these other forms of rhetorical thought. Some scholars believe that rhetoric actually began in Africa around 3100 B.C. with the Nubian society and its economic and cultural influence in the region (Campbell, 2006). In 751 B.C.E., the Napatan Empire was the focal point of the Nubian civilization and briefly controlled Egypt. King Piye ruled over the empire and derived his authority from divinity and took it upon himself to set an example for his soldiers and his kingdom as both a political and religious leader (Campbell, 2006, p. 261–262). In ancient Ethiopia around 500 B.C.E., the Axumite kingdom, a combination of cultures from Africa, the Mediterranean region, and southern Arabia, was founded (Hooker, 1996a). King Ezana took a different tack than some of his geographical contemporaries. Continuing the tradition of divine justification for the king's actions, Ezana suggested that both this divine influence and the wisdom of the king were responsible for the empire's successes. Moreover, in matters of combat he saw himself as a reluctant participant reacting to the poor decision-making of others—essentially, it was the other country's fault they went to war in the first place (Campbell, 2006). Again, we see here the traditions of epideictic rhetoric were around before Aristotle started lecturing on them. In 1230 A.D., the kingdom of Mali was founded, introducing the concept of **griots**, individuals who acted as orators that roused the public and also acted as advisors and spokespeople for the monarch (Campbell, 2006; Hooker, 1996b). Griots were often charged with rousing both the monarch and the public, using pathos appeals aimed at encouraging both parties to leave behind a powerful legacy.

Rhetoric was an issue of concern in ancient China as well, and it was tied just as deeply to philosophy as Aristotle's rhetoric was. Chinese scholars were concerned with questions of what makes a good state and a good ruler, as well as how a ruler leads and how human culture should interact with nature (Lyon, 2010). The Confucian tradition, which began around 479 B.C.E., focused on the interrelationship between members in a society and focused on self-improvement—in this view, rhetoric is based on building connections between people through clearly defined language tied to the rhetor's actions (Lyon, 2010). In 300 B.C., the *Daodejing* challenged Confucian ideals by suggesting natural communication and respecting differences were better than an artificially constructed means of communication; this perspective also suggested that there was no one concrete definition for words and concepts (Lyon, 2010). In the later Legalist tradition, human nature was seen not as desirable but "evil" and rhetoric should be built around developing and maintaining authoritative rule and law to manage this (Lyon, 2010, p. 360). While these three schools of thought were very diverse and different in nature, they, nonetheless, offer interpretations of rhetoric that are unique to the culture and have influenced other cultures around the world.

These diverse approaches to rhetoric add additional facets to the discussion of what rhetoric is and how we can use it in communication. The Aristotelian traditions of rhetoric are based on using logic and rational evidence to prove arguments, while the African tradition is focused on establishing balance and harmony (Atwater, 2010). Chinese rhetoric, by comparison, is focused more on establishing the proper means and actions of living life (Mao, 2010). It is important to note that there were other non-Western cultures investigating the questions of rhetoric and that many of these traditions inform how our cultures act today. While these approaches may have arrived at some different approaches from Aristotle, they are no less valid and indeed are quite useful for developing a practical approach to rhetoric.

Rhetorical Criticism

In order to be an effective communicator, it is important to understand both how to use rhetoric and how others may use it. This is where the concept of **rhetorical criticism** comes in. Rhetorical criticism is the procedural study of rhetoric, analyzing rhetorical artifacts and acts to determine their purpose and how they use rhetoric to attain that purpose (Foss, 2009). There are many different ways to conduct rhetorical criticism, and the actual critical study of rhetoric is a complex task to which countless scholars have devoted their lives. This is an introductory text, of course, so for the sake of simplicity, let's look at two forms of rhetorical criticism, one using Aristotle's definitions of rhetoric and the other using a model described by Kenneth Burke.

First, think back to the elements of Aristotle's rhetoric discussed earlier. We have a model for how communication occurs—person speaking, subject addressed, and the audience to whom they are speaking. Each of these elements will carry with it specific rhetorical payloads that influence the effect of the discussion, as will the specific rhetorical appeal a speaker uses. Given a particular rhetorical artifact, we can identify each of these components and use it to draw some conclusions about the effectiveness or purpose of the rhetorical artifact.

Say for example, we look at this following hypothetical public service announcement message:

> Moms! Don't play games with your child's life. Buckle their seat belt!

> —*A Message from the Everytown Police Department*

A few things are immediately apparent. First, we know the person speaking—it is most likely the Everytown Police Department. The Everytown Police Department, of course, has specific interests and reasons for creating this message—presumably, it is to cut down on the number of injuries and deaths sustained by children in an automobile accident. The subject of the rhetorical message regards the importance of wearing seatbelts. We also know the audience to whom this message is addressed, because it specifically mentions "Moms" in the text. It is curious that fathers are not included in this message, which may be an interesting starting point for analysis. In terms of the appeal used, we could argue that it is both a *pathos* appeal (appealing on a specific emotional level to parents to protect their children) and an *ethos* appeal (based on the presumed credibility of the Everytown Police Department). The former is probably more important than the latter, especially given the relatively widespread acceptance of seatbelt use—this message could come from anyone and not specifically appeal to the credibility of the speaker. Based on these criteria, we can start to make some assumptions about the effectiveness of the message. The pathos appeal probably works, because parents generally care very deeply for their children. However, the message being aimed exclusively at mothers could have a negative impact on the audience reached and may even potentially alienate or offend male parents. Therefore, through (very rudimentary) rhetorical criticism, we can unpack what a message means and whether it is effective.

A more complex form of rhetorical analysis involves the work of Kenneth Burke. Kenneth Burke is one of the most established and widely read rhetoricians in all of communication study. His claim to fame is his concept of **dramatism**, or the theory that all of communication can be likened to a dramatic play. From a rhetorical standpoint, this means that communication acts can be broken down into five component elements, called **Burke's Pentad**—the *act* (what is actually taking place within the context of the communication over time), the *scene* (the context or setting in which said act occurs), the *agent* or *agents* (those involved in the act), the *agency* (what processes, artifacts, or situations allow the act to occur), and the *purpose*, or why the event occurs (Burke, 1969). In some writings, Burke suggested a sixth dimension of *attitude* that represents the underlying feelings of the agents participating in the act (Burke, 1961). While determining the attitudes and motivations of participants in a communication act can be useful for determining its intent and purpose, there are certain obvious challenges to doing so—we cannot always look into the minds of people, and it may be difficult to ascertain attitudes from passive artifacts such as pictures and written texts. For our purposes, we will stick to the original five elements of the pentad.

It is also important to note that in dramatism, all the elements of a communication act must be taken together, and examining how these elements interact with each other and the relative importance of each can provide further insight into the motivations of the speaker and what causes things to happen in the communication activity (Burke, 1961, 1969). For example, if we spend the most amount of time focusing on the agency granted to an actor and how the actor uses it, the communicator most likely wants us to consider the relationship between actor and agency and why it is used. For the purposes of this text, we will stick to the original five elements of the pentad, though you are encouraged to investigate it further for your own research and inquiry. To see how this form of rhetorical criticism works, look at the image below from a fast-food workers' strike in New York City.

Let us consider this protest in its pentadic elements. The *act* is very clearly one of protest—we have individuals marching, carrying signs, and probably chanting messages in unison. From context clues, we can ascertain the *scene* of this protest is New York City and clearly outside on the street. The *agents* are those individuals involved in the protest—they may be fast-food workers based on the location and the signs, and they are diverse in age, ethnicity, and gender. We may also consider those watching but not engaged in the protest as agents as well. *Agency* is often nebulous, especially based on a photograph, but we can assume the signs and apparel of the protesters offer agency in delivering their message, as do the protestors' numbers and matching clothing. In a more abstract sense, we could also argue that the First Amendment of the Bill of Rights allows the protestors to assemble peacefully to protest (more on that in a later chapter). Finally, the *purpose* of the protest is most likely to demand higher wages and bring awareness to the issue of underpaid employees.

Knowing these components, we can begin to perform some critical analysis of the rhetorical action. What are the benefits of dressing in a similar, unified fashion? Why choose to demonstrate on a crowded city street instead of online or using a restaurant sit-in? If the intent is to advocate for higher pay, does the execution of the act match the purpose? These are all questions you may answer based on your own analysis and understanding of the situation, but understanding these modular components of rhetorical acts—whether Aristotelian, Dramatist, or otherwise—can further your own understanding of how to construct and (perhaps even more importantly) critically analyze and understand the rhetorical messages you receive every day.

Bringing It All Together

Rhetoric is at its core about the use of strategic communication to achieve determined ends. Understanding your audience and knowing how to convey ideas in a way that encourages participation or a change in belief or attitudes is a major component of being an effective communicator. These principles have been at the core of communication study and practice since the beginning, and while they may take different forms or represent different component variables, they are fundamental to how we think about and define communication. Now that we understand the beginnings of communication, we can start to develop a working definition and models to analyze how it is used every day.

References

Adler, M. J. (1978). *Aristotle for everybody: Difficult thought made easy.* New York: Touchstone.

Atwater, D. F. (2010). Review of the African origins of rhetoric by Cecil Blake. *The Howard Journal of Communications, 21*(1), 92–95.

Burke, K. (1961). *The rhetoric of religion: Studies in logology.* Los Angeles: University of California Press.

Burke, K. (1969). *A grammar of motives.* Los Angeles: University of California Press.

Burton, G. O. (2007, February 26). The canons of rhetoric. *Silvia Rhetoricae.* Retrieved from http://rhetoric.byu.edu/Canons/Canons.htm. Accessed 14 April 2015.

Campbell, K. E. (2006). Rhetoric from the ruins of African antiquity. *Rhetorica, 25*(3), 255–274.

Cooper, L. (1960/1932). *The Rhetoric of Aristotle.* Englewood Cliffs, NJ: Prentice-Hall.

Foss, S. K. (2009). *Rhetorical criticism: Exploration and practice* (4th ed.). Long Grove, IL: Waveland Press.

Hooker, R. (1996a). Civilizations in Africa: Axum. *World Civilizations.* Retrieved from http://public.wsu.edu/~dee/CIVAFRCA/AXUM.HTM.

Hooker, R. (1996b). Civilizations in Africa: Mali. *World Civilizations.* Retrieved from http://public.wsu.edu/~dee/CIVAFRCA/MALI.HTM.

Losh, E., Alexander, A., Cannon, K., & Cannon, Z. (2014). *Understanding rhetoric: A graphic guide to writing.* New York: Bedford St. Martin's.

Lyon, A. (2010). Writing an empire: Cross-talk on authority, act, and relationships with the other in the Analects, Daodejing, and Han Feizi. *College English, 72*(4), 350–366.

Mao, L. (2010). Searching for the way: Between the whats and wheres of Chinese rhetoric. *College English, 72*(4), 329–349.

Plato. (360 B.C.E.) *The Republic* (B. Jowett, Trans.). Retrieved from http://classics.mit.edu/Plato/republic.8.vii.html. Accessed 14 April 2015.

Stuart, E. (2010, March 3). "Jon Hamm of 'Mad Men' is becoming the voice of Mercedes-Benz". *The New York Times.* Retrieved from http://mediadecoder.blogs.nytimes.com/2010/03/03/talk-about-an-actor-getting-into-a-part-jon-hamm-is-becoming-the-commercial-voice-of-mercedes-benz/?_r=0. Accessed 17 April, 2015.

Welch, K. E. (1987). Ideology and freshman textbook production: The place of theory in writing pedagogy. *College Composition and Communication, 38*(3), 269–282.

Components of Interpersonal Communication

Christa Tess Kalk

Students sometimes wonder why they are asked to take this class as part of the curriculum of their degree choice. The soft sciences like Communication Studies can get a bad rap, but if you are using communication all of the time, wouldn't you want to do everything you could to be the best communicator you could be? Those in hiring positions are clearly stating more and more that good communication skills are the most important attributes of the applicants they are looking for. Are you able to work well with others? Are you able to clearly articulate goals and identify ways to attain them for yourself and the company? Do you handle conflict between yourself and others well? How do you step in and help others who are experiencing conflict handle the situation? Are you an effective listener and able to recall everything said in a meeting with a potential client in order to meet all of their needs? The workplace is just one area where interpersonal skills are crucial and this is the primary reason why colleges are requiring this course more and more. However, interpersonal communication happens in other crucial areas of your life as well. When you can apply what you learn in a class to so many contexts and people in your life, well, the benefits far outweigh the costs.

Communication is happening all the time. Messages can be sent intentionally and unintentionally. Intentional messages are obviously those we mean to send. When I send a text message to someone, I intend that they will receive it and consequently act on the communication I sent. Other messages are sent unintentionally. I might be sitting in a coffee shop reading a book or typing on my computer. I am not intentionally sending a message to anyone in the coffee shop. However, people in the area might notice me and interpret messages being sent from me to others in the area. By seeing me reading a book or typing on my computer, they might interpret that I am busy, interested in my book, writing a paper for school, or that I do not want to be bothered. The list of possible interpretations is endless, really. Many researchers agree that we spend between 80-90% of our waking hours communicating with other people (Klemmer & Snyder, 1972). Consider the time you spend talking to your friends and family, posting and reading on Facebook or other social media sites, listening in class, interacting with coworkers and classmates, etc. With the increase in technology that allows us to connect with others in new and innovative ways, how we communicate is changing as well.

Defining the Varieties of Communication

In order to better understand how communication works, it is a good idea to provide some definitions. This will assist you in identifying the similarities as well as the differences in the various types of communication. **Human communication** is the process of making sense out of the world around us (essentially perception) and sharing that sense with others through verbal and nonverbal messages. As humans, we need to communicate in order to have understanding, to learn and come to know things about each other that we can't tell simply by looking at each other, and to create relationships. **Relationships** are the ongoing connections you have with others. There are varying levels and types of relationships including acquaintances, close friends, romantic partners, family, work, school, and many more. Each relationship can have differing levels of communication, depending on how long you have known each other or your level of commitment and cohesion to each other and the relationship. The longer you know the person and the higher the level of self-disclosure you have with each other, the closer the relationship will likely be.

Interpersonal Communication is a distinct transactional mode of communication involving two people for the purpose of creating, maintaining, and affecting a relationship. There is often a seemingly natural volleying back and forth of conversation and self-disclosure: you give a little, I give a little, you give a little, I give a little, and so on. We use this type of communication to begin, maintain, or even end relationships. We also use this type of communication to influence others. For the purposes of this course, influence will often be used similarly with power and control. While there are certainly some negative connotations to those words, we are using them mostly to mean the attempt to get others to do, think, feel, or change something. In the simple persuasive aspect of it, influence can be attempting to convince someone of where you should meet for lunch. There is not necessarily any threat in the communication and no control or power as we typically think of those terms, rather, the communication can be used for simple influence to get someone else on board with your thoughts.

Impersonal Communication occurs when someone communicates with another as if they are objects or they are simply there to fulfill some need without any personal interaction. Consider going to lunch with a friend. As you are both engrossed in conversation, the waiter comes over to the table to take your order. While looking at the menu, you order your meal choices. Perhaps you never really look at the waiter much or interact with him beyond his job—which is to get your order and then deliver it to you. After he walks away, your attention goes back to your friend and you resume conversation. Your communication with the waiter is impersonal—there is nothing personal about it.

Small Group Communication occurs when 3-8 people communicate with each other. You can find these groups at home, with friends, at work, school, and organizations you become involved in, as well as many other places. The key to this type of communication is that the participants are striving for effectiveness in their communication with each other. To be an effective small group, the participants would feel a sense of belonging. They would feel cohesion with the group. They would be able to assert their opinions and be heard. In an effective small group, there would be a sense of mutual influence, which involves attempting to get others on board to make changes. You may be wondering why the range of people involved is 3-8. When you have that amount of people, there is less likelihood for cliques to form. A **clique** is a small group within a group, usually with an exclusive nature. While cliques often have a negative connotation and can cause problems for the group and their productivity, they are not always detrimental to the success of the group. As a member or leader of the group, you would need to keep an eye out for any cliques forming and make sure they are working for the best interests of the group. **Large Group Communication** occurs when 8-15 people communicate with each other. Again, the key to this type of communication is that the participants are striving for effectiveness in their communication with members of the group. While this size of people is still manageable and they might all feel like they belong and have cohesion, there is more likelihood for cliques to form. With that amount of people, some of them are sure to find areas where they connect on a smaller, more personal level. However, if handled well, everyone can still have a great group experience.

Modeling the Communication Experience

So often when discussing communication, there will be hypothetical examples or illustrations. Sometimes it is nice to visually see what the concepts we are talking about look like. Human Communication has many parts to it and we can map them out to be illustrated for visual effect.

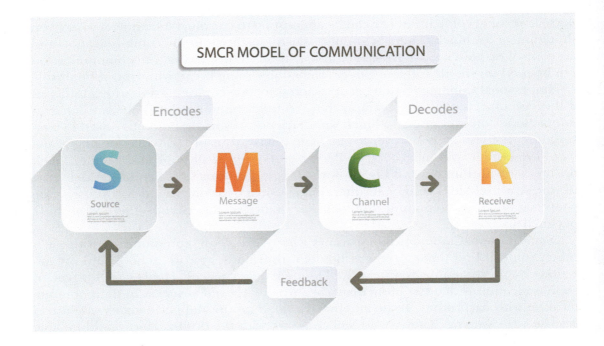

The **source** is the person starting the communication or message on its way, either through verbal or nonverbal means. The **receiver** is the person the message was received by, either intentionally or unintentionally. The **message** is what is being communicated, either verbally or nonverbally, which is encoded (created) by the source and decoded (understood) by the receiver. The **channel** is the mode through which the message was sent. The channel can be face-to-face, text message, Facebook post, telephone, etc. The **noise** is anything that gets in the way of the message being sent properly or received properly. Noise is basically anything that interferes with the message. This can be noise you hear, see, or feel—anything in the environment getting in the way of the message being sent from the sender to the receiver. The **feedback** is when the receiver responds and thus becomes the sender and sends a message back to the source of the initial message, who then becomes the receiver. This can again be verbal or nonverbal. The **context** relates to the entire area surrounding both communicators during the communication situation.

Verbal Communication and Symbols

Verbal communication occurs when we use an agreed upon symbol system to communicate with others. The language format for verbal communication can be written or oral. Most people think or consider verbal communication to be only spoken, but it can be written as well, as in text messages, email communication, letters, and social media posts. Language has a few basic characteristics: it is symbolic, it is governed by rules, it is flexible, it is cultural, and it evolves over time.

Languages are **symbol systems** that have been agreed upon so we can communicate with each other. For the purposes of this course, we use the English language. Words are symbols for something; the word "book" does not look like a book or feel like a book, it simply symbolizes the object that is a book. Even though the word might not look like or even sound like the thing it represents, the word comes to stand for the thing it represents. This is the principle of **semiotics**—that we assign particular **signified** means to **signifiers** such as words and visual shapes in order to create **symbols** that allow us to share a system of meaning. The word is the mutually understood representation which allows us to have a common communication ability. Whichever language system we have in common allows us to communicate with each other about objects, people, places, ideas, etc. we need language in order to do more than guess what each other is thinking or feeling. Self-disclosure relies on verbal communication and is necessary to further relationships with other people. When asked if sign language would be considered verbal or nonverbal communication, many students will say nonverbal. Due to what are perceived as gestures used in sign language, it can be mistakenly associated with nonverbal communication. However, sign language is actually considered verbal communication. Rather than just a bunch of gestures, sign language has standard language systems that allow people to communicate with each other. All languages; spoken, written, or signed; are basically giant collections of symbols that help us communicate with others who share the same language.

Language is governed by rules. Rules for language use can be explicit or implicit. Rules might relate to how language is to be used, contextual or situational changes, or depending on with whom we are communicating. One rule might apply to the way in which we arrange sentence structure; for example, the verb-noun placement in a sentence. For the English language, the noun comes before the verb, but in the Spanish language the noun comes after the verb and perhaps is even embedded into the verb. Another rule might apply to the logical flow of the messages being created and delivered, the levels of formality or ability to be informal, and rules for what is communicated with whom and where. **Constitutive rules** relate to the definitions or what a word means. To be discussing the nature of a stomachache, you would refer to the abdomen area of the body to help the other person understand. **Regulative rules** relate more to the relationship or how words are used with different people. You may need to code switch or change the way in which you tell someone something depending on who they are. For example, you might use different language when you tell your parents or friends what you did on Friday night.

We use language to do so many things and it is flexible. We share our thoughts, dreams, wishes, considerations, and we personalize it. We have the ability to use words and change how we use them so that they stand for many different things. Perhaps you have noticed that while we are adding some words to the English language over the years, we are also creating new and multiple meanings for the words that already exist. Of the 500 most commonly used words in the English language, there are over 14,000 meanings. Consider the word "cat." In a quick rundown of definitions of this word, you might come up with feline, cool cat, Cat (like the construction equipment), a name short for Catherine, among others. We use language and words for personal reasons as well. Personal idioms, pet names, and nicknames are ways in which we do this. Calling your significant other by "baby," "honey," "sweetheart," or "boo" are all ways in which we use language for personal means.

Culture has a large impact on language. For example, how to use language, how much language is used, and even who uses which language. **Context** in communication relates to the environment, and not just environment but the nonverbal communication that occurs in interactions. **High context** cultures are those that place more emphasis on nonverbal than verbal, traditions, a usual way of doing things, and expectations. China and many Asian countries would fall under a high context culture. **Low context** cultures place more emphasis on the verbal over the nonverbal. The United States falls under a low context culture because we love to talk. For example, if I didn't explain it well, I will do it again. Still not? I will offer yet another explanation. Consider how we are constantly bombarded by messages. Advertisements are all around us, on billboards, the radio, television, and ads on social media.

Language evolves and changes. Over time, the language itself and how we use it changes. Consider just how computers have changed our language over the past 30 years. You can access documents from our founding fathers online, but can you easily understand what they say? Those documents, letters, and written communication are incomprehensible for many people today. It takes a lot of effort to get through them without a dictionary and even looking up what some of the concepts mean, like "four score and seven years ago." Do you know what that measurement of time is? Swearing on television has come a long way as well. The word "bitch" was never used in the 1950s on television. Now it is commonplace during daytime soap operas to hear swear words. Depending on the knowledge of the language system, certain people can participate in conversations and others cannot. How many of you can discuss the inner workings and problems with your computers with your grandparents? Just like many young people not being able to read the documents of the founding fathers, some of the languages we have created and use now have generational gaps in access and understanding for older folks.

Functions of Verbal Communication

Having a common language system allows us to share meaning with each other. There are two different types of definitions we use to share meaning with others; denotative and connotative. **Denotative definitions** are the literal or dictionary meaning of the word. They are the words we can find in a dictionary, such as Webster's or Oxford Dictionaries, and are also often commonly known. **Connotative definitions** are the more personal or subjective meanings of the words. This would be what that word means to you based on your own experience, knowledge, or understanding. Consider the word "teacher." For the denotative definition, you might look in the dictionary and find something like "one who teaches." For the connotative meaning you might have an association with the word that relates to a personal story or experience. Perhaps you recall your second grade teacher who was so kind and sweet. Or maybe you think of your accounting teacher who gave you a poor grade. Your connotation might be positive or negative depending on your experience or perception of the word's meaning.

When communicating with others, you will need to know which definition type is best to use. There will be times where one might be more appropriate than others. In interpersonal relationships, people might get annoyed if you walk around talking like a dictionary so connotative meanings might be more appropriate there. If you are in a factory where production is very important, it will be necessary to use denotative meanings so all of the workers have the same understanding of what they are doing and how to do it.

Linguistic Relativity, also known as the **Sapir Whorf Hypothesis**, is the idea that words have the power to create reality. The words we use serve as the tools to name and label what we are doing and experiencing. Imagine you are getting together with your new business partner and figuring out what you will be doing in your new business venture. As you discuss and share ideas, you are creating the name of the business, the agreement of how things will be done, and all of the other details of the business partnership. These are all being created through language, which is thus creating the reality that you mutually understand.

Humans have the profound ability to name things and seem to love the naming process. We create labels and names with symbols for objects, animals, and children. Each year, there are lists released with the most popular baby names due to the trends of similarities in naming. Varieties in spelling are also used by many in an attempt to make the name slightly different than the norm. If you are a scientist or explorer, you might also get naming rights of what you create or discover. Did you know that if you were walking around South Dakota and stumbled on the remains of a dinosaur that hadn't been found yet, you would get the naming rights? An interesting naming situation occurred quite a few years ago when a company began selling naming rights for stars in the universe. It may be difficult to figure out who gave that company the ability to sell the stars and naming rights, but since they are still in business, you can imagine they sold quite a few already.

Roadblocks to Effective Verbal Communication

Many issues can occur and get in the way of effective verbal communication. They include mispresentation, misunderstanding, and the need to strive for careful language. **Mispresentation** of information can be unintentional or intentional. If you misspell a word by accident, it might be an unintentional mispresentation of what you meant to say. For example, in an online discussion board for class, the instructor might ask a question like, "which kid of the soda do you prefer?" versus "which kind of the soda do you prefer?"—which can mislead the students in how they answer the questions. You might also unintentionally miscommunicate a message in giving directions to a location as taking a left at 99th Street instead of taking a right, thus leading the person in the wrong direction. To intentionally mispresent verbal communication, it would include blatant lies and deception. Giving untruthful, vague, or irrelevant language to intentionally mislead others would be intentional.

When one person misperceives or misunderstands what the other person said, it can lead to ineffective communication. This can also be unintentional or intentional. **Misunderstandings** would be unintentional if someone wasn't listening well and missed a crucial part of the message. Another way misunderstandings can be unintentional are if the listener has a dislike of the speaker which could get in the way of effective listening or lead the listener to misinterpret what was said. To be an intentional misunderstanding, the listener could be listening for specific details so they could use them against the other person or twist them to be what they want them to be. If the person is listening to make something small have more meaning than it should with overgeneralization, this would be intentional misunderstanding as well.

Careful language can be tricky. It is not always easy to know what are the most acceptable terms or labels for people or objects. Some labels, titles, and names change so often it can be difficult to keep up. Consider the person who takes your order at the restaurant. We refer to them as "servers" versus "waitresses" or "waiters" these days. This allows the terminology to be used for gender-neutral positions, since many positions that were once only held by one gender, are now held by both. Some of the best advice is to stay away from the "-isms" like racism, sexism, and ageism in communication. Anything that demeans or attempts to belittle a group of people is usually a "no-no." **Jargon** is also something to be careful of. Jargon is language-specific to a group of people. If you meet someone who is intentionally using language that others cannot understand, or jargon, they are bad communicators. After all, if other people cannot understand them, then the communication is ineffective. Finally, slang is something to be careful of as well. **Slang** is lazy, blended speech. Instead of saying, "I am going to go to the store," you might use slang and say, "I'm gonna go to the store." This example may seem slight and yet not everyone will understand slang. We are changing how we use language with slang all of the time. For current examples of slang, you can listen to most songs on popular radio stations as they are filled with slang.

A theory that applies to verbal communication is the **communication accommodation theory**. This theory suggests that people are more likely to adapt their language in order to gain social approval. Moving from person to person or culture to culture, we adapt our language to be accepted. If you are going in for a job interview, you will change the language you use so you will be seen in a different way. You will likely use language that would be considered more business oriented, professional, and intelligent. We would strive to use the language that is acceptable for people in that work environment. Social approval will also require language changes on occasion.

Keep in mind that verbal communication has a lot of **power**. Language and how we use it can change relationships. We use language to begin, maintain, or end relationships. What we say can make and break relationships. **Polarization** is using language that is this way or that way, black and white, or ultimatums. Polarization leaves no room for gray area or middle ground. The outcome may not be favorable if you verbally back someone into a corner.

Finally, when dealing with issues or conflict with others, we should try to strive for **constructive** comments rather than evaluative ones. Being constructive means the communication you choose helps to bring the relationship closer. This would allow the person to address the concern without forcing them to get defensive. Again, using "I" language or "us" or "we" language will help here. To be **destructive** in your verbal communication would mean what you say would likely damage the relationship. Being aggressive or demeaning in your communication would surely fall under destructive communication.

Nonverbal Communication

We rely on nonverbal communication to predict and see how others feel about and react to us. In fact, nonverbal communication is more accurate in showing our true emotions when we talk or listen to others. **Nonverbal communication** includes anything that helps interpret a message in not so much what is said, but how it is said. Not only do we have more meaning in our nonverbal communication, but it tends to be more believable than verbal communication. We base more of our perceptions and reactions of a person on what they do as opposed to what they say. Imagine that you see your friend walking down the hallway and ask how they are. They respond with, "I'm great," but their shoulders are slightly sagging, their posture is hunched, they are looking down, and their voice sounds sad. You are a lot more likely to believe the body language and paralanguage over the words, "I'm great." When everything, or even just a few things, are saying the opposite of your friend's words, you are more likely to believe the nonverbal over the verbal. The old adage of "actions speak louder than words" typically holds true.

Nonverbal communication often occurs subconsciously. We don't think much about the messages we are sending off with our eye gaze when we are alone, but if others are around us, they could be interpreting what our eye gaze means. If you are sitting and flipping through a magazine at a coffee shop someone might interpret your level of interest in what you are reading, your level of interest in your surroundings, or if you are open to someone initiating conversation with you.

Verbal and nonverbal communication really do go hand in hand. Nonverbal communication accents and complements the verbal communication. What you are saying will gain meaning because of how you are saying it. The nonverbal cues can substitute for verbal—waving hello across a busy room rather than shouting it. They can contradict the verbal—saying, "I am fine…" while hunching over and pouting would contradict the verbal message. They can also regulate the verbal messages—when in conversation, we might nod excessively when we want the other person to stop talking.

Forms of Nonverbal Communication

Nonverbal messages are continuous. They are fluid and can flow quite easily from a happy moment to a serious one. Along with the emotions in those moments may be differences flowing in how we use hand gestures, facial expressions, and voice. Actions often continue from one moment to the next without thought. This is why conducting research on nonverbal cues can be difficult—finding the starting point or stopping point can be very tricky. Therefore, it can be difficult to classify certain nonverbal cues in isolation from others.

Much like verbal communication, nonverbal communication is guided by rules about when and how it is appropriate—there are circumstances in which it is okay to hug someone (they are your friend or loved one) and circumstances where it is not (you're passing a stranger on the street). Much as verbal communication is split into written and unwritten forms, nonverbal communication also varies in its type. **Static nonverbal communication** is nonverbal communication that does not change over the course of an encounter, such as one's clothing or hair color. **Dynamic nonverbal communication**, like gestures and facial expressions, change as the communicative event goes on—we don't maintain the same facial expression the entire time we're talking to someone, generally speaking (Duck & McMahan, 2009). These dynamic forms are built around a number of factors.

The study of body movements, posture, and gestures is called **kinesics**. Within the kinesic area of study are other subdivisions as well. They include emblems, illustrators, affect display, regulators, and adaptors. **Emblems** are nonverbal cues that have specific and generally understood meanings for many people. These could be cultural and often could substitute for a word or phrase. An example is holding up two fingers. In America, we would understand that to mean "peace." However, because the meaning can be cultural, you have to keep in mind that the meaning probably won't be the same everywhere you go. The "peace" sign with the palm facing your own body is an offensive gesture in other countries like Australia, where it closely relates to giving someone the middle finger in America. Knowing the acceptable and unacceptable gestures in the place you live or are traveling to is a good idea. Nonverbal behaviors that can accompany verbal messages to accent them or complement them are called **illustrators**. Fishermen will often hold their hands up a certain distance apart to illustrate the size of the fish they caught. This might also happen while trying to illustrate how high something was. Illustrators help us do just that, illustrate to the listener what something looked like.

To assist in control of conversation, regulators are used. **Regulators** are those non-verbal cues we use to send messages to others that we want to say something, that we are coming to the end of what are saying, or that we want things to change in the conversation somehow. We will often use things like nodding or eye contact to send these messages. Did you ever try to interrupt your mom when she was talking to someone and she gave you that look that said, "stop it right now"? Many students can identify that look with common understanding. Finally, the nonverbal behavior that helps satisfy a personal need or helps you adapt or respond to the situation you are in, are called **adaptors**. Adaptors could be twirling your hair when you are nervous, shaking your leg when it is crossed, or biting your nails. These things can help you burn off the excess nerves that you are feeling or simply make you feel more comfortable wherever you are or whoever you are with causing your reaction.

The eyes have been said to be the window to the soul. That said, it is clear that eyes tell a lot about us. Looking at the eyes of the person you are conversing with can help you monitor if they understand what you are saying or are confused. From the other perspective, using eye contact with the person you are talking to sends the message that you are interested and paying attention to them. Diverting eye contact can send the message that you are not interested and not paying attention. The actual meaning of **eye contact** might not always be as clear-cut as this, but in America, we consider eye contact to be important. Some other countries consider prolonged eye contact to be challenging and disrespectful, so again, it will be important to know the cultural norms for nonverbal communication. The eyes also allow us to express emotion. As was described in the area on facial expressions, the eyes go along with them. Wide eyes might indicate fear or surprise, perhaps even happiness if considered in combination with the other aspects of the face. Narrow gaze or tears might indicate sadness.

Another way to express emotion is with your voice. The tone, rate, pitch, volume, and intensity all provide indicators of emotion in the words you are using. Where you place emphasis on the words in a sentence can drastically change the meaning of what you are saying. Consider the sentence: "I didn't say she stole the money." Now read the sentence out loud placing a lot of emphasis on the word "I." That would mean that "you" didn't say she stole the money. Now read the sentence out loud again and place a lot of emphasis on the word "say." The meaning of the sentence changed slightly to mean that you didn't "say" she stole the money, but might have implied it. Read the sentence out loud again and overemphasize the word "she." The meaning changed to mean someone else might have stolen the money. With the emphasis on "stole," the meaning changes to the possibility she "borrowed" the money. And finally, with the emphasis on "money," it sounds like she may have stolen everything else. The old adage of "it's not what you say, it's how you say it" works here.

Consider how your voice changes when you are certain of something. Even if you don't know much about something, if you have confidence in your answer others can likely detect it. Have you ever had someone try to sell you something and when you asked a question, you knew they were really unsure about their answer when they responded? Confidence is especially important when you go to a job interview; you have to "fake it to make it" sometimes. Some emotions are easily detected in paralanguage. Joy and anger are easily identified when heard as they are quite different in tone. People often confuse fear with being nervous and love with being sad. Shame and love are often the most difficult to identify.

The study of personal space in nonverbal communication is referred to as proxemics. This relates to how far or close to other people we allow ourselves to be. One of the most prominent researchers in the study of proxemics is anthropologist Edward T. Hall (1966). He created the four zones of space. They are:

- **Intimate Space**—This is the zone of personal space most often used for very personal or intimate interactions. It ranges from 0 to 1.5 feet from the individual.
- **Personal Space**—This is the zone of personal space most often used for interpersonal conversations. It ranges from 1.5 to 4 feet from the individual.
- **Social Space**—This is the zone of personal space most often used for group interactions or acquaintances. It ranges from 4 to 12 feet from the individual.
- **Public Space**—This is the zone of interaction most often used by public speakers or anyone speaking to many people. The instructor of your course will typically fall under this zone. It ranges from 12 feet and beyond from the individual (Hall, 1966).

Many students will not have a problem allowing very close loved ones to be in their intimate space. Other students prefer most of their close loved ones to be within their personal space with only a select few in their intimate space area. Social space seems to be acceptable to many students as a comfortable distance from people they just met or don't know well. Public space will include anyone you don't know at all, so those people you encounter in public places. Territory is also a concept that falls under the area of space studies. **Territoriality** is the study of how people and animals use space and objects to communicate occupancy or ownership of space. People announce ownership of space with territorial markers permanently like fences around their property or temporarily like a jacket on the seat beside you.

The study of touch in nonverbal communication is called **haptics**. Touch can indicate a form of intimacy that can make people very uncomfortable if experienced without intent. However, many studies show that intimate touching is important in personal development and well-being. Before ethics were clearly established in the medical field, studies were conducted that attempted to find out if human touch was needed in infant and child development. By not allowing human touch of newborn babies, researchers found out very tragically that human touch is crucial for human development. Touching has a huge influence depending on whom it comes from. We are influenced most by the people who raised us. If your family greets you with hugs, you will most likely do this with others. Your level of acceptable touch will likely be more open with others as your family was more open with touch. If your family was not very open with touch, you may be hesitant to do so with others.

Society puts a lot of importance on physical appearance and personal relationships. Media helps spread awareness of what the ideal man and woman should look like in America. If asked to consider what that is, you might think about the woman being tall, thin but with an hourglass figure, with large breasts, and a pretty face. For the man, you might think he should be tall, dark, and handsome with six-pack abs and a full head of hair. Many of the images we are bombarded with in the media have been enhanced in numerous ways with Photoshop. In fact, if you input "before and after celebrity Photoshop photos" into a Google search, you will find many examples of what celebrities look like in real life and what they look like after being "perfected."

Most people can agree that the clothes they wear can affect how they feel as well as how others view them. If you wear a suit to a store one day and sweatpants and T-shirt the next, you will likely feel differently in the store and you may even be treated differently by those working there. This is one reason we dress differently when we go on a first date or job interview. Another interesting concept that falls under the area of attraction is if someone tells you that they think someone else is attractive, you will be more likely to accept that person being attractive rather than coming to your own conclusion. There are many celebrities who might not be considered very attractive if you saw them walking on the street, but because they were chosen to be on the cover of People Magazine in the "Sexiest People" edition, you will think otherwise. The accessories or things we carry with us say a lot about us too. These are referred to as **artifacts**. Having a purse, bag, jewelry, name brand clothing or shoes are all part of this area within nonverbal communication. Seeing someone with a wedding ring on may stop you from flirting with them. Seeing someone wearing a certain team's football jersey may have you starting up a conversation about the most recent or upcoming game. Artifacts are a way in which we show others what we like or even who we want to be like.

The study of time is called **chronemics**. A culture that is very time-oriented in calendars and appointments would be referred to as **monochronic**. The culture that sees time as more loose and fluid would be referred to as **polychronic**. How you value the importance of time can say a lot about you. If you were 20 minutes late for a business meeting in America, you would likely feel the eyes of disdain on you as you walked in. Good business etiquette in America indicates that you would need to offer an apology for being more than 5 minutes late to a meeting. Since we are monochronic in our time, there is not much leeway for being late.

The concepts covered in this chapter should help to serve as a foundation for us to build upon. How we use verbal and nonverbal communication to convey ideas and meaning is an important part of critical and strategic communication regardless of professional discipline. Being aware of them—both in your own communication and when you attempt to decode the communication of others—will help to make you a more effective and conscientious communicator.

References

Duck, S. & McMahan, D. T. (2009). *Communication in everyday life.* Thousand Oaks, CA: Sage.

Hall, E. T. (1966). *The hidden dimension.* Garden City, NY: Doubleday.

Klemmer, E. T. and Snyder, F. W. (June 1972). Measurement of Time Spent Communicating. *Journal of Communication* 20: 142.

Mehrabian, A. (1981). *Silent messages: Implicit communication of emotions and attitudes.* Belmont, CA: Wadsworth Publishing.

CHAPTER 4

Relationships and Conflict

Adolfo J. Garcia

The interdisciplinary nature of conflict resolution continues to emerge as one of the most interesting, diverse, and complex fields of study. New things are learned every day, yet other pieces of the puzzle have been known for millennia. The purpose of this chapter is to give you, the reader, an overview of the most important concepts in which to further your study. The chapter is only the beginning, however, and the reader should remember that communication, with all its interlocking pieces described in this book, serves as a backdrop to conflict resolution. At the outset, it is imperative that the reader also recalls that communication is a never-ending process, with no beginning or end. The same is true with conflict resolution.

This chapter is an interpersonal communication perspective on conflict resolution. As such, communication and messages are stressed and the most important components. Concepts that can help the reader to make good and informed communication choices in tough situations, with competence, are presented. I will come back to the concept of communication competence, but for now, let me just say that conflict resolution is a "give-and-take" process that involves introspection, intelligence, and a bit of luck and engaging in the messiness of human communication without fear uncertainly, so dive in, and don't fret, life will continue if you engage in conflict!

As with most encounters in our lives, conflict is interpersonal and "acted" on the stage of life. As you read this chapter, imagine you and your choices are being performed on stage, with an audience. This performance has scenes, and characters, and drama. And all the characters have motivations and goals and personalities. These characters all unfold through the interpersonal choices that they make. The "stage" analogy is a good way to describe what we do in conflict, because what we do is perform and represent versions of ourselves in front of our adversaries. And so do the other characters in the performance. Consider that communication is not just the vehicle by which the script is read but also the choices and meaning associated with choices (Goffman, 1990). In one sense then, conflict is a specific communication encounter or set of encounters that are performed, with informed or uninformed choice. The advantage that the reader is that herein contains the most relevant and up to date information about informed choices during conflict.

In another sense, the stage analogy describes the hopes for peace that are inherently represented in the study of conflict resolution. As a scholar in conflict resolution, my hope is always that the play will end well, with everyone getting along. I seek harmony for these characters, yet I also understand that any successful play includes building drama and conflict. Perhaps a difference between scholars in other disciplines and conflict resolution is that we wish for some return to normalcy through their empowerment to act in their best interest, without violence. I would hope that if people are able, the actors could end the play with resolution of their troubles and bring in third parties whenever necessary. Yet, trials and tribulations are part of life and should not and cannot be eradicated. Drama, conflict, or disputes are part of what make us human. We need tumult and change to grow and develop. So, **conflict resolution** is ironically not about eradicating conflict from the face of the world, because that is impossible; it is about engaging in helpful or appropriate strategies for handling or managing conflict, on the stage of life.

This chapter is built around the idea of appropriate and informed interpersonal communication choices. I understand that the interpersonal arena of communication is just one angle on human conflict, yet I will assume in this chapter that the interpersonal encounter, if handled well, is the "gold standard" toward resolution of some kind. This gold standard necessitates communication competence. Choices can range from doing nothing at all (which can be very appropriate indeed!) to engaging in constructive conflict. Although conflict can involve violence, the topic of violence is its own and not discussed further. Instead, I seek to represent conflict in this chapter as normal, episodic, ever-present, *and* positive.

First, we define conflict and conflict resolution. A little knowledge goes a long way, because simply reframing conflict can help us to reframe the negative connotation that we often attach to our experiences with conflict: a positive mindset and a positive framing of the experience of conflict can be a giant step toward engaging in conflict. Second, I describe specific choices a person can make in preparation for conflict encounters. These choices are good listening, a spirit of dialogue, and contemplative practices. Third, culture and conflict are explored through the lens of "face," along with our predisposition toward certain ways of managing conflict: conflict modes. Next, we examine well-worn, yet tried-and-true, techniques for choice making in conflict: negotiation and mediation. Finally, communication competence is used to weave together the chapter.

Defining Conflict and Conflict Resolution

Defining conflict and conflict resolution helps us establish common understanding of the topic. **Conflict** is a discord or barrier that two interdependent people perceive and communicate to each other. These barriers often present a challenge to communication.

Conflict, however, has been around as long as the earth itself and cannot be escaped or discounted as a powerful force in our lives. If we look to the natural world, conflict is all around us. When tectonic plates crash together and new islands form out of the depths of the Pacific Ocean, when creatures in the wild battle over limited food resources, and when the human body combats a virus, conflict is happening. Yet, humans seem to think that we can escape conflict in our relationships with other people! Conflict is all around us, and inescapable. I believe that this confusion stems from past negative experiences with conflict. We think we need to avoid it at all costs because it will always be negative outcomes (or so we believe!). There is confusion as to when conflict is happening among humans. We are so used to seeing conflict's many ugly faces that we forget that conflict is a normal and often nondestructive force in everyday life. Since conflict is normal, we can *choose* to think of it as a positive evolution of an ongoing relationship between people who genuinely care about each other's needs.

So, *when* is conflict present? Often conflict is perceived as a purely negative experience. That can be true, depending on the choices used and the mindset, but often conflict simply involves engaging in a certain type of communication. If we think of conflict as positive, then the choices we make can be geared toward understanding what the other side has to say, rather than fervently avoiding the situation. Conflict, however, does not exist, unless it is communicated between the two parties in some fashion, whether verbal or nonverbal, direct or indirect communication. So, conflict *is* discord, but *it is not* simply disagreement from one side. Conflict *is* the communication of barriers, but *it is not* simply one person perceiving these barriers. It must be communicated outwardly, whether constructively or otherwise. Conflict is also distinguished from disputes. Disputes are singular occurrences of disturbances or communication difficulties between people, while conflicts can be ongoing (Mayer, 2009). Also, conflict in this context does not mean physical violence.

Conflict is also about human needs. Abraham Maslow, a well-known psychologist, represented them in a pyramid structure as the "hierarchy of needs." Human needs are inherent motivations that every human seeks to fulfill in their lives (Maslow, 1943).

According to Maslow and in order of from the most basic upward are physiological, safety, love and belonging, esteem, self-actualization, and intrinsic values. In conflict for example, we seek to ensure that our need for safety is met by the other person. We may feel compelled or motivated to protect ourselves by doing all manner of things. If a roommate is smoking in your shared apartment, the need for safety may compel you to speak with the roommate about the merits of smoking outside or quitting. So, human needs are central to why conflict begin. Conflict can be over tangible or intangible scarce resources. Examples of tangible resources are time and money. Examples or intangible resources are trust and respect. Trust and respect can be thought of as human needs too. These resources can all seem to be scarce or missing during conflict.

In most conflicts, power is also an important factor. **Power** involves "the ability to get another person to do something that he or she would not otherwise have done" (Dahl, 1968, p. 158). Power is relational because it "is determined not only by the characteristics of the person or persons involved in any given situation, nor solely by the characteristics of the situation, but by the interaction of [the] two" (Coleman, 2000, pp. 111–112). Power imbalances occur because individuals perceive an unequal distribution of tangible or intangible resources, such as status and self-esteem (Walther, 2000). I now have established that conflict is defined as human needs and power differences that is distinct from conflict resolution because people may not seek to resolve conflict in any capacity. Progress may stop here, or there may be some work to do to prepare people to build up their capacity to engage in conflict resolution, or there may not be any incentive to engage in conflict at all.

Conflict resolution, however, is any process of communication that is undertaken to help improve communication between individuals and meet the needs of one or both parties. Conflict resolution can begin at any time, but the aim of conflict resolution is always to improve what has come before. Conflict resolution is meant to target the ill effects of conflict situations, but people can choose to avoid or negate the possibilities for constructive communication and so "conflict resolution" doesn't always "resolve" the dispute at hand. If, for example, there is an ongoing conflict between two neighbors about property lines, one neighbor could simply put up a fence. Adding a fence may settle, in one person's mind, where the plot lines should be, but the fence is not conflict resolution because there was no improvement in the communication between the two neighbors, and there has been no mutual understanding of needs or power differences.

Conflict resolution, therefore, *starts* when both parties seek to improve the conflict. For example, in property lines, Neighbor A could talk with Neighbor B about where a fence was placed. Now the process of conflict resolution has begun, but it may abruptly stop if Neighbor B wants nothing to do with conversation. Or, conflict resolution continues if Neighbor B agrees to talk further, perhaps about the noise that Neighbor A produces, which initiated the fence building. The neighbors may come to some resolution that solves the current dispute (e.g., noise reduction) but the resolution may only resolve just one portion of the overall conflict. For example, if we consider the needs of both parties, it is conceivable that some physiological or safety needs were met for both Neighbor A and B, but Neighbor B was also concerned about his need for self-esteem, or perhaps some power difference exists, like one neighbor is an police officer and seems to exert his status when confronting the other neighbor.

Conflict resolution is further distinguished from conflict management. With conflict resolution, there can be several agreements or resolutions that materialize between the neighbors. **Conflict management**, however, is a broader term that describes the real possibility that not everything will be resolved (and that is ok) but simply "managed" over time, as conflicts arise, as they always do. Conflict management has become a better term to describe the realities of conflict resolution, yet the term conflict resolution is so pervasive that we continue to use it. Bernard Mayer (2009) in his book "staying with conflict" contends that conflict management involves a realization that conflict is ongoing and that avoiding tactics seem to get in the way.

Therefore, conflict resolution can have a clear beginning (when the two parties communicate to improve the situation) and a clear ending (the settlement of a dispute) but may carry on past the current resolution into infinity, or as long as the two parties are interdependent. Conflict is natural and ongoing, and so can be the management of conflict.

Listening

Listening is defined as an individual who is partaking in shared communication with another with the intent of understanding what the other is saying. Good communication involves, in large part, good listening, because without listening, we are simply talking heads. This can be contrasted from hearing, since hearing is simply gathering or recognizing auditory signals from the environment. As time passes, and conflict becomes more entrenched, the harder it is for people to listen. It becomes easier to avoid conflict than to confront it, which in many cases is the opposite to listening (Mayer, 2009). Our so-called modern society at times seems to have forgotten that fast communication facilitated by texting, e-mailing, and its variants cannot come close to the quality of old-fashioned slow communication by listening face to face.

Active listening happens when an individual makes a concerted effort to step into the other person's shoes and suspend, at least temporarily, their own needs. So, improving listening first of all needs to happen face to face. This is where we can gain the most immediate and unhampered feedback from the person we seek to understand. So, active listening is just that active. As such, good listening involves a good bit of talking, but only during appropriate times that serve to understand the other side. Being an active listener involves listening in the ways that another person would want you to listen to them and there are some principles that help the listener.

First, point yourself at the other person with your full nonverbal attention, which includes choosing an appropriate amount of physical space, eye contact, and possibly touching. Nonverbal communication also will include a good amount of affirmation, like shaking one's head up and down. Paraphrasing is one way to ask good questions and listen. Paraphrasing is when a person summarizes or condenses what someone else has said with the express purpose of trying to understand what the other is saying, without interjecting one's own values. When someone paraphrases, they are asking not if they have "heard correctly." They are asking if they have "listening correctly," according to the wishes of the other person. Paraphrasing may start with "let me see if I heard you right" and end with "was that your intended meaning?" Take good notes, so that you are not compelled to monopolize the time.

Finally, to complete active listening, finish by asking the person if they said everything necessary. These steps are then carried forward as many times as is necessary to get all the issues out on the table, but it also serves another purpose. Active listening actually allows the listener to pick up more information than they normally might have done because of the systematic way in which active listening is done. It also allows the listener to ask questions about emotions and arguments, which is often left of out heated conversations. Active listening is particularly difficult in conflict situations but more can be achieved by remembering these basic principles.

People can listen for message content, argument, or emotion. And the speaker may want to be listened to for content, argument, their emotion, or a combination of the three. Has anyone ever said to you, "I just want you to listen!"? This simple statement should be a cue to you to start active listening. As a simple rule-of-thumb, start with listening for content. Listening for content means that the listener is looking to understand, and not simply hear, the messages that are transmitted. For example, if a roommate has politely asked you to explain how you can contribute to cleaning a shared bathroom, were you able to respond adequately and mindfully to the request? If not, you may have been led astray by our natural tendency to lose focus, and revert to simply hearing (versus listening).

People can also listen for argument. By "argument," I do not mean to suggest the negative connotation of argument (sometimes equated with conflict). Listening for argument is whether you were able to hear the claims and evidence that were communicated (the Rhetoric chapter has content about this). So, if the roommate claims that "you do not do your share of the cleaning duties" and presents some pretty compelling evidence to support the claims, like the vacuum hasn't left the closet in two months, was the listening able to paraphrase what and select claims and support, without getting derailed and revert to poor listening.

Finally, people can listen for emotion. Emotions are defined as the feelings that we attach to your our perceptions of the world. Feelings such as sadness, anger, and disappointment are common in conflict, yet seldom does a person reflect or paraphrase our feelings back to us. This can go a long way toward feeling some empathy for the other person. Empathy is a mental state where a person can step into the other person's shoes and feel as they feel, without judgment. An example of listening for emotion, a difficult task indeed since we're often driven by own emotions in a conflict, is to put aside how the listener feels (what emotions they have) and communicate back what they think the other person is feeling.

In practice, people are listening for content, argument, and emotion simultaneously. Yet, it is uncommon to actively listening for these. A listener, for example, could say "I sense that you're really hurt" (emotion) "and you think that I need to be more conscious of our shared living space by cleaning once a week" (argument—claim and support). This ability to paraphrase well, without our emotions driving us away from the goal, is good practice.

Active listening, then, is when someone listens with both good verbal communication (paraphrasing) and also with good nonverbal communication, such as good eye contact, body positioning toward the other, and choosing an appropriate private space.

Dialogue and Positive Intent

Dialogue happens when people choose to view the situation or conflict through a new lens, through the lens of positive intent. When people move beyond "what was said" to "what was intended" dialogue is in process. Conflict resolution may be in progress, as is often the case when people show up to mediation, but dialogue could still be missing. Dialogue is what all of us should strive to achieve with other human beings. Some consider the experience of having dialogue as transformative and sometimes spiritual, since through dialogue we strive to understand the unsaid by recognizing the underlying connections that bind all humans together.

Martin Buber, a well-known proponent and scholar of dialogue, wrote a book named "*I and Thou*" (1971). He described the conditions for dialogue compared with monologue. **Monologue** is when we treat each other as "objects," a sort of one-way conversation where we treat the other as a tool to get a particular task completed. Perceiving others as objects dehumanizes them. If we collectively create a wall of distrust to block the world out, we stand to create a world monologue. Buber have called this the "I/It relationship." Consider the example of ordering food at a drive-through window. We may approach the outside menu with food on our minds and with little concern or worry about the person who is on the other side of the speaker. We may feel urgency or uncertainly by the unnatural nature of the situation: an illuminated screen with food and drink options, a hollow and monotone voice asking for your order. The environment almost predetermines our response: we respond to the request for help with a shallow and disconnected tone, almost as if we were tapping at our keyboard rather than talking to another human. We order, pick the food up at the next window, and move on with our less-than-fulfilling interaction. We may or may not say thank you, make eye contact, or otherwise recognize the other person as nothing more than a necessary part in an assembly line.

What if we extrapolate this example to all other interactions and communication encounters, and yet further to conflict situations when our mental abilities are strained the most: in a conflict? Buber has said that the lack of dialogue, which he called monologue is the single most dangerous and fatalistic lens that people could have toward each other. The horrors of World War II and the genocide against the Jewish people by the Nazis were the product of Monologue. Imagining a life of monologue is not too far-fetched. Our modern lives bombard us with media messages where it is almost appealing to shut out the outside world.

Carl Rogers (1995), a psychotherapist, have said that having an "**unconditional positive regard**" is possibly the best strategy to take and is a state of mind where a person puts aside their own preconceived negative notions in order to listen. Buber have called this having an "I-Thou" relationships with the other. Having unconditional positive regard for others means that you, at least temporarily, can suspend judgment and have positive intent in your communication with them. We can choose to treat each other as objects, the reverse, as worthy intact humans. The *intent* is to achieve dialogue with this person. Dialogue, therefore, is the state of mind where we make an effort to exude or represent a more caring version of ourselves. Through the transformative power of dialogue, conflicts have the potential to be resolved amicably and with respect and kindness. The question can be asked, "How do I attempt to reach this state of dialogue?" Contemplative practices can help.

Contemplative Practices and Mindfulness

Contemplative practices are a set of focus-oriented techniques that can help to quite the mind and allow a person to gain a greater awareness of their surroundings. Only recently, we have started to see substantial scientific inquiry into contemplative practices, and the results have startling relevance to conflict resolution. We need new techniques for resolving conflict and thinking in new ways about conflict is relevant. Mindfulness and contemplative practices help establish new ways to connect what may have been missing, the essential connection between cognition and affection.

New evidence has found that the brain itself changes in shape and structure from practicing contemplation. In his work at the University of Wisconsin, Richard Davidson has argued that our brains are like clay, a concept called "**neuro-plasticity**." What this literally means is that we can train our brains through practice, even for compassion toward others. One study found that compassion training [through contemplative practice] physically changed the brains of the study's participants to respond to human suffering more altruistically (Weng et al., 2013). Training one's brain has also been found to regulate people's emotions and reduce stress (Ricard, Lutz, & Davidson, 2014). Our brains are like clay or muscle, waiting to be sculpted and exercised.

Yet people in the western hemisphere have associated contemplative practice with meditation, which brings certain connotations. I am not recommending that you move to Tibet, give up all your worldly possessions, and live a life of piety (although that may solve some of the world's conflict problems), yet there is a real benefit to reflecting and contemplating one's actions before doing them. Contemplative practices can *lead to choices* that peaceful, caring, respectful, which is exactly what we would want when people experience conflict. Meditation although popularized most recently through Chinese and Japanese Buddhism have been familiar to many cultures and religions as a contemplative practice for thousands of years. Hindus, Buddhists, Jews, and Christians (to name a few) rely on contemplation. "*Orison,* the repetitive and devotional meditation on Christ, repetition of the Holy Names, the spiritual teachings of St. Ignatius, and the Eastern Orthodox practice of the *philokalia* are examples from the Western contemplative tradition that come nearest to meditation as it has been cultivated in Asian countries" (Murphy, Donovan, & Taylor, 1997, p. 2). So, contemplation has been around for a very long time, even outside of meditating monks in Tibet.

In the communication discipline, contemplation has been associated with mindfulness. **Mindfulness** refers to "active and fluid information processing, sensitivity to context and multiple perspectives, and ability to draw novel distinctions" (Burgoon, Berger, & Waldron, 2000, p. 106). This can be compared to the concept of mindlessness, which is communication that is "reactive, superficially processed, routine, rigid, and emotional [as opposed to rational thinking]" (p. 116). Of course, we understand that conflict resolution isn't as simple as saying, "let's be mindful of what we're saying to each other" because that negates our talents for improvisation (we can all seem sincere without feeling it). That is not what I'm proposing at all. Instead, I suggest something more revolutionary that that: *let's mean what we say* (see section on Dialogue) by practicing mindfulness. I wholeheartedly believe that practice is necessary with all things, including communicating in conflict situations. So, how do we become better at "drawing novel distinctions" from what someone we dislike may be saying? The answer is by using contemplative practices to achieve a more stable mindset, and we can ask others to do the same, if they are willing.

There are three kinds of contemplative practices that have benefits for conflict resolution. Although original conceived through the Buddhist tradition, these techniques are used by hospitals and schools internationally (Ricard et al., 2014). The first is called **focused-attention meditation**. The purpose of this practice is to train one's mind to concentrate on the present moment, while learning to return to one's breath. This research has found that experienced meditators were able to stay focused, regardless of distraction. In the context of conflict resolution, distractions are evident, especially from the noise that can be attributed to one's own emotional distress in a conflict situation. This kind of contemplative practice can help us to stay alert to our senses and how they may be deceiving us into interpreting unintended messages. It is a practice we can do *before* engaging in conflict. If we're able to simply control our attention and keep it from wandering, we may not be at the mercy of our reactive brain.

The second practice is called mindfulness, or **open-monitoring meditation**, which is a technique that can help us get unstuck from our emotionally attachment to without much preoccupation. It is a practice we can do *during* a conflict. The technique teaches the mind to strays less away from the present moment. Mindfulness can help people to not "get stuck" and can people to control their emotions and alleviate anxiety and depression (Hanh & Vo, 1987). Certainly, as disputants are entangled in the messiness of conflict mindfulness can be an especially useful skill. Let me give an example. Let's say you are having an argument with a roommate about the state of the kitchen (in disrepair, in your opinion). If you were to practice focused attention mediation, your mind would not wander to "what I want to say next" and instead, your senses could be available to "what is she trying to tell me."

Finally, the third practice is called **compassion and loving-kindness**. The purpose of this training is to gain a greater appreciation in the form of altruism toward others. **Altruism** here means a sense of well-being toward others that transcends one's own needs. Altruism is the opposite of selfishness. Generating a compassionate connection with others can mean more than simply feeling empathy, but it may even call for the person to actively alleviate someone else's suffering. The benefit of this practice is that it can alleviate what some call "empathy fatigue." Third party mediators can experience empathy fatigue since they interact with conflict often. Showing compassion and loving-kindness is something we can all hope to achieve, but in the context of conflict resolution, it is an essential skill for any good mediator.

Therefore, the kind of interaction we hope to achieve through contemplative practice should lead to *better* communication. In this sense, better communication means using a mixture of contemplative skills that enhance our abilities to be aware of our *mind and body* and interact in a way that is nuanced and appropriate to the people and situation at hand. It can help to reduce the emotional stresses of conflict if we're able to be more competent in our communication. We could call this a cultivation of the heart and mind. "In a world beset with conflicts, internal as well as external, isn't it of equal if not greater importance to balance the sharpening of our intellects with the systematic cultivation of our hearts? Do not the issues of social justice, the environment, and peace education all demand greater attention…?" (Zajonc, 2006). Zajonc has called this "**contemplative inquiry**" (p. 3).

In some ways, this is not new knowledge, as people have been extolling the benefits of contemplation for millennia. Rationally, it makes sense, that the more mindful someone is, the more aware they become of their actions, and the perception of others' actions. Anyone can tell you acting before thinking is foolish yet not until recently has scientific evidence been found that being more mindful actually changes our brain, like a muscle. If that is the case, that we can train the muscle, even for those that don't seem to have a natural bend for empathy or understanding.

Grossenbacher and Rossi (2014) pointed out, however, that mindfulness alone isn't enough: "Mindfulness emphasizes observation while de-emphasizing the interpretation of observations." With conflict resolution, we also need the ability to organize the information into a useful form with which to make appropriate choices. The first three steps are noticing, slowing, and reflecting that helps the individual notice their surroundings more clearly, which align nicely with what Zajonc (2006) called "contemplative inquiry." The next three steps are distinguishing, recalling, and describing, which help a person make choices within the conflict situation—in essence to work through the conflict in a reflective and constructive manner.

I picture a scenario where people have come primed to discuss their grievances. Perhaps they are given "homework" by a mediator or third party. Practice is, however, necessary, along with knowledge about conflict modes.

Conflict Modes

Broadly speaking, **conflict modes** or conflict styles are predispositions that an individual has to manage conflict in a given situation (Folger, Poole, & Stutman, 2009). A predisposition or tendency means that a person may react in a certain way most of the time, if faced with similar people or circumstances. There are three basic conflict modes: avoiding, competing, or collaborating.

When someone avoids conflict, this means that that they generally care less about the outcome of the conflict or their own needs but may care very much about the other party's needs. Appropriately avoiding a conflict means that the individual selectively weighs the pros and cons of avoiding the conflict and realizes that they stand to lose little, so it may not matter if it is avoided. Inappropriately avoiding conflict is when a person decides to disregard the needs of someone else in a passive aggressive fashion.

When someone competes during a conflict, they care more about their own needs than the other person's. For example, consider a young woman who has had a child. If a conversation ensues where another person belittles young mothers, the women may feel entirely compelled to defend her lifestyle—this is using the competitive conflict mode. It may be entirely possible that at that particular moment, she is acting appropriately in a competitive way. Conversely, an example of inappropriately competing is lying to gain an advantage over someone else.

When someone uses the collaborative conflict mode, they seek to balance their own needs with the needs of the other party. In practical terms, people communicate collaboratively by giving the other side ample speaking time without interrupting and with concern for their points of view. Active listening and dialogue (see those sections in this chapter) can occur with collaborative conflict. An example of appropriate collaboration is when both sides have the best intent to solve a shared problem because they recognize that it is in their best long-term interests. Inappropriate collaboration is when a person pretends to have the best intent, but with hidden motives. For example, imagine that a team is working to solve a public relations crisis and the PR person has information that he knows will negatively impact the client. If he chooses to work out a solution but does not share the information, perhaps because he has a negative past experience with the client, then he is inappropriately collaborating.

Face and Culture

We now turn attention to the importance of culture in conflict resolution. We can express culture through the concept of "face." **Face** is the identity we claim for ourselves in public situations. We communicate face through our verbal and nonverbal communication and through our culture beliefs (Ting-Toomey, 2005). We seek to present a certain version of ourselves based on the social situation, and we may have different face needs, depending on the people that are present. For example, in a classroom, you may want to be perceived as an intelligent and studious person. Your "face" is that perception that you wish other's have of you. Yet, in another context, say with a romantic partner, your "face" may be of a loving and nurturing partner.

Face is important to the discussion of conflict because we all seek to have our "face" validated. We all seek to be respected. Yet, our "face" can be one of the most fragile parts of our identity in a conflict. For example, if a fellow student disrupts you in class while you're attempting display your abundance of knowledge, then they may be "threatening your face," or simply exerting a "face threat" (Brown & Levinson, 1987). A conflict can occur. Face is situational, however, because it a threat based on the relationship you have with the others in the room who are watching, and the initiator of the interruption.

Facework (Oetzel, Garcia, & Ting-Toomey, 2008) ensues when people seek to uphold and/or respect another's face or, the opposite, insult or diminish another's face. Facework also has some parallels with conflict modes, since they are specific culturally specific behaviors. For example, facework can be either "self-oriented" or "other" oriented. When other-oriented facework is in progress, a person may seek to repair or uphold the face of another by complimenting them or apologizing about any disrespect. When self-oriented facework happens, the individual's goal is to present a positive view of one's self by asking others to see the merits of their argument on a topic or by pointing out how someone else is wrong vis-à-vis themselves.

Face Negotiation Theory (Ting-Toomey, 2005) is a prominent culture-based theory that explains conflict through a theoretical framework involving face and how it is negotiated in different cultures. The theory is a helpful organizational framework to understand how culture helps to influence the ways that conflict is resolved or managed. The heart of the theory uses face, face concerns, and facework, as variables in the ways that individuals work through conflict. For example, people from a collectivistic culture have higher other-face concerns (upholding others' face is more important relative to their self-face) and, therefore, may use collaborative facework to establish rapport with the other person. Conversely, someone from an individualistic culture is often more concerned with self-face concerns (upholding one's own public persona) and, therefore, may be considered to use more competitive facework strategies. The most recent work on the theory (Zhang, Ting-Toomey & Oetzel, 2014) links emotion into the theory. The empirical investigation showed that Americans and Chinese nationals managed anger, compassion, and guilt differently.

Negotiation and Mediation

The choices or behaviors that we exhibit are the actions that others see. Making these choices explicit, for example, by describing the process in which you want to resolve conflict is an important step toward resolution. Two important choices are negotiation and mediation, which are only two formal processes in the spectrum of conflict resolution options. Other options are doing nothing (which is different than avoiding conflict), arbitration, litigation, and violence, which are not discussed in this chapter.

Making the first move toward constructive communication involves negotiation. **Negotiation** is the bargaining process that we engage in to figure out a solution to a conflict. Negotiation happens whenever we commit ourselves to engaging in conflict resolution. Negotiating doesn't just happen at the farmer's market haggling over the price of a tomato or on the used car lot bargaining over the price of a used car. People can negotiate over all manner things including concrete resources such as money or time, and also negotiation happens over less tangible things, like respect and honor (see Face Negotiation Theory). Negotiation also happens regardless of our wishes because even when we decide *not* to negotiate, that can be interpreted by the other side that the issue is settled (when it may not be at all). So, we cannot simply bow out of negotiating in conflict resolution because, in a sense, bowing out is negotiating by sending a message of avoidance. Let me explain. Let's say you have upset your neighbor by disregarding her pleads to keep the noise level at a minimum after 9 pm. If you choose to do nothing (keep playing loud music), then you are choosing to not negotiate. The choice to not negotiate is just as destructive as turning the music louder!

People explain what they *want* in negotiation through positions and what they *need* through interests. When someone states, "turn the music down," they are expressing their position in the conflict. They are saying that they *want* peace and quiet, but what they *need* underlies they want. An interest, then, answers the question "why do you want me to turn down the music." Negotiating over interests is much more fruitful to conflict resolution because it helps uncover the "whys" of conflict without getting stuck on the hardline positions that people often express in frustration. This is called interest-based negotiation (Fisher, Ury, & Patton, 1983).

Thankfully, there are other productive choices that can still be made, even when people cannot negotiate directly and alone. We call this mediation. While negotiation affords an individual the most decision-making control (by communicating directly with the other party), mediation offers somewhat less control, but still the most control without being alone. Formal **mediation** is a facilitated process of conflict resolution where a third party creates a structured environment where parties can discuss the conflict and come to a self-determined solution (Moore, 2014). **Self-determination** is at the heart of mediation practice because mediators believe that successful solutions to conflicts should be determined by those deeply involved in that conflict (the two sides). Mutually acceptable solutions are derived with the help of a trained mediator using a particular process of mediation. Mediation in the United States has become commonplace and is considered a quicker and cheaper alternative to litigation and trials. Mediators can be found working in community mediation centers, nonprofits, business, and government agencies throughout the country (Herrman, 2009) and is an up-and-coming career for students in communication.

Communication Competence

Communication competence (Cupach, Canary, & Spitzberg, 2009) stresses the dual importance of effectiveness and appropriateness in our communication. This concept helps us to merge together the concepts addressed in this chapter. **Effectiveness** answers the question, "were you able to reach your goals in the conflict interaction?" Notice that being competent does not involve giving up your own needs and opinions. No one should ask you to give up the goal you had in engaging in the conflict in the first place, unless it is meant to harm others. Martin Buber have said that giving up your own goals does not achieve Dialogue, but it prohibits it. A person must exert their will upon others to feel as if the conflict is being solved and the other should strive to succeed at meeting their goals, too, and reach them. We call this **assertiveness**. Active listening, a spirit of dialogue, and contemplation help us reach our goals and be effective.

Appropriateness answers the question, "did you manage the conflict in a way that was satisfactory to others?" Reaching one's goals misses half of what is important to the endeavor of conflict resolution—the other side. Getting good at resolving conflict, therefore, is also about *how* the conflict is handled. So, appropriateness involves skill in managing the people and situations that are part of the conflict. Including their preferred conflict modes, face needs, and available options for settling the dispute through negotiation and mediation. Before interacting in conflict resolution, people can consider, for example, the impact of acting competitively (if their need is great) versus collaboratively (if the need of both is important). Contemplative practices remind us that one cannot reach settlement without some proper preparation for an upcoming interaction. By training ourselves to be aware of our present environment, we're less likely to be driven by our misguided emotions. We can change our very brain structures by *practicing* compassion. We can still, however, be compassionate even when we cannot face the person alone, which may mean enlisting the help of a third party mediator. We can still reach self-determination, but with the help of a third party.

In all, the process of conflict resolution is about making informed choices. We started the chapter by explaining conflict on the stage of life. I encourage the reader to continue their exploration of conflict by getting involved in the messiness of life, which includes engaging in conflict in mindful and respectful ways. I guarantee that this will enhance, rather than detract, from your life.

References

Brown, P., & Levinson, S. C. (1987). *Politeness: Some universals in language usage.* New York: Cambridge University Press.

Buber, M. (1971). *I And Thou.* New York, NY: Touchstone.

Burgoon, J. K., Berger, C. R., & Waldron, V., R. (2000). Mindfulness and interpersonal communication. *Journal of Social Issues, 56*(1), 105.

Coleman, P. T. (2000). Power and conflict. In M. Deutsch & E. C. Marcus (Eds.), *The handbook of conflict resolution: Theory and practice* (pp. 108–130). San Francisco, CA: Jossey-Bass.

Cupach, W. R., Canary, D. J., & Spitzberg, B. H. (2009). *Competence in Interpersonal Conflict* (2nd ed.). Waveland Press.

Dahl, R. A. (1968). Power. In *International encyclopedia of the social sciences* (Vol. 12). Old Tappan, NJ: Macmillan.

Fisher, R., Ury, W., & Patton, B. (1983). *Getting to yes : negotiating agreement without giving in.* New York, NY : Penguin Books, 1983.

Folger, J. P., Poole, M. S., & Stutman, R. K. (2009). *Working through conflict: Strategies for relationships, groups, and organizations.* Boston: Pearson Education.

Goffman, E. (1990). *The presentation of self in everyday life.* New York, NY: Doubleday.

Grossenbacher, P. G., & Rossi, A. J. (2014). A Contemplative Approach to Teaching Observation Skills. *The Journal of Contemplative Inquiry, 1*(1). Retrieved from http://commons.suny.edu/wp-content/uploads/group-documents/170/1409326439-Grossenbacher-Rossi-ContemplativeObservation.pdf.

Hanh, T. N., & Vo, D. M. (1987). *The Miracle of Mindfulness: An Introduction to the Practice of Meditation.* Boston: Beacon Press.

Herrman, M. S. (2009). *The Blackwell handbook of mediation: Bridging theory, research, and practice.* Hoboken, NJ: John Wiley & Sons.

Maslow, A. (1943). A theory of human motivation: *Psychological Review, 50,* 370–396.

Mayer, B. S. (2009). *Staying with conflict: A strategic approach to ongoing disputes.* San Francisco, CA: Jossey-Bass.

Moore, C. W. (2014). *The mediation process : Practical strategies for resolving conflict* (Vol. 4). San Francisco, CA: Wiley.

Murphy, M., Donovan, S., & Taylor, E. (1997). The physical and psychological effects of meditation: A review of contemporary research. *Published by the Institute of Noetic Sciences.* Retrieved from http://www.chinabiofield.com/wp-content/uploads/2012/04/The-physical-and-psychological-effects-of-meditation-Michael-Murphy-et-al.pdf.

Oetzel, J., Garcia, A. J., & Ting-Toomey, S. (2008). An analysis of the relationships among face concerns and facework behaviors in perceived conflict situations: A four-culture investigation. *International Journal of Conflict Management, 19*(4), 382–403. Retrieved from http://doi.org/10.1108/10444060810909310.

Ricard, M., Lutz, A., & Davidson, R. J. (2014, October 14). Mind of the meditator. *Scientific American, 311*(5), 38–45.

Rogers, C. (1995). *On becoming a person: A therapist's view of psychotherapy* (1st ed.). New York, NY: Mariner Books.

Ting-Toomey, S. (2005). The Matrix of Face: An Updated Face-Negotiation Theory. In W. B. Gudykunst & W. B. (Ed) Gudykunst (Eds.), *Theorizing about intercultural communication.* (pp. 71–92). Thousand Oaks, CA: Sage Publications Ltd.

Walther, G. M. (2000). Power imbalances in divorce mediation. *American Journal of Family Law, 14*(2), 93–101.

Weng, H. Y., Fox, A. S., Shackman, A. J., Stodola, D. E., Caldwell, J. Z. K., Olson, M. C., … Davidson, R. J. (2013). Compassion training alters altruism and neural responses to suffering. *Psychological Science, 24*(7), 1171–1180. Retrieved from http://doi.org/10.1177/0956797612469537.

Zhang, Q., Ting-Toomey, S., & Oetzel, J. G. (2014). Linking emotion to the conflict face–negotiation theory: A U.S.–China investigation of the mediating effects of anger, compassion, and guilt in interpersonal conflict. *Human Communication Research, 40*(3), 373–395. http://doi.org/10.1111/hcre.12029.

CHAPTER 5

Communication Theory and Criticism

Part of being an effective applied communicator is understanding how to communicate effectively. This is hardly a new concept at this point—we've already discussed communication models and rhetoric in this book, and these ideas at their core are about understanding the most effective way to communicate. Yet this is only part of the equation. If we are to understand communication and how it can be applied across many different disciplines, we must also start to try to make some predictions about how communication happens. How do we make communication decisions? How do we use communication to resolve tensions or create the world around us? In some cases, could we even try to predict a desired outcome or effect for communication?

The need to understand and make predictions about communication in all its forms is what has led to the development of **theory**. We generally consider theory to be the domain of the hard sciences, the practice of scientists in laboratories and out in the field trying to find patterns and connections in the natural world. Communication theory operates in much the same way, though it has as its focus a significantly more intangible and assumedly much less predictable phenomena than rocks or electromagnetic waves. After all, humans are the source of communication, and humans vary and change in ways that cannot be taken for granted. How can we develop a consistent, dependable means of predicting and observing communication when the people who originate it are anything but?

As it turns out, much the same way we generate theory in any of the hard sciences. We will discuss the specifics of developing and testing theory later in this chapter but for now understand that the theories we discuss in this chapter are the sum total of years of testing and observation in many different places and situations. From these tests and observations, we start assembling patterns and making connections, then seeing if those patterns and connections apply in a different situation, and repeating the process until we see significant evidence that a pattern exists. No one theory can explain all communication phenomena, but each theory should carry with it the possibility and potential to help us understand a little more about how and why we communicate, and even how that communication may impact us.

Understanding and Building Theory

It first behooves us to understand what a theory is. A theory, in simple terms, provides us with a means or in some cases a direct prediction of something in terms of how it works, what it does, and how it can potentially be changed or altered (Wood, 2004). A theory is generally focused on a single **phenomenon**, which can best be described as an event or happening. For example, our increasing dependence on mobile devices is a phenomenon that theory might study. We can think of theory in scientific terms, and we often in fact do—though it should be noted that communication, as a **social science**, has different goals than the so-called "hard sciences." These differences will be illustrated throughout the chapter. Fundamentally, theory of any stripe has four main objectives: describing, explaining, predicting/controlling/understanding, and reform.

The **descriptive** objective of theory is quite straightforward—it is essentially trying to label often complex phenomena in a way that we can "get our arms around it" by assigning meaningful distinctions and symbols to its parts (Wood, 2004). Take, for example, the model of communication discussed in Chapter 3—it describes the component parts of communication by identifying that communication must come from a source, take the form of a meaningful message, go through a particular channel, and be accepted by a receiver. Later scholars built upon that theory by introducing other descriptive elements such as noise and feedback. Note that this theory does not do anything to predict the outcome of communication, rather it simply describes the phenomenon.

The **explanatory** objective of theory happens when theory attempts to clarify *why* something is happening or why it works; this part of theory cannot happen until after we describe the component parts of the phenomenon (Wood, 2004). If we can identify communication as having the aforementioned elements, we can start to ask questions about how the parts work together. Obviously, communication cannot work without a source from which it originates or an audience to receive it, and a message must be conveyed, but what of the channel? The channel carries the message to the receiver, and this process may be interrupted by noise that makes feedback difficult. Each part of the model has an impact on the overall product and an effect on the other parts.

The third objective of theory is a multipart one and which part is at the forefront depends on the goals of the theory itself. Some theory attempts to **predict** what will happen in a phenomenon, given the manipulation of particular variables—if we change the channel of message delivery, for example, can we potentially cut back on interfering noise? Similarly, we may try to use theory to **control** phenomena by identifying the dependent variables and specifically manipulating independent variables to reach a desirable outcome—we can choose which receivers receive our message in order for it to be most effective, or we can change the message for it to be received more effectively by our intended recipients. This is, however, not the goal of all theory, and in some cases, prediction and control are unattainable or even undesirable. For most social scientists, theory is there to help guide **understanding**—specifically, it is valued for its ability to demonstrate why something is happening. This may seem to be very similar to the goal of prediction, which is why Wood (2004) offered this helpful distinction—we can think of understanding as more inherently subjective than prediction. It is concerned more with *why* things are happening than *how* things will happen.

Finally, theory often has the objective of **reform**. When we use theory for reform, we are attempting to use theory to identify social ills and work to challenge those ills (Wood, 2004). Effectively, this objective uses theory as a tool for the repair of social problems. Keeping in line with our SMCR model, we could use that model and find that certain channels are disproportionately available to particular audiences over others; assuming that these channels are the primary means through which a message is transmitted, that lack of equal access can be a problem for some audiences. Not all researchers approve of this approach, arguing that theory should try to remain objective and in line with the Scientific Method, but an ever-growing number of researchers are acknowledging that application of reform-based theory is necessary to break down the wall that often goes up between communication study and practice (Wood, 2004). We will discuss several reform-oriented theories later in this chapter.

There are two main ways we can think about developing and testing theory—**induction** and **deduction**. To demonstrate, picture an hourglass—wide at the bottoms and narrowing as it approaches the center. Let's start at the top of the hourglass with the process of deduction. You may be familiar with this term through mystery stories (your author is a particularly big Sherlock Holmes fan). Yet, when it comes to theory, the meaning is somewhat different. Deduction is perhaps best understood as the process of starting with a broad general theory or question about a particular phenomenon, developing a guess about how that theory might apply to a situation, then making observations that confirm or disprove that theory (Trochim, 2006). In short, we are starting big and going small as we head toward the narrow center of the hourglass. Induction, by comparison, is closer to what Sherlock Holmes and his crime-fighting ilk actually do—we start small, with individual observations. From those individual observations, we start to examine and find patterns that allow us to develop a potential **hypothesis**, or predictive statement of a relationship, between the variables at play. We can then test that hypothesis to see if it is in fact predictive and from those tests can potentially develop a theory that can explain the broader phenomenon—in short, we start small and go big as we go down the hourglass to the bottom (Trochim, 2006). These are both valid means of building and testing theory—rather than saying one is preferable to the other, instead we need to continue thinking in terms of what we are trying to ask or find out.

Regardless of whether you are deducing from an existing theory or inducing a theory based on patterns of observations, it is important to understand that theory at its core is philosophical—it is concerned with questions of human nature and how we know things. Every theory has a specific **ontological** perspective or assumption about our human nature. Some theories suggest that human beings have **free will** to communicate and choose in whatever way they see fit while others are based on **determinism**, or the idea that human behavior is guided by forces beyond our direct control (Wood, 2004). Theory must also have a clear **epistemological** approach or understanding of how we obtain and process knowledge. A theory may be based in **objectivity**, which suggests that there is a measurable truth outside of our perception that is true in all cases, or it may be based in **postmodernism**, which suggests that truth is inherently socially constructed and dependent on the observer (Wood, 2004). Objectivity tends to be the domain of hard sciences and predictive theory, but reform theory is generally postmodern in nature. Finally, we must also identify the theory's focus—is it **behavioral** and focused on studying what people do, or is it meanings based and concerned with our motives and drives? As Wood (2004) suggested, behavioral theory tends to be focused on objective recounting of the execution of a phenomena—for example, we can survey students and find that most of them communicate via text. Therefore, a behavioral analysis would suggest that texting is the most popular form of communication among college-age students. However, this analysis tells us nothing of *why* students prefer texting. Through interviews with students, we may find that most of them text because they like the immediacy or the ability to communicate using images or maybe even that they are too shy to talk on the phone. Some theories lend themselves better to objective behavioral analysis, while others thrive on meanings-based inquiry.

Communication theory is often in a difficult spot because unlike theories based in the hard sciences, it is not always concerned with **causality**. For most hard science endeavors, through experimentation, we can discover that the manipulation of an independent variable will cause a dependent variable to happen, creating a causal relationship between those two variables. We determine these relationships through repeated observations and experiments that are categorized by the **Scientific Method**;

while social science inquiry like communication research cannot always show direct causality, it still follows the same general process of theorization, testing, and retesting (Baran & Davis, 2015). It is also important here to note the difference between causality and **correlation** or a relationship between two variables. This distinction is vital to our understanding of science and theory, but it is also very rare that the distinction is actually made. Consider a study in which we find that as cell phone usage goes up among our participants, attention spans go down. While it may seem that one is causing the other, there could be any number of other factors that contribute to these facts. Determining causality happens over a long period of time and research, and just because two variables go up or down in relationship to each other does not automatically mean one is causing the other.

Evaluating Theory

There are hundreds of communication theories, each with their own assumptions and expectations. As a student, you may be wondering how we can possibly determine which theories are the best or most useful. In general, there is no one theory that is better than all other theories, and there is no one universal theory that can explain everything. Moreover, just because a theory exists does not necessarily make it valid or useful. I could theorize, for example, that eating hamburgers makes one more likely to wear blue hats because I induced from a trip to Burger King that many of the people enjoying burgers were in fact wearing blue hats. This theory cannot really be tested, we learn nothing from it, and there is no real relationship between these two variables—which means that it's a bad theory. Learning how to identify good theory, or at least the theory that is most useful and constructive for your purposes, is necessary to be an effective communication researcher.

There are a multitude of different ways we can analyze theory, and in general, which theory is best is the one that suits your needs and most effectively guide you to answering the question you are asking. We can start by looking at the **scope** of a theory or the breadth of what the theory tries to explain or describe (Wood, 2004). Some theories are very broad and they can be expanded upon to explain or describe a number of different phenomena. However, this breadth can be a double-edged sword of sorts. As we will find in our later discussion of **uses and gratifications theory**, some theories are so broad that any description of a phenomena can fit into them, which makes strategic inquiry and generalizability difficult. Generally, a good theory should clearly and thoroughly explain the phenomena with which it is concerned (Baran & Davis, 2015). Consider the SMCR model—it has four elements, each one clearly distinct from the others, and the interaction between those elements can be applied to many different communication forms. The theory itself is not broad, but its applications are. Therefore, we see SMCR coming back again and again throughout communication study.

Second, we can evaluate theory based on its **testability** or its ability to be investigated through empirical observation (Baran & Davis, 2015). If a theory is too vague or does not provide enough information to guide the necessary scientific inquiry, then it is not testable and its worth as a theory is lower than one that can be more easily tested. A testable theory should clearly define its variables. For example, the theory "communication is important in the workplace" is not testable because it is too broad—we have no idea how to measure importance, "workplaces" are all generally different—as a result, we cannot develop a study that would investigate that claim. It may be a good starting point, however—if we replace "important" with "necessary to facilitate productivity", that might be an easier thing to measure.

Third, theory can be evaluated based on **parsimony**, or how simple and straightforward it is (Wood, 2004). It is important to note that this quality of theory does not necessarily mean that theory cannot be complex or applicable to a myriad of situations. On the contrary, many parsimonious theories are in fact very complex and broad. To understand what it means to be parsimonious, it is helpful to consider the concept of **Occam's Razor**, a principle introduced by the fourteenth-century Franciscan friar and logician William of Ockham. Occam's Razor suggests that when we are faced with two competing perspectives or theories, the one that makes things simpler—or more parsimonious—is better (Gibbs and Hiroshi, 1997). SMCR is a parsimonious theory because it consists of four parts that describes how communication works, but Harold Lasswell's "who says what to whom through which channel and to what effect" model is also parsimonious, as it explains an additional layer of communication (effect) in a direct and simple way (Shoemaker & Reese, 1996). When we evaluate a theory for parsimony, we should be careful to see if there are any extraneous or unnecessary details that can be removed from the theory without hurting its overall predictive or descriptive ability.

The fourth and fifth principles of theory evaluation are closely related so we will discuss them together. In order to determine the value of a theory, we must critically analyze it in terms of its **utility**—its practical value and usefulness—and its **heurism**, or ability to encourage new thinking and inquiry (Wood, 2004). These two are relatively self-explanatory principles. If a theory does not describe the phenomenon we are interested in studying, then it is not a useful theory on its face. If we are studying behavior patterns in social media communication, it is relatively unlikely that a theory built around face-to-face communication would apply. Moreover, if we cannot use the theory to guide scientific inquiry, experiments, and the like, it is not heuristic and therefore not useful. Remember that science—social or otherwise—relies on the concept of replicating and building upon findings that have come before. Therefore, if a theory does not encourage the further development of science by inspiring new questions and new theories, it is not useful.

It is important to note that a theory does not have to excel in all of these categories to be considered good or useful. As Wood (2004) suggested, a theory can be highly heuristic but not terribly focused in scope. Uses and gratifications theory, a mass communication theory we will discuss later in this chapter, is incredibly parsimonious but falters in its scope—it is concerned with how people use media, and because people can use media for any number of reasons, there have been numerous permutations of the theory that occasionally makes it difficult to have a consistent discussion. It is better, in general, to simply keep these principles in mind and evaluate theory less in terms of whether it meets all of them and more in terms of whether it describes a phenomena and answers the questions you want to answer.

Testing Theory

So far in this chapter, we have discussed how we can develop theory as well as how we can evaluate it. However, we have yet to discuss how theories are actually implemented and tested. After all, one of our evaluation criteria for theory basically suggests that a theory is only as good as one's ability to use it. There are a plethora of ways to evaluate theory, and we will cover several of them very briefly—as you go on in your communication study, you will have the opportunity to delve into these research methods in more depth (as well as the ability to delve more specifically into theory itself). For now, we will just hit some of the most common ways of testing theory.

When discussing research methods, it is important to note that the method is often chosen both in terms of the theory and also in terms of the question it is intended to answer. Some methods are better at getting **quantitative** data, or data that is primarily numbers driven and can be analyzed in terms of trends and patterns. When we deal with quantitative data, we are generally dealing with large amounts of data derived from **samples** of a target population—if we are trying to analyze social media habits, we could ask the millions of people who live in America to tell us how they communicate using social media … or we could choose a smaller group of a few hundred or a thousand people who would be representative of the larger group. The process of obtaining such samples can often be intricate and there are numerous ways to do it (as you will learn in later courses) but generally you want to make sure that the sample is representative so you can generalize your findings out to the larger population.

Qualitative data, on the other hand, is much more narrowly focused on the reasons and motivations behind actions and trends—if quantitative data tells us what is happening, qualitative data tells us why it is happening. Unlike quantitative data, we cannot always draw larger trends from qualitative data, and it is often comprised of data that is not easily converted to numbers and graphs (though it is not necessarily impossible, and some forms of qualitative analysis do require looking for recurring patterns and numerical repetitions in the data). Qualitative data is generally used when you want to find out the deeper underlying reasons for why something is happening, or how people think and feel about a phenomenon. Some researchers see quantitative and qualitative data and methodical approaches as antagonistic and oppositional, but in reality, quantitative data can actually be a great starting point for qualitative inquiry and vice versa. For most communication problems, the willingness and ability to conduct and analyze both forms of research is vital.

Generally, quantitative methods are aimed at gathering large amounts of data. The most popular is the **survey**, a list of questions with objective options for answers that is distributed to a large sample of a population. There is a good chance you have yourself taken a survey—perhaps someone called you aside at the mall to answer some questions. Maybe someone called you at home and asked what you thought of the political candidates. Perhaps you received a request to fill out a survey online. Regardless of form, surveys generally have questions that are designed in accordance with the principles of a theory. From the data obtained in surveys, we can get a good snapshot of what a sample population is feeling at a given moment in time, or learn about behavior patterns and activities. The data, however, remains inert until we analyze it by looking for correlations between factors (Wood, 2004). Moreover, because these are not open-ended questions, we cannot get much qualitative data. We can also get quantitative data by conducting **experiments** where we attempt to find how a dependent variable is or is not influenced by the manipulation of an independent variable (Wood, 2004). Experiments are conducted generally in closed environments that control for **confounding variables**. For example, if we want to find out how nonverbal communication affects attention, we could have two people communicate in a room free of distractions and compare it to a room full of distractions. Experiments are powerful for determining causality, but the data can sometimes be skewed because they are inherently synthetic environments—it is unlikely we will ever have a room fully free of distractions. We can also gather quantitative data about the effectiveness of online communication from **Web analytics**, a growing form of quantitative analysis that uses Web-page-based code to track how long users stay on a page, where they come from, how often the Web page is viewed, and a number of other factors (Kent et al., 2011). This data, incredibly useful for marketers and public relations professionals, can tell us a lot about how audiences use a Web site (even if it cannot always tell us why).

Qualitative data can be gathered using a variety of methods. One of the most prominent is the **in-depth interview**, which is a structured conversation with a respondent aimed at exploring their involvement with and feeling toward a subject or phenomenon (Lindlof & Taylor, 2011). Because they are conversations, in-depth interviews can allow us to develop a deeper understanding of an issue on both an objective and a subjective level while helping respondents feel comfortable—someone who might be hesitant to reply to a survey about their workplace communication habits may open up at the chance to share their particular experiences or concerns with an interested party (Seidman, 2011). Similarly, **focus groups** allow us to have in-depth conversations with a larger group, generally around 6–10 people. A moderator asks the panel questions and encourages them to explore particular perspectives or ideas, as well as examine how the group communicates together—essentially, it is an interview on a larger scale

(Lindlof & Taylor, 2011). Focus groups are used quite often in product testing and marketing in order to find out how a panel of targeted customers react to a product or marketing campaign.

Qualitative researchers can also engage in **ethnographies**, where they embed themselves in a population and take careful notes about how that population operates. This perspective is aimed at gaining deeper understanding of a culture with which the researcher is unfamiliar, meaning the researcher may often take part in the culture's activities and rituals without assigning value judgements (Wood, 2004). Ethnographies are useful for getting in-depth information about a culture or a phenomenon but it can be difficult to extrapolate your findings beyond your observations; moreover, it is not always practical for all communication research. An updated form of the ethnography, called a **netnography**, allows researchers to delve into online communities with relatively little investment. Researcher Robert Kozinets (2002), who created the method, suggested that a researcher who wants to study the behavior of online communities needs to find a place where a large amount of community members congregate and directly and openly engage with community members. This has been especially useful for marketing research, as marketers and academics can examine customer behaviors and spending patterns simply by reviewing and participating in online discussions. Netnography combines elements of ethnography as well as another method, **textual analysis**, which involves the theory-driven close reading of communication texts in order to ascertain their dynamics and symbolic resonance (Wood, 2004). Textual analysis is quite often used in critical and rhetorical research and is not necessarily limited to text as we know it—indeed, textual analyses can analyze everything from the rhetorical dimensions of speech to the symbolic power of comic book superheroes. Textual analysis, though qualitative in nature, can also be quantified in **content analysis**, where recurring ideas, symbols, and patterns in a text are counted in order to derive patterns and trends in the text.

Regardless of the method chosen, any test of theory requires a few specific assessments of the questions asked and the hypotheses posed, as well as of the research itself. The two main criteria any test of theory (whether it is an experiment, textual analysis, survey, or any other form) must pass are **reliability** and **validity**. Validity refers to the ability of a test to truly and accurately measure what it intends to measure—for example, we know a study of teenage cell phone habits should involve people between the ages of 13 and 18 years, even though that range may hold a number of different uses and expectations of cell phone technology. If a test is reliable, the same test will return the same or similar results consistently over time (Wood, 2004). To understand how validity and reliability work, picture a target. Now imagine firing volley after volley of arrows at it. If you hit everywhere on the target without a consistent pattern, you are not a reliable shot. If you hit an area well above the bullseye consistently, you are reliable but not valid. However, if you group your shots in the center of the target every time, even with some variance that keeps you from hitting the bullseye dead-on, you are both reliable and valid and (by any standard) a good shot. The same principle applies to testing theory (Shoemaker & Reese, 1996). Consistency is important in the testing and the construction of theory, for if we cannot return the same results when we test a theory in different situations, the utility and heuristic capabilities of that theory will be in doubt.

These principles and methods for testing theory have been vital to the construction of communication theories that guide us through all aspects and levels of communication inquiry. In the next sections, we will delve briefly into some specific and applied forms of theory to give you a brief overview of how theory can be used to explain, predict, and, in some cases, critique communication phenomena. Please note that this is nowhere near an exhaustive list, but it will hopefully act as a way to spark your interest in studying theory further and seeing how it can apply to a variety of different communication situations.

Theories of Interpersonal Communication

Interpersonal communication, as discussed earlier in this text, is essentially any form of communication between individuals. Therefore, theories about interpersonal communication are primarily focused on the ways in which people communicate and interact with each other. Because the concepts of symbolism, interpersonal interaction, and communication dynamics are explored in great detail throughout this text, we will instead focus directly on some of the specific theories that we can apply to make sense of interpersonal communication.

Have you ever met someone for the first time? You are generally not really sure what to think of that person. Do they like you? Do you like *them*? Over time, you start to get to know the other person, and they start to seem less ambiguous and more personable. This is at the core of **Uncertainty Theory**, a theory that suggests communication is built around managing this ambiguity (Wood, 2004). Uncertainty Theory suggests a causal relationship between the level of communication in a situation and the level of uncertainty, suggesting (among other things) that as our communication with strangers increases, our level of uncertainty goes down; as our level of uncertainty goes down, we tend to like and trust people more. While this seems like an obvious idea, it, nonetheless, is powerfully heuristic and raises the question of how we might be able to manage uncertainty effectively to inspire greater affection; this could be applied to everything from interpersonal interaction to business communication.

A slightly more cynical view of human interaction comes to us through **Social Exchange Theory**, a theory that suggests that we make decisions in relationships based on the economic principles of maximizing rewards and minimizing costs (Wood, 2004). Generally, we tend to view rewards as those things that benefit us or have a positive impact—companionship, acceptance, loyalty—and costs as those that have a negative impact—time spent, lack of ability to participate in other relationships, abuse, or anger—and select those relationships that lean more heavily toward the former via an unconscious form of cost–benefit analysis. This (quite parsimonious) theory suggests that individuals are rational actors who will compare relationships against each other to find the most desirable outcome. You might at this point argue that people are not always rational when it comes to relationships, but this comparative property could suggest why people may stay in harmful or one-sided relationships—they may not see any better alternatives (Wood, 2004). Again, this theory can be quite heuristic—maybe you are already thinking of ways you could use it in class or in your everyday life.

Finally, let us consider **developmental theory**, a school of interpersonal theory that is interested in how relationships between people are formed over time (Wood, 2004). This theory began with the notion that there are multiple layers that must be penetrated in order for relationships to grow stronger, or what is known as the **social penetration model**. For relationships to grow stronger, the model suggests that we must go beyond the initial or superficial layers of likes and dislikes to find a middle layer of political and social views and attitudes; this middle layer rests atop an inner layer of spiritual beliefs and deep-seated dreams and fears and then finally at the core of the human being is their most basic self (Wood, 2004). Such penetration takes time, and as theorists discovered, human relationships are rarely if ever so linear. The next generation of developmental theory focused on how our individual perceptions of people and what they communicate to us, and the trajectories of our relationships are inspired by **turning points** that mark changes in the nature of a relationship—saying "I love you," having someone not show up for your birthday party, or any number of things (Wood, 2004). Instead of layers, contemporary developmental theory is more focused on **stages** or steps through which a relationship goes. These stages are generally organized in a trajectory or narrative, but that trajectory will differ for every relationship, and what trajectory the relationship takes will determine whether it becomes more or less intimate in nature.

Theories of Mass Communication

Mass communication theory moves its sights away from one-to-one or interpersonal communication to the one-to-many approach favored by broadcast and other forms of mass media. As we will discuss in later chapters, communication on the mass level is generally mediated in nature, which means that they are facilitated by some form of technology or medium. Theory in this area is often concerned with the effects of mass communication, due in no small part to the work of Harold Lasswell, who modified the traditional SMCR model by referring to mass communication in terms of this:

Who says **what** to **whom** through **which channel** to **what effect**?

Again, you can see the correlation between this model and the SMCR model, but it is Harold Lasswell's addition of an "effects" component—that the combination of these factors may lead to a particular or desired effect in the audience—that changes the dynamic and acts as a starting point for many of the theories we will discuss in this section. Generally, theories fall into one of the two categories—they are either **active media** theories, which suggest audiences are largely passive and influenced by powerful media, or they are **active user** theories, which suggest users are critical and powerfully engaged in their media decisions. Lasswell in particular advocated for one of the most potent active media theories, the **hypodermic needle theory**. The hypodermic needle theory suggested that the media were so powerful they affected all audiences equally and significantly with little ability for the audience to challenge the messages they received; therefore, messages could be explicitly tailored to get audiences to feel certain ways or do certain things. This perspective takes a pretty dire view of the media, viewing it less as a means of conveying information and entertainment than as a means of thought control (Harris, 2004). The idea that the media can effectively control the minds of the audience uniformly has more or less died down, though echoes of this theory still appear today—consider how many members of the media seem to think violence in the media will cause people to commit violent crimes, despite the lack of a conclusive causal link.

Mass communication theory has become much more complex since the days of the hypodermic needle theory and early propaganda-based research, and the relationship between audiences and media content has been explored in more nuanced ways. One of the most commonly used theories to understand media usage is the active user-focused **Uses and Gratifications** theory, which suggests that people use media to gratify particular needs—it accomplishes something for us (Baran & Davis, 2015). The theory breaks from the active media approach in some significant ways—it assumes that the audience is active and critical and will choose the media that best suit them from an open marketplace (Baran & Davis, 2015). Uses and gratifications theory, as it is built around the uses we find for media, is rather broad in scope and studies using the theory will often vary in terms of what elements they find most important. Some of the core or recurring gratifications include surveillance (the media tell us what is going on around us), interpretation (the media helps us analyze and make sense of what's happening), transmission of culture (the media convey norms and expectations of our society to us), and entertainment (the media act as an amusing diversion) (Baran & Davis, 2015). I may choose to watch the nightly news because I need to be informed, but I will select a comedy program like *Archer* if I wish to be entertained. This theory is powerfully heuristic and descriptive but is difficult to be parsimonious simply because there are so many uses for media.

This is not to say the active media approach has gone away—far from it. It has simply evolved into other forms. Researcher George Gerbner discovered that repeated and heavy exposure to television affects audience perceptions of the real world, particularly when it comes to crime and violence (Harris, 2004). This **Cultivation Theory** suggests that the repeated cumulative effect of exposure to violent media leads to what Gerbner called "Mean World Syndrome," in which people begin to think the real world is as mean and nasty as it often is on television (Harris, 2004). Interestingly, Gerbner's theory has been applied to media other than television and to issues such as the portrayals of race and gender and consistently found that heavy media consumers' worldviews tend to be more closely aligned with what they see in the media. Similarly, Albert Bandura's **Social Cognitive Theory** suggests that the media are one of many agents in our lives (along with our families, schools, churches, etc.) that serve to socialize us into the world and teach us how to act and behave; we pattern ourselves and our perspectives in part on what we see in the media (Harris, 2004). I may decide to dress like a character I saw on television or may use the relationships I see between parents in sitcoms as a yardstick for measuring the relationships in my own life. While these theories are certainly active media theories in nature, they offer slightly more complexity when it comes to the role of the audience and how the audience interacts with the media.

Many of the mass communication theories we have discussed so far have their roots in old media—radio, television, film, and broadcast. These theories are vibrant and potentially still useful but they do not account for the interactivity and greater social relation afforded by digital and interactive media. We will cover two of these theories here—the narrative database, online anonymity, and social network theory. The **narrative database** is a theory introduced by Lev Manovich (1999), who suggests that new media communication is best conceived as using an interface to interact with various **databases** of options and information. Manovich's definition can be applied to a variety of new media contexts, from Web sites to video games, which are databases which we use in a variety of interfaces to navigate through. The navigation through the database creates an individualized narrative (or **syntagm**) using the **paradigm,** or the options, language, and form provided to the user through the database. For example, think of Wikipedia—you may start out trying to conduct research for a communication theory paper, but you could click on a link for an important theorist, then discover that theorist had an interest in xylophones, then click on the link for xylophones, then expand your inquiry to percussion instruments in general, and so on. This theory is particularly heuristic because we can start to ask questions and conduct research into how the theoretical limits of the database influence what kind of syntagms are created.

Online communication is characterized in part by its ability to foster and facilitate relationships between individuals. **Social Network Theory** is concerned with how those relationships form and seeks to analyze how relationships between individuals influences the spread of social capital, or influence and power. While this theory has actually been around well before the popularization of social media, it has become much more popular because it offers a useful means of describing how social media connections operate. This theory comes with a set of variables and metrics that describe the facets of a social network, including **mutuality** (reciprocation of friendship or following), **density** (how many connections there are in a network), **centrality** (where an individual is located in a network), and many others, all built around the idea of understanding how social connections are maintained (Reid & Smith, 2009). Social network theory and its associated analysis can tell us a great deal about who the significant **nodes**, or individuals, are in a network; the commonality of connections between disparate groups can help to seek out opinion leaders and influencers. This can be especially useful for applied communication—if I am a marketer, I can look at a social network and find those people who have the most connections and specifically target them in the hopes of reaching the people to whom they are connected as well.

Critical Communication Theory

The final main branch of theory we will discuss in this chapter most closely aligns with the "reform" objective of theory we discussed earlier. **Critical theory** casts itself in opposition to what it views as inequality and oppression present throughout society and attempts to unveil and counteract these trends (Wood, 2004). In a communication context, this means that critical theorists attempt to find the **ideologies**, or recurring and ingrained patterns of belief, that drive and guide communication in a variety of ways (Althusser, 1965/1969). Critical theorists suggest that communication does not happen in a vacuum, but rather is highly influenced by ideology. Ideologies go beyond belief because they generally guide and control our perspective and social activity—moreover, we may not even consciously hold them! Often, ideologies are vaguely considered in terms of "just being the way things are," a sort of underlying social foundation that shapes our world through ritual and repetition while promoting particular forms of understanding and value relationships that go unquestioned (Croteau & Hoynes, 2003; Ferguson, 1998; Marcuse, 1964). Through ideology, we see ourselves a certain way, and we often see other groups in a way specifically proscribed by that ideological perspective. If this is somewhat confusing, don't worry. Critical theory is fundamentally complex and largely intangible in nature, so we will try to cover it very simply here with the understanding that you may delve into it in more detail in future classes.

Generally, the form critical theory takes is influenced by the ideology it identifies and is in opposition to. For example, a **feminist** critical theory would suggest that society is driven by the ideology of patriarchy or a system that espouses a very particular form of gender roles in which men are expected to be masculine and superior to women. Feminist critical theorists would argue that these roles are harmful to women and men alike by oppressing individual freedom and achievement. A **Marxist** critical theorist would identify capitalism as the ideology that drives society, creating distinct socioeconomic classes and promoting inequality that puts the upper class in power. Some critical theorists may well combine both of these theories, some will identify completely different ideologies, and some may even have a critical theoretical approach that is in direct opposition to these approaches.

One way we can take a critical approach to communication is through a critical approach to rhetoric. Raymie McKerrow (1989) suggested a critical approach to rhetoric seeks to reveal and identify discourses of power through how that power influences the way we communicate. McKerrow identified this less as a method and more as a state of mind that opposes powerful interests and proposes solutions. The goal of a critical approach to rhetoric is to find how communication justifies and normalizes the imbalance of power (Wander, 1988). Essentially, anyone analyzing a culture's rhetoric from a critical perspective is tasked with reconstructing it from a multitude of communication acts and texts across many different practices (McGee, 1990). Think of communication in this perspective as a vase that has been knocked off its shelf and shattered—we can take all the parts and glue them back together to create the form of a vase, even if that form is not perfect.

In our case, those pieces may include things like the pronouns we use when referring to people, episodes of *Family Guy*, the rhetoric used by our politicians, and countless other shards that make up our cultural communication. A critical approach to communication focuses on both the **epistemic** (immediately obvious) level of communication as well as the **doxa** (underlying and often subconscious) level (McKerrow, 1989). Is *Law and Order* a television series about police detectives and lawyers (epistemic), or is it a means through which we see the power granted to our legal system as legitimized, natural, and not to be questioned (doxa)? The goal of a critical approach to communication and rhetoric is to understand and analyze the function and meaning our symbolic communication has in a society (Biesecker, 1989; Foucault, 1980; McKerrow, 1989). Those symbols, of course, take many different forms, and it is the goal of the critical communication theorist to identify what those symbols are and how they replicate and transmit systems of power.

Because critical theory is somewhat broad in nature, there are not as many named and specific theories to discuss, but we can identify a few. **Muted Group Theory,** for example, suggests that language is primarily driven by the Western male experience, and the power given to language to name our experiences means that people who do not fit in that experience are often marginalized and "muted"; this in turn takes away their ability to express themselves in a meaningful way (Wood, 2004). You can see how this fits into a critical approach to rhetoric, as it demonstrates how these systems of power construct discourses and in this case also discuss who can contribute. Similarly, **Political Economy Theory** suggests that the control of the economy by powerful elite groups has a spillover effect that influences forms of communication, particularly the mass media (Baran & Davis, 2015). Critics using this theory suggest that the experiences and stories discussed in the mass media are limited and biased in order to support the interests of these groups (Baran & Davis, 2015). This is similar to Horkheimer and Adorno's (1944/2002) theory of **culture industries**, which suggests that these powerful elites construct popular culture and hand it down to a passive audience; this culture creates a skewed version of reality that supports the interests and values of a powerful cultural elite. In this theory, the masses are kept placated by a constant loop of new diversions, products, and entertainment that keeps them from questioning their situation; therefore, the media does not only sell products and experiences but it also acts as a form of social control (Horkheimer and Adorno, 1944/2002; Storey, 2009). As you can see, many critical theories are focused more on heurism rather than parsimony, which means that they can be used to flavor and guide more regimented theoretical approaches and inspire inquiry. They are also generally and closely related in a way many other forms of theories are not.

Wrapping It Up

Regardless of your personal theoretical perspective, it should be clear by now that there are a wide variety of approaches to thinking about communication on many different levels. There is no one theory that is the best or most descriptive, just as there is no one answer to every question (at least, not that we would accept). Part of being a successful communicator is understanding where and how you situate yourself in a communication context, and how your perspective may influence the way you communicate. You may not use theory in a direct way every day in your career, but it can be a useful guidepost to help guide effective communication and decision-making.

References

Althusser, L. (1969). *For Marx* (B. Brewster, Trans.). New York: Pantheon Books. (Original work published 1965).

Baran, S. J., & Davis, D. K. (2015). *Mass communication theory: Foundations, ferment, and future* (7th ed.). Stamford, CT: Cengage.

Biesecker, B. A. (1989). Rethinking the rhetorical situation from within the thematic of différance. *Philosophy and Rhetoric, 22*(2), 110–130.

Croteau, D., & Hoynes, W. (2003). *Media/society: Industries, images, and audiences.* Thousand Oaks, CA: Pine Forge Press.

Ferguson, R. (1998). *Representing race.* New York: Oxford University Press.

Foucault, M. (1980). *Power/knowledge: Selected interviews and other writings* (C. Gordon, ed.). New York: Pantheon Books.

Gibbs, P. & Sugihara, H. (1997). "What is Occam's Razor?" Retrieved from http://math.ucr.edu/home/baez/physics/General/occam.html.

Harris, R. J. (2004). *A cognitive psychology of mass communication* (4th ed.). Mahwah, NJ: Lawrence Erlbaum Associates.

Horkheimer, M., & Adorno, T. W. (1944/2002). *Dialectic of enlightenment.* (E. Jephcott, Trans.). Stanford, CA: Stanford University Press.

Kent, M. L., Carr, B. J., Husted, R. A., & Pop, R. A. (2011). Learning Web analytics: A tool for strategic communication. *Public Relations Review, 37,* 536–543.

Kozinets, R. V. (2002). The field behind the screen: Using netnography for marketing research in online communities. *Journal of Marketing Research, 39*(1), 61–72.

Lindlof, T. R., & Taylor, B. C. (2011). *Qualitative communication research methods* (3rd ed.). Thousand Oaks, CA: Sage.

Manovich, L. (1999). Database as symbolic form. *Convergence, 5*(2), 80–99.

Marcuse, H. (1964). *One-dimensional man.* Boston: Beacon Press.

McGee, M. C. (1990). Text, context, and the fragmentation of contemporary culture. *Western Journal of Speech Communication, 54*(3), 274–289.

McKerrow, R. E. (1989). Critical rhetoric: Theory and praxis. *Communication Monographs, 56*(2), 91–111.

Reid, N., & Smith, B. W. (2009). Social network analysis. *Economic Development Journal, 8*(3), 48–55.

Seidman, I. E. (1991). *Interviewing as qualitative research: A guide for researchers in education and the social sciences.* New York: Teachers College Press.

Shoemaker, P. J., & Reese, S. D. (1996). *Mediating the message: Theories of influences on mass media content* (2nd ed.). White Plains, NY: Longman.

Storey, J. (2009). *Cultural theory and popular culture: An introduction* (5th ed.). New York: Pearson.

Trochim, W. M. K. (2006). Deduction & induction. *Research methods knowledge base.* Retrieved from http://www.socialresearchmethods.net/kb/dedind.php.

Wood, J. T. (2004). *Communication theories in action: An introduction* (3rd ed.). Boston, MA: Wadsworth.

Wander, P. (1962). The ideological turn in modern criticism. *Central States Speech Journal, 34*(2), 1–18.

CHAPTER 6

Identity in Communication

Meta G. Carstarphen

Quickly—ask yourself one question: *"Who Am I?"* Now, if I asked you to describe this "identity" in just one word, would you be able to do so easily?

No doubt, like the rest of us, you might be able to immediately think of a dominant identity, or a description that leaps to the top of your mind first. It might, for instance, include any one of the following: male, female, student, instructor, blonde, redhead, Ghanaian, Swedish, athlete, scholar, parent, sibling, and so on. You get the picture. We tend to identity ourselves by roles that we play or by an overt characteristic or role that we play. The problem is that when you select one identity, you leave out many more. In my short list above, for example, it is possible that one person could claim to identify with nearly every one of the descriptive terms used above!

Identity and the Communication process

Identity plays a vital role in the communication process, even when we do not think it does. But one reason it does is that we all process messages we receive from a variety of information sources through the filters of our identities. Some will mean more to us than others at any given time, in part because the information we are receiving "triggers" some aspects of our identities more than others.

For instance, you are a student of a specific institution of higher learning. Imagine that you are now browsing your favorite news Web site and you see an article link about your school and its plan to adopt an important new measure that will affect all students. How likely would you be to at least scan that article for more information? Probably, you would be very likely. Now, imagine that same news about an institution several states away from where you live. How likely would you be now to read it? Probably, you would not be very likely to read past a glance, unless you had other compelling reasons to explore more. If your best friend, for example, attended that school you might very well want to learn more. In this case, your identity as a "best friend" might compel you to read an article that you would otherwise ignore.

These simple examples should help you begin to think about the complexities of identity construction and why identity is crucial to communication processes and institutions. This chapter will

- define identity,
- review key identity theories,
- discuss the applications identity for communicators and communication professions, and
- highlight strategies for applying an understanding of identity to communication in diverse and global contexts.

Defining Identity: Three Factors

Trying to find a commonly shared definition of identity may be the most challenging pursuit of all. By one measure, some researchers have counted a dramatic increase in the sheer number of written materials about the subject between the 1960s until now (Vignoles et al., 2011). Part of the challenge in wrestling to the ground a neat, concise meaning for the word "identity" is the fact that people have tried to analyze it from multiple viewpoints within the social science disciplines. We would look at a few of these perspectives but will not be in any way comprehensive. But a great way of thinking about identity is expressed in one singular question: "Who are you?" (Vignoles et al., 2011, p. 2). Although there are many ways of tackling possible answers to this question, we will define identity by looking at three factors: individual roles, social contexts, and time.

Figuring out who you are as well as who others are in your circles of influence and interactions involves some understanding of the external as well as internal identity cues that we all carry. In very general ways, it will be helpful to think of identity as comprising a sense of oneself as both an individual and as part of a community. Early research, for instance, connected identity experiences within family relations as adapting meaning through role performances (Stryker, 1968; Stryker & Burke, 2000). In other words, we first learn to formulate a sense of identity as individuals. And, individual roles are often the first way in which we think about identity.

So, a woman who chooses a role as a wife has added layers to her identity, not simply collapsed these two into one state of being. While this line of thinking highlights individual choices and personal role choices, there are social expectations that influence all of us in how we might perform a role (Burke & Reitzes, 1981). These expectations would normally have to do with our understanding of societal norms, or the "rules," about any number of roles we might play, including such as "wife," "husband," "student," and "teacher,".

Secondly, social expectations are part of the external influences of identity construction. A set of ideas about how group affiliation affects our sense of who we are central to social identity theory (Tajfel & Turner, 1986, 2004). So, for instance, research in this area explores how shared relationships in social and cultural groups, such as race and gender, affect our sense of identity. Is there an identity difference, for instance, between Chinese Americans, Latinos, Anglos (Whites), and African Americans women born in the United States, simply because of the racial category they were born into? Social identity theory invites us to connect whatever significance there might be in these group identities to an individual's thoughts, actions, and feelings.

As we think about identity in terms of answering the question, "Who are we?," it is easy to understand that this is no longer a simple question. And should we add the factor of time, we can see that even who we think we are can shift from one set of circumstances to the next. Think back to the type of person you were at age 6 and how you might have thought of your identity compared to now. Next, imagine your future 40 years from now. Can you even begin to think about the new identity roles you will have added by then, or even anticipate how your current sense of self might change? The music you listen to now might no longer be pleasing to your ears, meaning that you could no longer consider yourself a member of that fan community.

Even views and experiences that you might now consider fundamental to your identity—gender, sexuality, and race—might occupy a less salient, or important, role in your life four decades from now. So this third broad aspect of identity—time—introduces the possibility of changes tour sense of who we are, when measured in either short-term or long-term shifts. If we consider the possibility of identity movement, then we enter into the debate about whether our identities are stable or fluid (Vignoles et al., 2011, p.10).

The range of possible factors influencing identity construction is vast. It is possible to conceive of the answer to the question—"Who am I?"—as a combination of factors that include personal choices and social expectations. Some researchers call these "domains" of identity, or central areas, where each of us forms an identity position. One approach identifies four such domains (Vignoles et al., 2011, p. 18):

- Moral and spiritual
- Family, gender, and sexual
- Economic and civic
- Ethnic, cultural and national identities.

In light of all of these factors, we can define **identity** as a sense of oneself, comprising influences from biological, personal, and social factors, which change over time, and which presents itself differently depending upon motivations and influences. We will explore the idea of the social construction of identity in more detail, as we examine and challenge our thinking about the domains of gender, race, and moral identities.

Social Construction and Biological Determinism

I hope this exploration about identity so far has prompted you to question the idea of what is fixed, as opposed to variable; what is "stable" about our identities compared to what is "fluid." Before we discuss the social contexts in which identities may be influenced and shift, let's consider biological determinism. As the name suggests, this concept states that biological factors, which contribute to our physical existence—such as hair, skin color, and sex organs—help decide our capabilities and future potential.

The belief that physical traits are evidence of profound, unchanging divisions among human beings has directly contributed to potent fallacies. This thinking in US history, for example, has generated a racial "science" that has tried to link observable physical traits with intellectual capacity and the aptitude for "civilization" among various ethnic groups (Mukhopadhyay et al., 2014, p. 23). Let's be clear, though. We do see physical differences among people. There are differences in eye color and shapes of the eye, hair color and texture of hair, and skin tone and hue. These are true biological variations, scientists now argue, existing within one (human) race, illustrating that as a species, we are "remarkably alike" to each other at a genetic level (Mukhopadhyay et al , 2014, p. 80).

Similarly, biological determinism would argue that the fundamental physical differences between men and women dictate the capabilities between the sexes (Gauntlett, 2008, p. 18). Of course, ever since you squirmed through your middle school health class when perhaps an equally uncomfortable teacher tried to coax you through the "birds and the bees" lesson, you knew that boys and girls were different. Truthfully, you realized it long before you learned about some of the biology behind these differences.

But when did you "learn" that these differences mattered in achievement, future careers, and personal choices? Boys are better at (fill in the blank). Girls are only good at (fill in the blank). Men cannot be good teachers because they aren't nurturing. Women cannot be effective business leaders because they are not logical. When biology becomes the exclusive tool to explain identity roles, the science behind human variation becomes blurred. Connecting genetic capabilities to social outcomes pushes identity definitions into less scientific areas—ones that have more to do with power, privilege, and the chance to manipulate individual choice and opportunity.

If one's identity is not purely a matter of biology, or personal choice, then other research has argued that it is **socially constructed**. As this term suggests, social systems and expectations help define identities in terms of hierarchies, or structures of power. Another view of social construction is that it is shaped by "society and culture" and that people "can adapt and change" (Gauntlett, 2008, p. 18).

Social construction can also idealize identities, giving all of us explicit and implicit messages about what we should value and what we should try to become. And these messages vary from one social setting to another. So, let's consider how this might work in gender identities. From a biological perspective, we might identity a person as belonging to either a male or female sex. From there, however, there will be many influences upon how that person is gendered; that is to say, how "one's future is structured within gendered norms and expectations." (Oyserman & James, 2011, p. 126).

Social expectations about gender identity influence not only the roles people choose but also the level of approval received. So, if a woman adopts a gendered role that highlights her physical attractiveness over her intellectual abilities, she may be seen as "more of a woman" than others. Similarly, males who emphasize physical prowess and aggressive behaviors may be celebrated as a "real man" over men who are not. Gender identity, ultimately, may include how we perform our roles to others as well as the levels to which we can represent ourselves to others (Carstarphen, 2016).

As we have seen, racial identities are constructs that may have begun with perceived biological differences but have been proven to inaccurate measures of human abilities. For instance, let's say African Americans are socially constructed as superior athletes. At first glance, this might seem to be a positive, and even complimentary, assessment. But if this perceived identity discourages recognition of, say, African Americans as scientists, then this "social construction" is limiting. Similarly, if Jewish Americans are constructed only as businesspeople, their participation in other fields might be obscured.

Socially constructed identities, especially when amplified through repetitive and frequent media portrayals, can easily carry the weight of truth. These can also be the basis of stereotypes or inaccurate portrayals of a person or group based upon an exaggerated negative trait (Bramlett-Solomon & Carstarphen, 2014, p. 156). In the media, stereotypes can be especially troubling, because they repeat themselves widely, over lots of screens and pages, and gain influence when people form groups around the same erroneous thinking (Bramlett-Solomon & Carstarphen, 2014).

Identity and Applied Communication Contexts

Communication and identity are so intertwined that it would be impossible to separate the two. Every day, we encounter messages that someone crafted with us in mind. And, if we are aspiring to professional communication careers, then we're developing those skills and abilities that will allow us to influence people using any number of communication tools. As you've learned in Chapter 2, rhetoric is the basis of strategic communication, and identifying your audience is key. It seems that communication messages can be powerfully influential in the ways that we see ourselves, the world around us, and each other.

Sometimes, these impressions can sneak up on us. For instance, ideal beauty standards in the media may prompt women to see their own bodies differently when they try to measure how they look, compared to the movie stars, models, and other glamorous females portrayed. Some research says that racial identity matters, as women of color with strong cultural ties may develop their own definitions of beauty based upon women who look like them in their communities (Sanderson, Lupinski, & Moch, 2013). Major advertisers who want to widen the base for their goods and services make strategic choices to display diverse images and welcoming messages.

In advertising, companies and brands do what they can to foster customer loyalty to their companies, continually learning how strongly groups can identify with a particular brand (Lam et al., 2010). And in the entertainment sphere, even the identities of the starring characters in superhero movies can communicate subtle messages about power and privilege (Carr, 2014).

In other instances, our identity frameworks cause us to choose communication messages that affirm our identities. This seems very pronounced, for instance, in political-oriented media. Consider "partisan media"—that is, mediated programs that intentionally target audiences belonging to one political party or another. Many observers believe that such media help create divisions based upon the strong opinions expressed. But research shows that people who already identify strongly with one party or another choose the media based upon that affinity (Levendusky, 2013). However, over time, audiences who support only like-minded media develop attitudes that are more negative toward oppositional views, making cooperation and compromise more difficult (p. 576).

In the rough-and-tumble world of political communication, candidates and their advisers know that their messages must connect with various "identity" groups in order to be successful. Perhaps, as this research suggests, the most important identity is political affiliation.

Another way that identity can impact working lives is through cultural background, ethnicity, and workplace communication, especially when organizations have diverse employees (Mannix & Neale, 2005). One study, for instance, sought to assess how employees for an international company from two countries were learning to work together. As employees formed groups around their shared national identities, **in-groups** and **out-groups** developed, pointing to boundaries that may need to be managed in order to strengthen overall "corporate" identity (Suzuki, 1998, p. 176).

These brief examples are all variations of how an understanding of group formations provides insights into individual and mass identities. These are often explained as "in-group" and "out-group" dynamics. In-groups are ways of classifying people who come together around shared interests and/or experiences and who form a majority in a given setting. Out-groups, in contrast, are excluded from the majority and are defined by shared traits that the "in-groups" believe to be negative (Tajfel, 1978; Tajfel & Turner, 1986, 2004). Importantly, for our study, these groups bond over shared communication—both positive and negative—about themselves and others.

In-groups became stronger as positive communication about them increased, as well as negative information about others seemed stronger, especially when the social and self-identifications seem mutual (Reynolds et al., 2000). For instance, if highly successful athletes who define their own identities solely by their competitive successes, they could form a group identity that believes that physical prowess makes them superior individuals. As a result, then they might be likely to put down others who are not athletic. But if these same successful athletes connect with other groups where there are people of mixed physical abilities, they are far more likely to communicate with less rigidity and less bias with those not like them.

Transactional Communication: Towards a New Identity Framework

Identity infuses every aspect of our communication processes, from speaker, message, to receiver. And, it is clear that all of us process and produce these messages from the perspectives of complex, and even competing, identity constructions. But in increasingly globalized and multicultural contexts, our biggest challenges may be to learn how to express ideas and to receive them, from multiple and diverse groups.

Perhaps it's time to think of such communication exchanges through what I call a **Transactional Communication Model** as a framework for communicating about difference. Transactional communication builds upon the rhetorical "exchange" that is at the heart of both the challenge and the opportunity to successfully engage with diverse publics. Rather than a set of prescribed tactics, Transactional communication bridges the seeming gap between publics by acknowledging, not ignoring, the identity differences that may be part of particular groups and individual networks. Defined, this transactional model that uses communication to represent a relationship between constituents where difference is strategically identified, expressed, and negotiated.

Making transactional communication work involves expressing a concept of value, perceived or actual, to the exchange between diverse groups. Without such strategic overtures, out-groups are likely to feel marginalized by in-groups, and such perceptions could undermine effective communication. Successes with transactional messages can perhaps overtake negative messages that reinforce rigid identity boundaries through extreme comparisons of which identity groups are inherently better than others.

Bringing It All Together

Communication and identity are intertwined. Who we are (or who we think we are) influences every aspect of the way we receive and interpret messages, construct them, or seek to influence others. Understanding what makes identity is multifaceted and involves understanding of individual and social contexts. We are, in the end, more than the sum of our biological DNA. What helps define us and each other involves traits that are indelible parts of ourselves, as well as the full range of individual and social agency we choose to employ.

References

Bhabha, H. K. (2015). "The Beginning of Their Real Enunciation": Stuart Hall and the work of culture. *Critical Inquiry, 42*(1), 1–30.

Bramlett-Solomon, S., & Carstarphen, M. G. (2014). *Race, Gender, Class and Media: Studying Mass Communication and Multiculturalism* (2nd ed.). Dubuque, IA: Kendall-Hall.

Burke, P. J., & Reitzes, D. C. (1981). The link between identity and role performance. *Social Psychology Quarterly, 44*(2), 83–92.

Carr, B. (2014). Reframing the secret identity of whiteness: The rhetorics of white privilege in superhero media. In M. Baliff (Ed.), *Re/Framing Identifications* (pp. 269–276). Long Grove, IL: Waveland Press.

Carstarphen, M. G. (2016). Historicizing sexual rhetorics: Theorizing the power to read, the power to interpret, and the power to produce. In J. Alexander & J. Rhodes (Eds.), *Sexual Rhetorics: Methods, Identities Publics* (pp. 72–78). New York, NY: Routedge/Taylor & Francis.

Gauntlett, D. (2008). *Media, Gender and Identity: An Introduction.* New York, NY: Routledge.

Lam, S. K., Ahearne, M., Hu, Y., & Schillewaert, N. (2010). Resistance to brand switching when a radically new brand is introduced: A social identity theory perspective. *Journal of Marketing, 74*, 128–146.

Levendusky, M. (2013). Partisan media exposure and attitudes toward the opposition, political communication. *Political Communication, 30*(4), 565–581.

Mannix, E., & Neale, M. A. (2005). What differences make a difference? The promise and reality of diverse teams in organizations. *Psychological Science in the Public Interest, 6*(2), 31–55.

McRae, L. (2003). Rethinking tourism: Edward said and a politics of meeting and movement. *Tourist Studies, 3*(3), 235–251.

Mukhopadhyay, C. C., Henze, R., & Moses, Y. T. (2014). *How Real Is Race? A Sourcebook on Race, Culture, and Biology.* Lanham, MD: Alta Mira.

Oyserman, D., & James, L. (2011). Possible identities. In S. J. Schwartz, K. Luyckx, & V. L. Vignoles (Eds.), *Handbook of Identity Theory and Research, Vols. 1 & 2.* New York, NY: Springer Science + Business Media.

Reynolds, K. J., Turner, J. C., & Haslam, S. A. (2000). When are we better than them and they worse than us? A closer look at social discrimination in positive and negative domains. *Journal of Personality and Social Psychology, 78*(1), 64–80.

Schwartz, S. J., Luyckx, K., & Vignoles, V. L. (Eds.). (2011). *Handbook of Identity Theory and Research, Vols. 1 & 2.* New York, NY: Springer Science + Business Media.

Stryker, S. (1968). Identity salience and role performance. *Journal of Marriage and the Family, 4,* 558–64.

Stryker, S., & Burke, P. J. (2000). The Past, Present, and Future of an Identity Theory. *Social Psychology Quarterly, 63*(4), 284–297.

Suzuki, S. (1998). In-group and out-group communication patterns in international organizations: Implications for social identity theory. *Communication Research, 25*(2), 154–182.

Tajfel, H. (1978). Social Categorization, social identity and social comparison. In H. Tajfel (Ed.), *Differentiation Between Social Groups: Studies in the Social Psychology of Intergroup Relations* (pp. 61–76). London: Academic Press.

Tajfel, H., & Turner, J. C. (1986). The Social Identity Theory of Intergroup Behaviour. In W. G. Austin & S. Worchel (Eds.), *Psychology of Inter-Group Behaviour* (2nd ed., pp. 7–24). Chicago, IL: Nelson-Hall.

Tajfel, H., & Turner, J. C. (2004). The Social Identity Theory of Intergroup Behavior. In J. T. Jost & S. Jim (Eds.), *Political Psychology: Key Readings* (pp. 276–293). New York: Psychology Press.

Vignoles, V. L., Schwartz, S. J., & Luyckx, K. (2011). Introduction: Toward an integrative view of identity. In S. J. Schwartz, K. Luyckx, & V. L. Vignoles (Eds.), *Handbook of Identity Theory and Research, Vols. 1 & 2.* New York, NY: Springer Science + Business Media.

Broadcast and Traditional Media

There is no question we live in an incredibly mediated world. Everywhere we go, there are screens and speakers blaring, telling us about important news events, entertaining us, and (often most importantly) trying to sell us things. For a fun experiment, try this—keep track of all your media usage for three days. Every time you turn on the radio, flip through the channels on television, check your Facebook or other social media, listen to a song on your MP3 player, or watch a movie, write it down. As you fill up those pages, you'll soon find that you are spending a lot of time with media, even when you think you aren't!

The **media** have been a huge part of our lives—it's hard to imagine a world without television, radio, or any of the other **broadcast media** we rely on to keep us safe, informed, and entertained. To put it in perspective, radio has been a viable commercial medium for nearly a century, television for over 70 years. And of course we've had the telephone and newspapers even longer than that. The rise of mediated communication forms also means a change in how we have come to understand and interpret communication—the standard one-to-one model that characterizes interpersonal communication needs to be reevaluated to accommodate this kind of **mass**

communication, where one speaker or source communicates the same message out to a wide audience. This has been the dominant model of communication in the mediated age; however, there are multiple technological and socioeconomic developments challenging that perspective. We will address some of those concerns later in this chapter and more thoroughly in the next.

This chapter is primarily concerned with traditional broadcast media—radio and television. You will learn more about newspapers and journalism in Chapters 9 and 10, and we will delve much more deeply into digital media in the next chapter. However, it is important to understand how radio and television have developed into such influential cultural forces, as well as unpack the societal forces that have shaped these media and the way we communicate across them.

A Very Brief History of Broadcast Media

When talking about the history of broadcasting, it is important to note that both radio and television influenced each other a great deal. Understanding the relationship between these two very different media will help shed light on the contemporary communication environment of which they are a part. An entire book could be devoted simply to the history of broadcast media, but for our purposes, a brief look should suffice.

In 1864, the Scottish physicist **James Clerk Maxwell** published a paper suggesting the existence of electromagnetic waves that traveled through air and space at the speed of light and could theoretically be used to transmit signals; two decades later the German physicist **Heinrich Hertz** would prove Maxwell's theory by demonstrating the existence of radio waves but ironically he did not think it was of any practical or commercial use (Maxwell, 1865; Keith, 2010). Maxwell and Hertz's work provided the scientific principles for radio upon which **Guglielmo Marconi** would later expand. Inspired by Hertz's work, Marconi had conducted experiments with wireless transmissions from a young age. By the late 1890s, Marconi was making breakthroughs in **wireless telegraphy** by sending **Morse Code** signals across increasingly vast distances without the need for the wires that had characterized the existing telegraph network (Campbell et al., 2013). Marconi opened his own company and installed wireless devices on land as well as ships at sea. It is worth noting that Marconi was not the only researcher working on wireless transmissions—a Russian researcher named Alexander Popov was doing similar experiments and the famous inventor Nikola Tesla had developed a device capable of sending electricity wirelessly as well (Campbell et al., 2013). Later, in the early 1990s, **Reginald Fessenden**, a Canadian engineer working for General Electric transmitted the first one-to-many voice broadcast from land to ships at sea and proved the idea of **wireless telephony** (or the wireless transmission of voice and music) possible. However, the practicality of radio as a home device would not truly be apparent until the devices were smaller and more affordable—the equipment needed to pick up and amplify signals was not convenient or practical for personal use. Around the time Fessenden was doing his broadcasts, **Lee De Forest** developed the **audion vacuum tube**, which was able to detect and amplify radio signals and boost their range. This device became an integral part of radio until the development of smaller, cheaper **transistors** in the 1940s (Campbell et al., 2013). However, radio was still largely an experimental medium, looking for a chance to grow.

In the mid-1910s, **David Sarnoff**, a manager at the American branch of Marconi's wireless company, supposedly proposed an idea that would revolutionize the growing radio industry—broadcast music and other content to radio enthusiasts and turn a hobbyist medium into an entertainment service that could be broadcast to any household that owned the right equipment. This idea not only represented a dramatic shift in how radio was used, but it is also argued to be the start of the concept of **broadcasting** (one source to many receivers) as a business (Benjamin, 2002). Later, as general manager of RCA, Sarnoff arranged for a live broadcast of a heavyweight championship boxing match between Jack Dempsey and Georges Carpentier, which proved to be a smash hit and put sales of RCA's radio equipment through the roof (PBS, 1997). Sarnoff rose through the ranks at RCA to eventually run the company, overseeing the rise of radio as an entertainment medium over which he happened to exert a great deal of legal control. Under Sarnoff, RCA focused primarily on acquiring patents for various radio technologies, as we will discuss momentarily.

The federal government became interested in the power of radio around this time, taking steps to address the chaotic "free-for-all" nature of the radio airwaves. The early days of radio were a cacophony of competing signals that regularly conflicted with each other, making many broadcasts inaudible as multiple broadcasters attempted to broadcast on the same signal. Moreover, the airwaves were full of broadcasters who were less interested in serving the public with relevant information than they were simply experimenting with the medium (Mullen, 2008). A series of radio conferences were called by then-President Herbert Hoover to address the problem, culminating in the **Radio Act of 1927** that created the **Federal Radio Commission,** an early governing body tasked with assigning licenses to prospective private broadcasters (Mullen, 2008). Later, the **Communications Act of 1934** replaced the FRC with the Federal Communications Commission, an organization that expanded on the FRC's power in two important ways—not only were they tasked with regulating other forms of mass communication (most notably television), but they also enacted specific policies requiring license holders to operate in the **public interest** by airing programs that met societal needs. We will explore the regulation of the broadcast industry later in this chapter.

Much of the technological development of television happened concurrently to radio. In the 1880s, German inventor **Paul Nipkow** experimented with turning images into a transmittable form and invented the **scanning disk**, a large metal disk that when spun turned pictures into points of light that could be transmitted electronically

(Campbell et al., 2013). Many years later, **Vladimir Zworykin** built upon Nipkow's idea of separating images into points of light with his **iconoscope,** a camera tube that converted those light rays into electric signals—Zworykin took a job with RCA, who helped him patent it. That patent would become a point of contention later, as around the same time Zworykin was working on his device, a young scientist named **Philo Farnsworth** had already transmitted the first electronic TV picture. In 1930, RCA attempted to sue Farnsworth for patent infringement, but the case was thrown out after Farnsworth's high-school teacher produced some of his student's original drawings (Campbell et al., 2013). Let Farnsworth's story be a lesson to you—be nice to your teachers, you might need them later! Later, RCA would demonstrate TV at the 1939 World's Fair, but it is important to note that Farnsworth had done a public demonstration prior to that in 1934. While there are many who could lay claim to being the "father of radio," Farnsworth is generally accepted as the "father of television."

The interplay between radio and television at this point is important to understand—most of the popular radio talent left that format in the 1940s and 1950s for the increasingly more lucrative field of television. Television had essentially usurped the position of "entertainment for everybody" from radio, and it is at this point their purposes diverge. Radios had become increasingly smaller and cheaper and, for this reason, were included in many cars at a time when the country was spending more time driving around. These programming and technological changes cause a shift in radio programming toward focusing on music. While the **AM broadcasting** standard had enjoyed a perpetual monopoly on the industry, thanks to Sarnoff's efforts, it also had significant weaknesses. The signal could travel vast distances, especially at night, but was prone to interference and had poor overall sound quality that only came through one channel. **FM broadcasting**, a standard Sarnoff had fought to keep from coming to market since 1933 because of the threat it posed to RCA's monopoly, offered two channels of audio and comparatively crystal-clear sound. Upon its approval in 1961, many commercial radio stations switched over to music-driven formats; the availability of left and right audio channels also changed the way music was recorded and produced. Ironically, despite Sarnoff's efforts, the FM standard brought his view of the "radio music box" to its fullest fruition.

The 1930s and 1940s saw the rise of television networks as well as the start of monetizing the industry. Television was largely an expensive theoretical medium largely confined to demonstrations like those Farnsworth and RCA were conducting until the end of World War II, when stations that had been temporarily suspended as part of the war effort resumed broadcast and returning Americans started investing in the new technology for their homes (Mullen, 2008). Much like the popular radio programs of the day, television programs were generally presented by a single sponsor who was given exclusive rights over the program, though this model would become less popular as networks sought more control (Campbell et al., 2013). ABC, NBC, and CBS all started around this time as outgrowths of their existing radio networks; these television networks offered programming to local **affiliates** who rebroadcast that programming into their respective markets. We will cover the affiliate system later on in this chapter, as it still endures today.

As television grew in popularity, the problem of how to get it into homes became a challenge for some areas where television signals did not reach. In the 1940s, this problem lead to the creation of small **CATV**, or cable TV networks, in areas around the country (Mullen, 2008). In these networks, a cable was run from a receiver that could receive network programming in one area to subscriber homes further away. Though cable was restricted from some of the largest media markets during the 1960s, the 1970s saw relaxed regulations and the advent of satellite technologies that allowed for the introduction of specific niche channels (Mullen, 2008). While over-the-air television aimed for the broadest possible base in its appeal, cable was able to create channels with specific and limited program types aimed at specific audiences. In 1975, Time Inc. introduced the Home Box Office channel, now known as HBO, which aired unique documentaries, exclusive coverage of boxing, and sporting events, and in 1977, began airing first-run Hollywood movies (Mullen, 2008). Other **basic cable** channels (which did not require the separate subscription fee of HBO and its competitors) broadcast religious programming (CBN), Congressional hearings and debates (C-SPAN), and sports and entertainment programming (ESPN) (Mullen, 2008). None of these channels would survive in the expensive terrestrial broadcast market but cable audiences latched onto them. This model of using narrowly focused programming, called **narrowcasting**, continues to be the de facto business model for cable systems today.

The **big three** networks—CBS, ABC, and NBC—operated mostly without any major competition apart from a few also-ran networks until 1985, when the Australian company **News Corporation** bought out the 20th Century Fox film studio at the same time they bought television stations in many markets. In order to provide programming to these stations, they formed the Fox TV network, which premiered in 1986 with a late-night talk show hosted by comedienne Joan Rivers (Harmetz, 1986). On the back of popular, edgy programming like *Married with Children, Cops,* and perhaps most important of all (at least, to your humble author) *The Simpsons,* Fox gradually moved from last place to a major player in the broadcast television industry. By 1993, they had enough clout to acquire the rights to NFL games and even outbid more established networks like CBS (Carter, 1993). Fox reached a milestone in the 2007–2008 TV season—for the first time, it had the most viewers of any of the broadcast networks, thanks in large part to its popular reality singing competition *American Idol* (de Moraes, 2008). Later, other independent networks would jump into the affiliate fray—competing youth-oriented networks UPN and The WB became The CW, and an increasing number of affiliates partnered with the Spanish-language network Telemundo to serve the growing Hispanic and Latino demographics (Warner, 2009). Despite the competition, most network television tends to be as broad-based in appeal as possible.

Increasing competition from the Internet and other sources as well as rising production costs sparked a revolution in television content toward the end of the twentieth century. While we often consider **reality television** to be a recent invention, the genre has been around in some form or another since the late 1980s due to its low production costs and relative lack of need for writers and other overhead—*Cops* was one of the many factors in Fox's success as a fledgling broadcast network specifically because it was compelling programming that was also inexpensive to produce. Reality television is characterized most often by its mixing of traditional forms of scripted entertainment—soap operas, comedies, and the like—into theoretically more documentary-like situations that are at least somewhat unscripted (Edwards, 2013). This lack of scripting has proven to be a matter of concern for television writers and also served television networks well during the 2007 writers' strike (Edwards, 2013). Some reality shows, such as *Survivor* and *American Idol*, also introduce a competition element in which competitors are "voted off" the show either by their fellow contestants or through the intervention of the home audience through text messages and Web site votes. The success of these programs is without question (put in some reality show ratings here) and reality programming now even has its own category at the Emmy awards (Edwards, 2013). While the genre fluctuates in popularity, in an uncertain media market, it is unlikely to go away any time soon.

Broadcasting in the Future

There is no question the Internet has changed the way broadcasting operates in terms of content production. Broadcasters can now take advantage of a myriad of different technologies in order to facilitate reporting and storytelling. The Internet allows for on-the-spot news reporters to record footage and transmit it wirelessly back to the station, and the **convergence** of multiple devices into fewer and fewer devices make it easier for reporters to not only gather and edit content but also post it to a variety of different platforms (Pavlik, 2008). A television reporter can use their cell phone to shoot video, edit it, transmit it back to the station, and also post it on the station's social media platforms without breaking a sweat. The news industry has already moved toward these so-called **one-man bands** for years, and new digital technologies are making it even easier.

Television, while still one of the most influential media and a major content generator, is no longer the dominant avenue for video consumption it once was. Services like Netflix, Hulu, and YouTube offer hours of video content; this combined with the increasing costs of cable and satellite subscriptions have led to the rise of the so-called "**cord-cutters**," or those people who elect to stream video from online services and use free HD over-the-air broadcast signals to get their entertainment and information rather than pay subscription fees for cable and satellite. Specialized content providers are also embracing the digital future and offering subscriptions for users to stream their content online—Major League Baseball, the National Hockey League, and World Wrestling Entertainment are just a few of the companies who have found success cutting out the distribution middleman and streaming directly to consumers. These services are referred to as **over the top services** specifically because they "cut out" proprietary cable and satellite equipment and services (Hall, 2010). Those who still watch television through cable or satellite services use technology like **digital video recorders**, or DVRs, to **time-shift** television programming to watch at a time convenient to the user. This is a dramatic shift in terms of how television is consumed—while viewers were once beholden to the schedules of broadcasters, now they can program their own schedule of shows they are interested in, even fast-forwarding past commercials. As you might imagine, being able to skip past the commercials that fund broadcast programming poses some interesting challenges to programmers and marketers alike—we will discuss some of these problems in the next section.

Radio has also experienced a great deal of competition from online sources. **MP3 players** have been providing listeners with self-selected, high-quality music content for years, and as multiple devices converge into one singular device—generally, the smartphone—they have gone from a luxury item to near ubiquity. **Streaming radio services** like Pandora and Spotify have proven to be incredibly popular with the younger audience advertisers desire. To compete, many traditional radio stations have begun offering live **simulcasts** of their over-the-air content online via their Web sites or branded smartphone apps; these simulcasts can be especially useful for reaching listeners in their workplaces and may also act as an important source of secondary revenue for the station.

New technologies have also created alternatives for radio. One of the most popular is **podcasting**, a form of broadcasting that utilizes digital media players and content aggregators such as Apple's iTunes to deliver narrowly targeted specialty programs on a direct subscription basis to listeners. Podcasts have proven to be an especially popular way for niche programming to find an audience and even become profitable in a way it could not through traditional media. One of the most popular podcasts in recent memory, National Public Radio's *Serial,* conducted an ongoing investigation into a closed murder case in Baltimore. The podcast became a major media event, spawning untold pages of online discussion and sleuthing as it became the fastest-ever podcast to reach five million downloads and streams (Dredge, 2014). However, this also belies the challenge of podcasting—because the barrier to entry is so low (anyone with a microphone and Internet connection can podcast), the number of shows is enormous, and the best way to find massive audiences is to have prior success in traditional media or be associated with a popular media brand. Often, it can be difficult for smaller podcasts to compete financially, so many podcasters view it as a hobby in the same way most early amateur radio operators did.

The **Satellite radio** industry began in the early part of the twenty-first century, promising commercial-free narrowcasted content beamed to users across the country and the world from satellites orbiting the Earth. Theoretically, this allowed users to listen to the same station without the loss of signal or quality anywhere they went, a selling point terrestrial radio could not claim (Campbell, 2013). Initially, due to its high-quality audio and lack of FCC restrictions (the FCC does not regulate satellite radio content, for reasons we will discuss toward the end of this chapter) as well as its sports programming and niche content, the service was popular. However, the services offered by chief competitors Sirius and XM were subscription based, and the number of people willing to pay to subscribe to a medium they were used to get for free was not big enough to sustain two companies. In 2008, Sirius and XM merged their operations and customer base into a single company called SiriusXM (Campbell, 2013). Despite the shaky start, satellite radio proved enticing for many terrestrial radio programs and their hosts. The early to mid-2000s saw the FCC take a significant interest in broadcast content, driving the likes of Howard Stern and Opie and Anthony toward SiriusXM's less regulated airwaves. Stern, the prototypical "shock jock" who had long been one of the most marketable names in radio, signed a deal with Sirius in 2006 worth $100 million a year; as of this writing, his current contract signed in 2010 is undisclosed but is likely still in that ballpark (Stelter, 2015). Exclusive programming like Stern and live broadcasts of major sports events from multiple markets continue to make satellite radio a viable option—and potential alternative to traditional radio.

Advertising and Programming

The first thing an aspiring broadcaster should know is that radio and television are fleeting media—a broadcast on either medium goes out over the air and dissipates when it is done, leaving behind little that is tangible (Moriarty et al., 2015). Compare this to say, a newspaper, which once published can be held, shared, or displayed in perpetuity or at least until you are tired of having it around. This makes advertising a tricky proposition at times.

Before we get into the specifics of marketing and advertising on radio and television, it is important to understand that each medium has its specific strengths. While they both serve to inform and entertain their audiences, radio is much more pervasive and can appear everywhere from cars to grocery stores. Virtually, every household in America has at least one radio or device capable of picking up radio signals, and almost everyone listens to at least an hour of radio a day (Moriarty et al., 2015). This means the potential audience for radio is massive. Moreover, radio can be used while doing other things; hence, its popularity as a medium people listen to while driving—it is hard to watch TV and keep your eyes on the road, after all! Radio is also generally more cost-effective and faster to change if necessary. However, television does a much better job than radio of attracting and holding our attention—we are a very visual society, and TV caters to that. Visuals are also incredibly powerful and allow for demonstrations and explanations that are much more effective than audio alone.

TV also tends to have the broadest reach in terms of its audience—nearly everyone watches TV and many people even plan their schedule around it, though again that is less common now with time-shifting (Moriarty et al., 2015). It is worth pointing out, however, that television audiences are often built around **seasons** or specific time periods in the year—fall and winter tend to be where the most new programming and returning favorites land so they draw the most audiences, leaving networks to try to find replacements for late spring and summer to maintain their audiences and ratings.

Most radio stations broadcast in specific **formats** that play a particular kind of music or programming; the stations do not deviate from these formats and they generally play a role in the station's marketing. While there has been an increase in popularity in recent years of the "we play everything" or **JACK-FM** format, most radio stations are targeted to specific niche audiences. In general, the most popular formats for radio are the Country, News/Talk, and Contemporary Hit Radio formats; Country and News/Talk in particular tend to have incredibly loyal listeners who spend a great deal of time listening to their favorite stations and format (Nielsen, 2014). In the late 1960s, the **Corporation for Public Broadcasting** was formed; shortly thereafter, the **public radio** format began, carrying limited-interest programming such as classical music and in-depth news reporting (Keith, 2010). Unlike commercial radio stations, which can sell advertising for profit, public radio and television stations are supported through donations from listeners and increasingly limited public funding. Such stations can also receive **underwriting** from corporate sponsors, though these messages cannot carry advertising slogans or **calls to action** that inspire the listener to purchase or do something. Whichever format a radio station uses, it generally broadcasts to a **targeted** audience made up of listeners that meet specific demographic and psychographic criteria.

Over-the-air television stations, like your local TV stations, generally do not broadcast in formats. Instead, they are **affiliates** who enter into contracts with network providers like CBS, ABC, Fox, and the CW. In exchange for carrying network advertising and in some cases sharing revenue, these affiliates get high-quality network-produced programming that can be very attractive to prospective local advertisers. Programs like *The Big Bang Theory* and *The Blacklist* attract massive audiences but are beyond the budget and production ability of local stations to produce, so this is a mutually beneficial arrangement. Depending on the affiliation, local affiliates can fill over one-third of their day with network shows from drama to news to sports, leaving the rest to be filled with lucrative local news and **syndicated** programming (Warner, 2009). Syndicated programming is programming that does not belong to a specific network and can be carried by any station. Such programming may be **first-run** original programming like *Wheel of Fortune*, which premieres in syndication, or it may be rebroadcasts of programs that originally aired on other networks (Warner, 2009). Regardless of what kind of programming they air, over-the-air network affiliates generally attempt to attract the largest audience possible, often by offering broad and inoffensive shows that most people can agree on called **least objectionable programming** (or LOP). By comparison, cable channels are much closer to radio stations in that they broadcast specific types of programming aimed at very specific and limited audiences—ESPN broadcasts specifically to sports fans, Comedy Central broadcasts specifically to comedy fans, and HGTV is particularly aimed at those interested in buying or renovating their homes. These forms of narrowcasting allow marketers to pick channels that most directly target the audiences they want to reach. This narrowcasting approach works for individual programs too.

In general, companies and agencies looking to advertise on broadcast media need to do their homework on the audience they want to reach and plan their strategy accordingly. Certain products are aimed at everyone and benefit from programming that reaches the broadest audience. Consider the Super Bowl—what kind of products do you see advertised there? Generally, you see products that are relatively broad-based in their appeal, such as candy bars, beer, and insurance. However, other more niche products may benefit from programming that reaches a smaller mass audience but is more likely to be watched by their target demographic. Try watching a golf tournament sometime—you are more likely to see advertisements for golf equipment, investment companies, and **brands** that specialize in office equipment and resources because the demographics that watch these programs are more likely to buy golf equipment, invest, and buy products for their businesses.

Advertising decisions are generally built around research, specifically into how many people are watching a program or channel at a given time. Media planners use a wide variety of different audience measures, but for the sake of this intro text, we will keep it relatively simple and talk about some of the most basic forms of audience measurement. Radio and television advertising rates are both built around **ratings**, which measure the percentage of the total audience that is tuned into a particular station (Moriarty et al., 2015). For television, we can also look at the **share** of a particular program or station, which is its percentage of the total audience that currently have their televisions on and are watching them—because this number is smaller, the share percentage is generally a larger number (Moriarty et al., 2015). There are more forms of audience measurement, but data like this is used to determine what stations to buy advertising on and when.

Broadcast advertising is also built around strategic timing. Both radio and television set their advertising rates in terms of **dayparts,** or specific blocks of time during the day. In radio, the "morning drive" daypart is the most lucrative, because people are in their cars driving to work and tuning in to the radio for weather, news, and traffic reports. In television, the "prime time" or "prime access" spot tends to be the most lucrative, as it takes place after people have come home from work, eaten dinner, and settling down to relax (Moriarty et al., 2015). Most high-end network programming is aired during the prime access daypart. Advertisers may also choose to air their ads during specific programming or, in the case of local affiliates and radio stations, buy **run of station**-type plans in which their ads will be placed in any available spots throughout the day (Keith, 2010). Both radio and television can carry advertisements from national companies as well as local businesses. These ads are often part of a **campaign**—it is common for most advertisers, especially at a national level, to use multiple channels to advertise their products and services.

Generally, broadcast advertising is brief in duration. It is very rare to see an ad on either television or radio run for more than 60 seconds. Generally, the longer the **spot**, the more is it costs an advertiser to place the ad on the station. Good advertisers know to tailor their messages to the medium. Radio, for example, is everywhere, but people often listen to it while doing other things. A good radio spot, then, should mention the name of the client's business several times during the ad and avoid complex addresses or phone numbers in favor of more generic directions or easy-to-remember Web site addresses. After all, if you are in the midst of traffic, it is difficult to pick up a pen and write down the phone number for the restaurant you just heard about! Television ads have the luxury of being able to more immediately grab the viewer's attention and can use visuals to more clearly and powerfully demonstrate the value and qualities of a product or service—therefore, **copywriters** should follow the "show, don't tell" model and let the visuals do most of the work. While the approach to these different media will vary, repetition is incredibly important—as a very general rule of thumb, it takes around 3–10 **exposures** to an advertising message for the average viewer or listener to remember it and potentially act upon it (Moriarty et al., 2015). This will vary depending on the number of factors, from medium to prior awareness of the brand (Moriarty et al., 2015). A good advertisement, regardless of whether it is on television or the radio, should strive to engage the audience as soon as possible or at the very least make it clear what the advertisement is selling.

Media Ownership and Legal Issues

The legal questions surrounding broadcast station ownership and licensing are enough to fill an entire course. For now, we will focus on the basics. First, over-the-air, terrestrial broadcasts of television and radio are governed by the **Federal Communications Commission.** This government agency is tasked with multiple functions from regulating the signal strength and broadcast range of stations to the content that goes out across the airwaves and regulates everything from telephone communication to the Internet. First and foremost, they issue **licenses** to prospective broadcasters—without an FCC license, a station cannot go on the air. The reason for this is straightforward. As discussed in the previous section, radio and television are broadcast over the air, across the electromagnetic spectrum Maxwell and Hertz discovered. Because the electromagnetic spectrum exists all around us in the air, U.S. broadcast policy dictates it belongs to the public and cannot be owned by anyone else. Space in the electromagnetic spectrum is also finite—there is only so much of it that is actually usable by broadcasters. Broadcasting only makes up a narrow part of the spectrum, as frequencies must be reserved for satellite transmissions, emergency communication, and other needs. This principle of **scarcity** suggests those who wish to broadcast on one of these limited frequencies must meet certain criteria.

Therefore, the FCC has derived its authority to license and regulate broadcasters by acting as a representative of the public. The FCC's role as public representative extends to many different tasks. For example, in 2009, the FCC successfully pushed for a transition to digital television after years of delays, in large part to alleviate scarcity problems that were arising due to the growing number of wireless phone users. Television owners across the country were able to sign up for vouchers to get free converter boxes that allowed their sets to pick up digital over-the-air signals (cable and satellite users did not need to, as their providers carried the digital signals for them). The primary reason for this is that analog television signals took up a great deal of space on the spectrum—by forcing the digital transition, the FCC was able to sell off some of that newly-freed spectrum space to mobile carriers as well as use it for public safety concerns. Modern televisions have these digital converters built in, and the more highly compressed nature of digital broadcasts has allowed broadcasters to pack high-definition signals into a much smaller amount of spectrum space (this in turn has led to more cord-cutters).

FCC licenses are mandatory and in part require that broadcasters must broadcast in the **public interest**. The public interest standard has changed over the years—in the 1940s, the FCC took a more active approach to enforcing the public interest through a report colloquially called the **Blue Book**, which suggested broadcasters must promote live programs of local origin, promote discussion of public issues, and limit excessive advertising (Riley, 2012). The Blue Book was controversial with advertisers and was eventually abandoned, but the public interest standard has remained. In broad, general terms, the public interest standard mandates that broadcasters offer informational programming that is acceptable in terms of language and content for the broadest possible sections of the audience (especially young children). There are exceptions—during the so-called **safe harbor** hours (generally between 10:00 AM and 6:00 PM local time), for example, broadcasters have slightly more freedom in terms of what they can air. A discussion of the legal issues of broadcast content could and does fill an entire textbook, but in general, **indecent** content can be aired during safe harbor hours, while **obscene** content cannot. Indecent content is also generally protected by the First Amendment, while obscene content is not. The difference between indecent and obscene content is based on the standard set forth in the Supreme Court case *Miller v. California* (1973). The so-called **Miller test** suggests that there are three main criteria that content must meet in order to be ruled obscene content that can be regulated by the FCC and the government:

1. The average person, applying *contemporary community standards*, finds the work as a whole appeals to the *prurient interest*

2. The work describes or depicts "in an offensive way" sexual conduct or excretory functions, as defined by applicable *state law*
3. The work as a whole lacks "serious literary, artistic, political, or scientific value" (*Miller v. California*, 1973).

In order for content to be ruled obscene, it must meet all three of these characteristics. A documentary on human sexuality would be acceptable for broadcast even if it depicted nudity or frank discussion of sexual intercourse because it could be ruled as having scientific value—its purpose is to educate. However, a shock morning radio DJ going on a tirade about a guest's sexual history may not be protected by the First Amendment because it would not have that same scientific value. As you can imagine, this standard can be difficult to pin down, as community standards vary from community to community and what is artistic versus what is obscene will also vary based on the individual and their definition. In general, these rules are left open to interpretation—as the Supreme Court justice Potter Stewart once said about pornography, "I know it when I see it" (Lattman, 2007). This ambiguity is why the FCC generally only acts upon complaints received from the public. The FCC has handed down fines in particular situations, such as Janet Jackson's infamous "wardrobe malfunction" during the 2004 Super Bowl halftime show—the FCC initially handed down a fine of $550,000 to the CBS network for airing the incident but the Supreme Court declared in 2012 that subsequent changes to FCC policy invalidated the fines; their refusal to hear an FCC appeal effectively closed the case (Cushman, 2012). This ruling also invalidated fines levied in similar situations, such as U2 lead singer Bono cursing during a speech at the Golden Globes.

Regulation of broadcasting has not always been restricted to bad language or nudity. The FCC defined the idea of equal access and time for differing sides of political arguments as part of the public interest relatively early on with the 1949 introduction of the **Fairness Doctrine**. The Fairness Doctrine held that FCC licensees must both devote programming to controversial public issues and air opposing viewpoints (Matthews, 2011). The Doctrine was unpopular with and faced legal challenges from many broadcasters, most notably in the *Red Lion v. Federal Communications Commission* (1969) case, wherein the Supreme Court famously ruled the FCC was allowed to enact such regulations as a result of the public ownership of the airwaves (*Red Lion v. FCC, 1969*). Following that case, however, the Fairness Doctrine standard was relaxed and eventually removed altogether in the 1980s as part of a gradual trend toward deregulation under the Reagan-era Commission; the end of the Doctrine arguably led to an explosion in conservative-driven AM talk radio after the decision (Hagey, 2011; Matthews, 2011). The Fairness Doctrine remains an issue of debate and discussion to this day.

The FCC also mandates specific limitations on station ownership, though these restrictions have relaxed significantly over the years and depends on the total number of stations in the market—for example, in a market with 45 or more radio stations, a single company can own up to eight stations, but that number decreases as the number of total stations in the market does (FCC, 2014). Television ownership by comparison is based on the total number of "media voices" in a market—radio stations, television stations, cable systems, and newspapers (FCC, 2014). A critical approach to mass communication begs the question—what impact might the ownership of multiple media outlets by a single company have on the quality of information provided by these outlets, or the content carried by them?

These changes in ownership are necessary to understand how media has developed since the early days of the twentieth century. Contemporary mass media is characterized by two major and opposite forces—**fragmentation** and **consolidation**. Fragmentation refers to the idea that we have a much larger number of media outlets than before, and the individual audiences for each different outlet are smaller—*fragmented*—in comparison to the much broader audiences of the traditional mass media model (Self, 2009). Contemporary mass communicators can still reach large audiences, but no one channel is likely to reach every possible audience because the audiences' attention is diverted between so many different outlets. Yet at the same time, because of the relaxation in ownership restrictions and merger and acquisition rules, our mass media is also becoming more **consolidated**. Despite the countless number of outlets and channels we can access as audiences, those outlets and channels are increasingly owned by fewer and fewer companies—just six companies control the vast majority of media we use (Lutz, 2012). For example, the Walt Disney Company owns not only the Disney theme park, film, and television interests but also other companies like ESPN, ABC, and Marvel Comics. News Corporation owns the 20th Century Fox TV and movie interests, as well as numerous newspapers in the United States and around the world like the *Wall Street Journal* and the *New York Post* (Lutz, 2012). The media that make up our mediated lives appear to be diverse in form and outlet, but in reality, we learn about the world around us from an increasingly smaller number of actual sources. This paradox is at the core of contemporary media and we will explore it in more detail in the next chapter.

References

Benjamin, L. (2002). In search of the Sarnoff "music box" memo: Nally's reply. *Journal of Radio Studies, 9*(1), 97–106.

Campbell, R., Martin, C. R., & Fabos, B. (2013). *Media essentials: A brief introduction* (2nd ed.). Boston: Bedford St. Martin's.

Carter, B. (1993, December 19). Pro football; Stunned CBS now scrambling for AFC. *The New York Times*. Retrieved from LexisNexis.

Cushman, J. H. (2012, June 30). Supreme Court rejects FCC appeal in Janet Jackson case. *The New York Times*. Retrieved from LexisNexis.

de Moraes, L. (2008, May 23). David Cook wasn't the only winner on Wednesday as 'Idol' ratings spike. *The Washington Post*. Retrieved from http://www.washingtonpost.com/wp-dyn/content/article/2008/05/22/AR2008052203719_pf.html.

Dredge, S. (2014, November 18). Serial podcast breaks iTunes records as it passes 5m downloads and streams. *The Guardian*. Retrieved from http://www.theguardian.com/technology/2014/nov/18/serial-podcast-itunes-apple-downloads-streams.

Edwards, L. H. (2013). *The triumph of reality TV: The revolution in American television*. Santa Barbara, CA: Praeger.

Federal Communications Commission (2014, July 30). FCC's review of the broadcast ownership rules. *FCC.gov*. Retrieved from https://www.fcc.gov/guides/review-broadcast-ownership-rules.

Hagey, K. (2011, January 16). Fairness doctrine fight goes on. *Politico*. Retrieved from http://www.politico.com/story/2011/01/fairness-doctrine-fight-goes-on-047669.

Hall, G. (2010, December 30). Why 2011 is being called the year of the "cable cut". *Business Insider*. Retrieved from http://www.businessinsider.com/what-will-it-take-to-make-over-the-top-video-successful-2010-12.

Harmetz, A. (1986, October 5). "Fox's Barry Diller gambles on a fourth TV network". *The New York Times*. Retrieved from http://www.nytimes.com/1986/10/05/arts/fox-s-barry-diller-gambles-on-a-fourth-tv-network.html.

Keith, M. C. (2010). *The radio station: Broadcast, satellite, and Internet* (8th ed.). Burlington, MA: Focal Press.

Lattman, P. (2007, September 27). The origins of Justice Stewart's "I know it when I see it". *The Wall Street Journal Law Blog*. Retrieved from http://blogs.wsj.com/law/2007/09/27/the-origins-of-justice-stewarts-i-know-it-when-i-see-it/.

Lutz, A. (2012, June 14). These 6 corporations control 90% of the media in America. *Business Insider*. Retrieved from http://www.businessinsider.com/these-6-corporations-control-90-of-the-media-in-america-2012-6.

Matthews, D. (2011, August 23). Everything you need to know about the Fairness Doctrine in one post. *The Washington Post*. Retrieved from http://www.washingtonpost.com/blogs/ezra-klein/post/everything-you-need-to-know-about-the-fairness-doctrine-in-one-post/2011/08/23/gIQAN8CXZJ_blog.html.

Maxwell, J. C. (1865). A dynamical theory of the electromagnetic field. *Philosophical Transactions of the Royal Society of London, 155*, 459–512.

Miller v. California, 413 U.S. 15 (1973).

Mullen, M. (2008). *Television in the multichannel age: A brief history of cable television*. Malden, MA: Blackwell Publishing.

Moriarty, S., Mitchell, N., & Wells, W. (2015). *Advertising & IMC: Principles and practice (10th ed.)*. Upper Saddle River, NJ: Pearson.

Nielsen. (2014, December 12). Tops of 2014: Audio. *Nielsen Media Research*. Retrieved from http://www.nielsen.com/us/en/insights/news/2014/tops-of-2014-audio.html.

Pavlik, J. V. (2008). *Media in the digital age*. New York: Columbia University Press.

Public Broadcasting Service. (1997). More about Sarnoff, Part One. *American Experience*. Retrieved from http://www.pbs.org/wgbh/amex/technology/bigdream/masarnoff.html

Red Lion Broadcasting v. Federal Communications Commission, 395 U.S. 367 (1969).

Riley, T. (2012, December 19). The FCC, the public interest and the Blue Book. *BillMoyers.com*. Retrieved from http://billmoyers.com/2012/12/19/the-fcc-the-blue-book-and-the-public-interest/.

Self, C. (2009). The evolution of mass communication theory in the 20th century. *Romanian Journal of Journalism and Mass Communication, 4*(3), 29–42.

Stelter, B. (2015, March 11). SiriusXM and Howard Stern in a contract 'dance'. *CNN Money*. Retrieved from http://money.cnn.com/2015/03/11/media/howard-stern-sirius-xm-contract-speculation/.

Warner, C. (2009). *Media selling: Television, print, Internet, radio* (4th ed.). Malden, MA: Blackwell Publishing.

CHAPTER 8

Digital and Online Media

In 2001, education specialist and author Marc Prensky coined the term **digital natives** to refer to those students coming through the educational system who not only have grown up with and fully understand the language of technology and new media but also do not remember a time before it (Prensky, 2001). If you are reading this, the chances are pretty good you too are a digital native. Ask yourself—do you remember a time before the Internet? How long have you had a cell phone, or a social media account? Do you post your pictures and experiences online? Do you expect to be able to find answers quickly and efficiently, for example, via a search engine? If so, you are a digital native and you are not alone—in fact, as Prensky (2001) suggested, there is a growing demand in the education marketplace to accommodate this unique way of thinking and experience to more efficiently and effectively teach material.

It is hard to look at digital media and not immediately see its importance and impact, as well as the necessity to reframe our old ways of thinking and communicating. In many ways, digital media has made our lives better or at least brought us closer together—think of how we may now connect via Facebook with friends and family we may not see often otherwise or how we can now collaborate and communicate with people in different countries and time zones as though they were in the room with us.

Think of the virtual worlds that allow us to explore different parts of our identities or the vast repositories of information online that have been indexed and are accessible with a few keystrokes. However, there is still room to question the effect digital media has on our sense of identity, empathy, and connectedness to others. While the world may be smaller as a result of the breakthroughs, the past few decades have provided in communication, so too may our perspectives have narrowed.

To start, let us first identify **digital media** as any sort of media that is transmitted primarily through digital means—the Internet, video games, social media, or any other form of mediated communication that comes to us via code and computer connectivity. You may have also heard the phrase "new media" used to refer to these technologies. This text prefers the "digital media" term for a very simple reason—while these technologies are certainly new and innovative relative to traditional and broadcast media, they are far from new themselves. The Internet has been around in at least some form since the 1960s. Cell phones have been around since the 1980s, and smartphones have been around since the mid-1990s. The earliest social networking sites are from the mid-1990s as well, and video games have been around in a commercial form since the 1970s and in experimental form since the 1950s. For these reasons, "digital media" is a more accurate term.

Of course, not all technologies take off. For every iPod, there is a Zune. For every Twitter, there is a Tout. We tend to adopt technologies because other people in our social circle adopt them—if you have a Facebook account, you have probably noticed how many of your family members have adopted one as well. We are more likely to adopt a technology if we can not only see others using it but also see how it might benefit our lives as well. Most technologies are adopted according to a pattern called the **diffusion of innovation**, suggesting that the majority of people adopt technologies or practices around the same time (Rogers, 2003). Essentially, technological adoption goes in distinct stages—from the **innovators** who adopt technology immediately despite potential setbacks and expense to the **laggards** who adopt technology more or less when alternatives are no longer available. However, we may be less inclined to adopt certain technologies than we are others, particularly if we do not find a technology useful, consider it to be too expensive or we are afraid of what it can do—think of how many people are still afraid their personal information is guaranteed to be stolen if they shop online, for example (Foote, 2014; Zickhur & Smith, 2012). It is important to understand when we discuss the practical applications of digital media and communication that they are not necessarily the right fit for all audiences at any given time. In fact, things like cell phones and broadband Internet often act as what Duck and McMahan (2009) call **relational technologies**, or those technologies that allow us to maintain our personal identities and relationships with others. Technology is so integral to our identities that we can even divide ourselves into **media generations** based on how the technologies we use have shaped our consciousness (Duck & McMahan, 2009). You are likely part of what we could call the Internet generation, because your knowledge and experience has been so shaped by that particular technology. Your parents were likely part of the television generation, your grandparents were likely part of the radio generation, and so on.

With digital media, we must also again revise our concept of what communication looks like. In the interpersonal model, we looked at communication as a one-to-one proposition, in the mass communication model, we looked at communication as a one-to-many proposition, and with digital media, communication is no longer just one-to-many but also **many-to-many** as audience members interact with, share, critique, and remix communication content. The audience acts as a sort of relay for a message, passing it on to other members of the audience and propagating it beyond its original reach—in marketing, this is called going **viral**—and acting in a way that was not possible with traditional media. We will explore this concept in more detail throughout this chapter. First, let us start with the origins of the system that makes digital communication possible.

Development of the Internet

Generally speaking, if you are an underclassman in college at the time of this writing you likely do not really remember a world before the Internet (an important quality of a digital native). When social commentators say things like this, they seek to point out how new the Internet is, but in reality, the Internet has been around for half a century. The Internet began as a government project by the U.S. government's Defense Advanced Research Projects Agency (or DARPA). The original Internet, or **ARPANet**, consisted of four computers linked together and was first switched on in 1969 (Curran, 2012; Leiner et al., 2012). The idea was to create a communications network that could survive a nuclear strike, a justifiable concern in the days of the Cold War between the United States and Russia. However, the network began to grow beyond its initial purpose with the development of a universal computer language and protocols. Soon, the network was being used for other applications, most notably **e-mail**. The sending of electronic messages across the Internet was first introduced in 1972; the first unsolicited advertising message, or **spam** message, is believed to have happened just six years later (Curran, 2012; Oberoi, n.d.). Around this time, the first use of the term **Internet** emerges, referring to the interconnected computers and networks that make up the backbone of our online communication (Curran, 2012). It is these connections that make many-to-many communication possible.

The philosophy behind the Internet was simple and yet radical at the time—rather than having one centralized network, the Internet would be comprised of multiple open networks that could spread out from the initial ARPANet. What that meant is if a university, business, or other organization wanted to create their own network and connect it to the main network, they could (Leiner et al., 2012). This led to the Internet being adopted very quickly around the world in the 1980s and 1990s, starting with the adoption of IP (or Internet Protocol) by CERN, the European Organization for Nuclear Research and culminating in the development of the **World Wide Web** in 1991 (Curran, 2012). Here it is important to note that the terms "Internet" and "World Wide Web" are related but not interchangeable. The World Wide Web refers to the graphical interface that makes navigating across the Internet simpler and more intuitive—the collection of graphics, hyperlinks, and Web site designs that organize and display online data. Think of it as the "skin" over the Internet's skeleton and nervous system (Unless you find that analogy somewhat unsettling. I'm not entirely sure *I'm* comfortable with it).

Several innovations in the early 1990s hastened the more widespread global adoption of the Internet. In 1993, the National Center for Supercomputing Applications at the University of Illinois introduced the first widely adopted **web browser,** Mosaic, which supported graphics, sound, and video and further simplified the process of browsing the World Wide Web. While not particularly easy to use, Mosaic was simpler than the alternatives and served as the backbone for a much more user-friendly browser, Netscape Navigator, in 1994 (Vaughan-Nichols, 2013). Around the same time the first search engines debuted, and the computer itself went from a niche commodity to a more affordable, practical device—the power of the Internet drove much of the adoption of personal computers at this time as well (Curran, 2012). Around this time, the Internet started becoming more commercialized, moving from relatively simplistic "banner" ads placed on Web sites to more sophisticated advertising based on users' keyword searches. No company profited from this more than the 1998 startup Google, which used its proprietary algorithms to offer faster, more intuitive searches and in 2002 introduced a service where advertisers could pay to have their Web sites associated with particular keywords—this turned Google from a startup into one of the most profitable companies in the world (Oberoi, n.d.; Rosso et al., 2009). In the late 1990s and early 2000s, the Internet would come to play host to a plethora of online shopping sites selling everything from books to dog food; while many such sites fell to the wayside following the burst of the "dotcom bubble," some like Amazon. com are not only still around but also act as flourishing examples of **e-commerce**. We will discuss e-commerce and online advertising later in this chapter.

Around this same time, many of the traditional media outlets discussed in the last chapter started establishing an online foothold as well, repurposing content from their print and broadcast outlets in an online space. While this was happening from the start, the move toward greater use of multimedia online correlated with the shift from **dial-up** to **broadband** Internet connections. Dial-up Internet connections are connections carried along the same lines as telephone communication, and while they are the slowest form of Internet connection, they are still ubiquitous in many areas where broadband is not available. Broadband Internet connections are higher-speed, "always on" connections that can be carried across DSL, cable, satellite, wireless networks, and even power lines (Pavlik, 2008). As Internet speeds became much faster and the amount of bandwidth available both to content providers and end users increased, **streaming** video in particular became a much hotter commodity—rather than downloading an entire video at once, users could now watch movies, television, and live events by downloading a few packets at a time from a centralized source. This development led to the success of several other companies, most notably Netflix, which offers streaming movies and television, and YouTube, which offers a community of online video creators. These two sites are so popular that, as of this writing, they can account for around 50% of the total Internet traffic in North America at peak times (Spangler, 2015).

However, it is this increased reliance on broadband that has given rise to concern over other issues—specifically, the question of access and literacy. This **digital divide** has long been an issue for tech companies, policymakers, and educators, though it has shifted from a question primarily of access to one that is more focused on literacy and navigation ability (Foote, 2014). This shift has been due in no small part to the increased prominence of mobile networks and wireless devices, as well as the decreasing costs and increasing speed of fixed broadband networks—the U.S. Census Bureau estimates that nearly 80% of U.S. households have access to high-speed Internet, though this varies significantly based on factors such as class and ethnicity; smartphone and mobile penetration is over 60% in the United States and around 70% in the Black and Hispanic populations (U.S. Census Bureau, 2014; Smith, 2015). However, that is not to say access is not still an issue. There is a clear and growing divide between higher-income and lower-income school districts in terms of technology, equipment, and access; lower-income schools in particular are struggling, with only half of teachers in the lowest-income districts reporting they have adequate resources and technological support (Foote, 2014; Xie, 2013). The Federal Communications Commission (FCC) estimates that 55 million Americans still lack access to advanced broadband, and over half of all rural Americans and two-thirds of Tribal lands lack access to reasonable broadband speeds (FCC, 2015). It is difficult to disconnect socioeconomic class and Internet access from each other; given that the Internet is increasingly a way for people to communicate, stay informed, and perform important life tasks, this disparity is problematic.

There is also an ongoing debate over how "free" the Internet should be. Most of the nation's Internet connections come through networks that are owned by telecommunications providers such as AT&T and Comcast. These providers argue that they should have the ability to restrict or slow down traffic in order to protect the integrity of their network. However, advocates for **net neutrality** argue that these providers may use the so-called **quality of service** (or **QoS**) controls to restrict or slow access to content or applications they find undesirable or may be able to charge specific content providers for faster access, as Comcast did with the Netflix streaming video service (Wyatt & Cohen, 2014). Providers argue that charging for higher quality access allows them to put more money back into the network and create better infrastructure, but

Net neutrality proponents argue the Internet should remain open and competitive regardless of financial access. In 2015, following years of debate and argument at the legislative and public policy levels, the FCC voted to reclassify broadband Internet as a utility akin to phone service that would allow the FCC to prohibit paid prioritization or arbitrary data restriction (Gokey, 2015). Mobile and telecommunications companies have argued such classifications will harm their ability to compete and have attempted to block parts of the ruling from taking place; while a significant victory for net neutrality advocates it is likely this debate is far from over.

Mass Self-Communication and Our Digital Selves

This disparity in access is also important in light of the fact the Internet is a source of information and expression for many young people. More than half of younger Internet users can be classified as **content creators**, people who post material to Web sites such as YouTube, Tumblr, and Instagram. Likely, you have done so as well even if you never thought of putting a picture on Instagram as creating online content. The Internet can often be a means of sharing personal identity and connecting with others through the writing of blogs and communication on social media (Duck & McMahan, 2009). Essentially, we can generate content driven by and defined by our sense of self to a mass audience, a phenomenon mass communication scholar Manuel Castells (2010) calls **mass self-communication.** The development of this phenomenon is something of a perfect storm. Castells identified four main attributes that have led to this change in communication behavior. First, he suggested the advancements in hardware, software, and networking as well as the ubiquity of online connections have made it easier for communication to become digitized and individuals to communicate anytime and anywhere. Second, Castells suggested that there are significant changes in the organization and infrastructure of the communication industry as a result of globalized media and increased convergence between the companies that create the networks and content as a result of changes in political policy and social expectations. Third, Castells suggested that the fragmented nature of global culture and powerful identity relationships have created a situation in which the media can both bridge cultures and also create more insular, narrow ones. Finally, Castells suggested the social and economic relationships that make up the communication industry are more prominent, with greater corporate influence and more audience targeting (Castells, 2010). Still, as Castells suggests, the new mass-self communication paradigm is thriving in this often contradictory climate. Not only do individuals share something about themselves in this mass self-communication paradigm, they also forge new social connections with family, friends, and other like-minded individuals.

The expansion of **social media**, or online services that allow users to connect with friends and family, has been a major driver in technological adoption. While the term "social media" is still relatively new, the concept of social media has been around for many years, dating back to the bulletin board systems and user networks of the early Web. Users seem to rapidly move from one network to another—Friendster, one of the earliest networks, faltered in the face of technical glitches and advanced competition, while Myspace went from being a popular online social hangout to a service used by the music industry to promote artists and albums (Holpuch, 2013; Liu, 2008). That is not to say that there have not been sites that are both successful and consistent. In the early 2000s, Facebook started as a way for Harvard students to connect with each other and gradually rolled out to other universities, then to high schools and finally the general public. Today, Facebook is worth hundreds of billions of dollars and has hands in everything from marketing to virtual reality. Twitter turned a side project about posting 140-character SMS messages online to a group into a massively popular online presence with millions of users; in addition to changing how politicians, celebrities, and their audiences communicate, it was also vital in spreading information and organizing protesters in Iran, China, and other countries (Miller, 2010). While we often view social media as an isolating element or a device that acts at best as a surrogate for real communication, in reality, social media may be doing more to strengthen human communication than we suspect. The Pew Research Center discovered that users of Facebook are politically engaged, use the site to keep up with others, have closer relationships, and are less likely to be socially isolated (Pew Research Center, n.d.).

However, not everyone agrees with those findings. In her book "*Alone Together,*" psychologist and digital media researcher Sherry Turkle (who had once spoken enthusiastically of the possibility of the Internet to foster expressions of identity) suggested the move to a more connected world "disrupts many of our attachments to things that have always sustained us" such as face-to-face communication and interpersonal connection (2011, p. 284). The "low-risk" nature of online communication, Turkle argued, provides attractive connections that keep us from exposing our vulnerable selves (2011, p. 295). Even though we have more ways of connecting than ever before, critics argue, these connections are synthetic and isolating. These social networks may also serve to reconstruct harmful real-world social hierarchies and narratives—consider that young women will often present themselves via sexually desirable poses and language on social networking sites in the hopes of attracting heterosexual male interest (Kapidzic & Herring, 2012; Wang, 2011). Some, like Nicholas Carr (2011), have suggested that the rapid response of online communication and the ability to access information easily and quickly have essentially "rewired" our brains and limited our ability to focus and concentrate. Think of how often we check our phones for the latest status updates from our friends or attempt to "multitask" such desirable tasks with undesirable ones.

In Chapter 6, we discussed the importance of self-concept and identity in communication. These ideas extend into the digital world, as well. From the moment you go online, you have begun constructing a digital "brand" or identity based on what you search for, what you post, and what you do. Some of this information is collected with your consent, while other information is not—for example, **cookies** are small packets of data gathered by the Web sites you visit to track your behavior and habits, largely for marketing purposes. When you go to a chat room or sign up for a social networking site, you may select a **screen name** or an online "handle" you go by to provide anonymity. Even your e-mail address can tell an astute observer a lot about who you are, delineating not only your name but also the place where you get your e-mail from and what kind of organization it is (Duck & McMahan, 2009).

We often go to great lengths to hide our identities online, and just as we do so in our real lives, we may have multiple "selves" we utilize in different situations (Turkle, 1995). In many ways, the Internet acts as a surrogate reality, in which we can experience and do things we may not do in the real world (Turkle, 1995). Key to this concept is the idea of anonymity discussed above. When we go online, we are anonymous, or at least more anonymous than we would be in the real world—though it is increasingly challenging to have a completely anonymous online life. John Suler (2004) suggested that this anonymity brings with it a form of **disinhibition**, or a lack of the restraints placed on us in everyday interaction. Such disinhibition, Suler argued, takes two forms—it may be **benign disinhibition,** wherein the user feels more comfortable about sharing their true self because they do not have a real identity attached to their words (such as in an online support group), or **toxic disinhibition**, in which the user becomes more hostile and aggressive because of the lack of consequences afforded by anonymity. Both are possible and likely, though the latter certainly seems more prevalent in most online activity. Because online communication is **asynchronous**—it does not happen in real time, and there is a delay—and because it is **dissociative**—it is separated from an actual physical or visual presence—such disinhibition is possible (Suler, 2004). It is again worth noting, however, that changes in social networking policy and privacy mean that screen names do not guarantee the same level of privacy they once did—so be careful with what you say and do online, as it can often be traced right back to you.

Cyberliteracy

The move to a digital world requires literacy, not only in terms of what it does to our identity but also how we access and trust information. Unfortunately, our collective skepticism has not seemed to keep pace with the plethora of news and information sources available to us. How many times have you seen a satirical article from a comedy Web site like *The Onion* passed around your online social networks as fact? In the last chapter, we discussed the importance of media literacy for critically analyzing and evaluating the media available to us. Let us now turn our attention to **cyber literacy**, or the ability to critically analyze the value and truthfulness of online content. As digital media scholar Laura Gurak (2001) suggested, it is not enough to simply understand how to navigate a Web page or decode emojis—instead, we must also be able to understand the social and economic factors that shape the Internet and its attendant communities as well as possess the knowledge and experience necessary to guide the development of such technology.

Part of this knowledge, Gurak (2001) argued, is the knowledge of how to critically assess a Web site and the information it contains. You may have heard of the **CRAP test**, which suggests that the quality of an information source is based on four points: currency, reliability, authority, and purpose (Gold, 2010). Currency refers to how recent the information is or how recently it has been revised or updated. Reliability is what kind of information is in the resource and whether that information is referenced or opinion driven. Authority is one of the most important sources, as it asks who wrote the piece and what their credentials are—are they knowledgeable in this field or just a spectator? Finally, Purpose asks what the true goal of the resource is—is it an impartial reporting of an event, or something specifically designed to get across a particular point of view or sell you on a concept (Gold, 2010)? For example, if you were writing a paper on the effects of fast food on the health of young people, it is probably a better idea to cite peer-reviewed research by dieticians than it is to cite a press release from McDonald's talking about how their food is part of a healthy diet.

The CRAP test is a good rule of thumb, but there are more specific things to take into account when it comes to online resources. As Gurak (2001) suggested, it is also important to analyze the **URL,** or Uniform Resource Locator, from which a source originates. The URL is an online address that can tell you a lot about the source of a message. I teach at the University of Wisconsin—Green Bay, and our acronym is UWGB. Therefore, our Web site address is http://www.uwgb.edu. I want to call your attention particularly to the last part of the URL—the ".edu" part, which signifies this is a Web site affiliated with an educational institution. There are many such **top level domains**—the most popular is ".com," which signifies a commercial site, but ".net," ".org," ".biz," and many others are also often used. A general rule of thumb is that if the top level domain does not match the organization, you should not click on the link or trust its contents. If you were a student and received an e-mail from "uwgb.com", for example, it is best not to give your e-mail password to whoever sent it (or more generally, it is not a good idea to give your password out via e-mail anyway). I have seen my fellow professors fall for articles from "nytimes.com.co", a Web site attempting to pass itself off as the trustworthy *New York Times* Web site as well. Gurak (2001) also suggested that the **hyperlinks** on a site—the lines of text or images you click on to navigate to other parts of the Web—should be present and working—if they are no longer active, the Web site may not be a good resource. Finally, when navigating through social media, it is a good idea to make sure the account you are looking at in fact belongs to the person to whom it is claimed to belong—on Twitter, you can usually rely on a small blue checkmark next to the user's name, but some enterprising hoaxers have embedded a fake version of that checkmark into their page. As always, it is important to double and triple check your resources—it's very easy to fake information online, so reading Web sites with a healthy dose of skepticism is key.

Online Advertising and Marketing

The speed, interactivity, and ubiquity of the Internet have made it an ideal forum for marketers trying to sell products. Marketers and advertisers can now sell to receptive niche audiences without the need for expensive physical overhead that comes with brick and mortar locations. Much like traditional advertising, Internet advertising reminds potential customers of products and brands and can also carry promotional messages. However, the interactive nature of the Internet allows for brands to attract consumers to their Web sites via links and promotions. For customers, the Internet offers a chance to research and connect with their favorite brands and products, creating a dialogue between both parties; in turn, this allows brands and businesses to collect data about their customers and provide more direct customer service (Moriarty et al., 2015). The form and function of online advertising has changed dramatically over the inception of the medium.

The **banner ad** is the classic example of online advertising. A banner ad is an image, generally placed in the margins of a web page; these images are either static or animated and when clicked upon, they direct a user to a sponsor link (Moriarty, 2015). Banner ads are still used on many Web sites to this day and can be tailored to the specific layout of the site. **Pop-up** ads are another, much more intrusive form of advertising—true to their name, they literally will "pop up" by opening a new window over the window the user is currently looking at. **Pop-under** or "pop-behind" ads work on a similar principle but open the new window "underneath" or behind what the user is currently reading (Moriarty, 2015). As rich Internet applications like Flash, Silverlight, and the HTML5 standard have become more commonplace, other more complex forms of advertising have also emerged. Some ads can expand beyond their initially designated space on the page and grow larger or smaller, or even play audio and video. **Pre-roll** advertising has also become incredibly popular as sites like YouTube have grown in audience and offer video advertising that is either skippable or unskippable depending on the length of the ad (IAB, 2014). While such ads can be narrowly targeted, users may often find them annoying and ignore the message altogether.

Even the searches users conduct online can be monetized. In 1998, Larry Page and Sergey Brin founded a company named Google. Thanks to a proprietary PageRank algorithm, which ranked Web pages based on how many other pages linked to them, Google offered faster searches than the competition and quickly became the preeminent search site. The company built on this in 2002 with AdWords, a service where advertisers could bid to have their Web pages associated with specific keywords and perhaps the best example of **search marketing**. As an example, let's say your humble author was in the market to buy a new flat screen television, and I typed "flat screen television" into Google. Companies like Best Buy, Wal-Mart, and Amazon could all bid with Google ahead of time to associate their ads with that search string, and the highest bidder gets more prominent real estate on the search results that come up after I hit the "enter" key (Warner, 2009). These ads are often set off from the rest of the search results and marked as advertising but can still attract numerous clicks and attention from searchers. The highly targeted nature of social networking sites like Facebook can also make them very attractive outlets for advertisers, who can pick and choose users with specific valuable characteristics and interests to push their ads to. Twitter also allows for Promoted tweets, where users and companies can pay to have their tweets automatically pushed to users, regardless of whether they follow the advertiser (Bennett, 2014).

Internet advertising works in part because it can be so specifically targeted through the gathering of unique user data, which leads to concerns over exactly how much data is out there and the level of privacy users can reasonably expect. Most Web sites gather only general information about consumers, but some less scrupulous advertisers may hide **malware** in their marketing that installs unwanted programming and trackers on the user's machine. However, relatively little enforceable legislation on user privacy exists—in 1998, the Federal Trade Commission passed the **Children's Online Privacy Protection Act** (or **COPPA**), which placed specific guidelines on advertisers to ensure the privacy of users under the age of 13 (FTC, 1998). Consumers are also generally protected from deceptive online advertising through the general policies put in place by the Federal Trade Commission for other forms of advertising. In 2003, Congress passed the **CAN-SPAM Act** to require online advertisers sending e-mail to clearly mark their messages as marketing materials and also give consumers the option to "opt out" of receiving such messages, but it has proven difficult to enforce and marketers continue to send out unsolicited marketing messages (Lee, 2005). Many users have also opted to use **ad-block** software that simply prevents unwanted advertising from appearing in their web browsing; however, since most advertising payouts online are based on this has led to criticisms from online content creators that blocking advertisements keeps them from receiving money for their work. As a prospective communication professional, these issues will be important to how you live and work in a digital media environment.

Video Games and Virtual Worlds

Perhaps one of the most popular outgrowths of the digital revolution is the video game industry. Once the domain of hobbyists and hackers, today, the video game industry has gone mainstream. Over half of American households own a dedicated video game console, and over 40% of Americans play video games for three hours or more a week (Entertainment Software Association, 2015). At the same time audiences are playing video games, they are spending less time with other media, particularly film and television. All told, the video game industry was worth over $22 billion in 2014, and that number is likely to increase as digital purchasing and mobile platforms are tracked more extensively (Entertainment Software Association, 2015). Not bad for an industry that started more or less as a lark from bored engineering students.

It is difficult to pinpoint exactly *where* the video game industry began, as different scholars will have different perspectives on what actually constitutes the first video game. Most of the earliest examples of video game technology were experiments and side projects on the mainframes of universities and laboratories, such as William Higinbotham's *Tennis for Two* game, played on the oscilloscopes at the Brookhaven National Laboratory (Herman et al., 2002; Nielsen et al., 2008). In the early 1960s, MIT student Steve Russell developed a game called *Spacewar!* on that university's mainframe—soon, other engineering students at MIT and on campuses around the country were tweaking the game, adding features and complexity, and even developing special controllers with which to play it (Kent, 2001). One of those students was the University of Utah's Nolan Bushnell, who worked on an unsuccessful commercial version of the game called *Computer Space*—it flopped, but Bushnell and associates found success years later at their new company, Atari, with a simple ping-pong game called *Pong* that effectively created the video arcade (Carr, 2014). Video games began to enter homes around the world with the development of new machines designed for the purpose, such as the Atari 2600 and Intellivision—these devices were not only entertaining but continued questioning the one-way relationship between television and its audience (Donovan, 2010; Kent, 2001).

Following an early 1980s "crash" in the American home video game market, Japanese toy manufacturer Nintendo revitalized the industry with its Nintendo Entertainment system, pitching it as a device that could do more than just play games (Carr, 2014; Kohler, 2004; Ryan, 2011; Sheff, 1999). Gradually, video games became closer to other forms of entertainment in terms of their content and audiovisual fidelity. Later consoles like the Xbox 360 and PlayStation 3 would even act as "Trojan horses" that served to bring high-definition disc-based media and streaming television and movies into many homes (Herman et al., 2002; Subramanian et al., 2011). Now, many players use their consoles as a "set-top box" that is part of their living room entertainment setup and allows them to watch movies and television as well as listen to music (Entertainment Software Association, 2015). Combined with the explosive popularity of games like *Clash of Clans* and *Candy Crush Saga* in the mobile space and the continuing popularity of games on PCs, it is not hard to see that video games are a communicative force to be reckoned with.

The popularity of video games and the deep connection that players often forge with the medium has led to a great deal of concern about their effects on players. Parents, researchers, and politicians have fretted over the impact of games on players (particularly children) since the inception of the industry, even bringing Senate hearings on the subject in the early 1990s. In 2011, the Supreme Court ruled in *Brown v. Entertainment Merchants Association* that video games were protected speech under the First Amendment, but concerns over whether they encourage or cause aggression and violent acts remain. The research on this subject remains inconclusive—while Miller (2010) found that video games have in fact gotten more violent over time, disagreements over the scope of effects research and concerns over methodology and moral panics have clouded the discussion (Jenkins, 2002; Ferguson, 2008; Ferguson, 2010; Gunter & Daly, 2012). While some studies have found a link between violent games and increased aggression in users, so far a direct link between violent gameplay and violent real-world acts has yet to be discovered.

From a communication standpoint, video games are being used in a variety of different fields. Video games have been found to be particularly effective as advertising tools, for example, because of their ability to utilize what games scholar Ian Bogost (2007) calls **procedural rhetoric**, or using actual activity to make persuasive points. Video games have been used to sell everything from movies to sound financial planning. Research has found that advertising in video games may lead to better perception and recall of in-game brands (Chang et al., 2010; Fogg, 1998; Hernandez & Chapa, 2010; Lee & Youn, 2008; Lewis & Porter, 2010; Mallinckrodt & Mizerski, 2007). Video games have also long been used for educational purposes—the so-called **edutainment** games use the trappings of video games to reinforce and drill students on topics from math to spelling to geography. Many businesses and other organizations are also using the process of **gamification,** or the application of game mechanics to real-world problems, to do things like increase employee satisfaction, teach complex lessons, or even lose weight. Scholar and game designer Jane McGonigal (2011) argued that the "fun" nature of the work that games make players perform and the immediate, tangible rewards are what makes this process feasible. As an example in her book *Reality is Broken,* McGonigal cited the game *Chore Wars,* which offers players "experience points" and other rewards for doing household chores like sweeping and taking out the trash as an effective way to encourage household members to take on undesirable activities. While you may not think about video games as part of our communication world, they are in fact an ever more significant component and are just one of the many different forms of digital media that are changing the way we think, act, and communicate both professionally and personally.

References

Bennett, S. (2014, October 20). A History of Social Media Advertising [Infographic]. *AdWeek.* Retrieved March 11, 2015 from http://www.adweek.com/socialtimes/social-media-advertising-timeline/502459.

Bogost, I. (2007). *Persuasive games: The expressive power of videogames.* Cambridge, MA: The MIT Press.

Brown v. EMA. 564 U. S. ___ (2011).

Carr, B. J. (2014). No quarter given: The rise and fall of the arcade empire. *Voyageur, 30*(2), 48–53.

Carr, N. (2011). *The shallows: What the Internet is doing to our brains.* New York: W. W. Norton & Company.

Chang, Y., Yan, J., Zhang, J., & Luo, J. (2010). Online in-game advertising effect: Examining the influence of a match between games and advertising. *Journal of Interactive Advertising, 11*(1), 63–73.

Curran, J. (2012). Rethinking Internet history. In J. Curran, N. Fenton, and D. Freedom (Eds.), *Misunderstanding the Internet* (34–65). New York: Routledge.

Donovan, T. (2010). *Replay: The history of video games.* East Sussex, UK: Yellow Ant Media Ltd.

Duck, S. & McMahan, D. T. (2009). *Communication in everyday life.* Thousand Oaks, CA: Sage.

Entertainment Software Association (2015). *Essential facts about the computer and video game industry.* Retrieved from http://www.theesa.com/wp-content/uploads/2015/04/ESA-Essential-Facts-2015.pdf.

Federal Communications Commission. (2015). 2015 Broadband Progress Report. Retrieved from https://www.fcc.gov/reports/2015-broadband-progress-report.

Federal Trade Commission. (1998). Children's Online Privacy Protection Rule ("COPPA"). Retrieved from https://www.ftc.gov/enforcement/rules/rulemaking-regulatory-reform-proceedings/childrens-online-privacy-protection-rule.

Ferguson, C. J. (2010). Blazing angels or resident evil? Can violent video games be a force for good? *Review of General Psychology, 14*(2), 68–81.

Ferguson, C. J. (2008). The school shooting/violent video game link: Causal relationship or moral panic? *Journal of Investigative Psychology and Offender Profiling, 5*(1/2), 25–37.

Fogg, B. J. (1998). Persuasive computers: Perspectives and research directions. In *Proceedings of the SIGCHI conference on human factors in operating systems* (p. 225–232). New York: ACM Press.

Foote, C. (2014). Multiculturalism, sexism, and online voices. In S. Bramlett-Solomon and M. G. Carstarphen (eds.), *Race, Gender, Class & The Media* (2nd ed., p. 211–231). Dubuque, IA: Kendall-Hunt.

Gokey, M. (2015, May 4). FCC Net Neutrality update: U.S. telecoms say reclassification will be 'crushing' to industry. *Digital Trends.* Retrieved from http://www.digitaltrends.com/web/fcc-reclassify-broadband-title-ii-explained/.

Gold, L. (2010, September 20). The CRAP test for evaluating resources. *Lisa Gold: Research Maven.* Retrieved from https://lisagoldresearch.wordpress.com/2010/09/20/the-crap-test-for-evaluating-sources/.

Gunter, W. D., & Daly, K. (2012). Causal or spurious: Using propensity score matching to detangle the relationship between violent video games and violent behavior. *Computers in Human Behavior, 28*(4), 1348–1355.

Gurak, L. J. (2001). *Cyberliteracy: Navigating the Internet with Awareness.* New Haven, CT: Yale University Press.

Herman, L., Horwitz, J., Kent, S., & Miller, S. (2002). The history of video games. *Gamespot*. Retrieved from http://gamespot.com/gamespot/features/video/hov/index.html.

Hernandez, M. D., & Chapa, S. (2010). Adolescents, advergames, and snack foods: Effects of positive affect and experience on memory choice. *Journal of Marketing Communications, 16*(1/2), 59–68.

Holpuch, A. (2013, January 15). Myspace publicly unveils its revamped site—to little excitement. *The Guardian*. Retrieved from http://www.theguardian.com/technology/us-news-blog/2013/jan/15/myspace-justin-timberlake-facebook-announcement.

Interactive Advertising Bureau (2014, May). "Digital video in-stream and metric definitions". *Interactive Advertising Bureau*. Retrieved from http://www.iab.com/wp-content/uploads/2015/08/DigitalVideo_MetricsDefinitions.pdf.

Jenkins, H. (2002, August 20). Coming up next: Ambushed on "Donahue"! *Salon*. Retrieved from http://www.salon.com/2002/08/20/jenkins_on_donahue/.

Kapidzic, S., & Herring, S. C. (2011). Gender, communication, and self-presentation in teen chatrooms revisited: Have patterns changed? *Journal of Computer-Mediated Communication, 17*(1), 39–59.

Kent, S. L. (2001). *The ultimate history of video games: From Pong to Pokemon.* New York: Three Rivers Press.

Kohler, C. (2004). *Power-up: How Japanese video games gave the world an extra life.* Indianapolis, IN: BradyGames Publishing.

Lee, M., & Youn, S. (2008). Leading national advertisers' use of advergames. *Journal of Current Issues and Research in Advertising, 30*(2), 1–13.

Lee, Y. (2005). The CAN-SPAM act: A silver bullet solution? *Communications of the Association for Computing Machinery, 48*(6), 131–132.

Leiner, B. M., Cerf, V. G., Clark, D. D., Kahn, R. E., Kleinrock, L., Lynch, D. C., Postel, J., Roberts, L.G., & Wolff, S. (2012). Brief history of the Internet. *InternetSociety .org*. Retrieved from http://www.internetsociety.org/sites/default/files/Brief_History_of_the_Internet.pdf.

Lewis, B., & Porter, L. (2010). In-game advertising effects: Examining player perceptions of advertising schema congruity in a massively multiplayer online role-playing game. *Journal of Interactive Advertising, 10*(2), 46–60.

Liu, L. (2008, January 29). Friendster moves to Asia. *Time*. Retrieved from http://content.time.com/time/business/article/0,8599,1707760,00.html.

Mallinckrodt, V., & Mizerski, D. (2007). The effects of playing an advergame on young children's perceptions, preferences, and requests. *Journal of Advertising, 36*(2), 87–100.

Miller, C. C. (2010, October 30). Why Twitter's C.E.O. demoted himself. *The New York Times*. Retrieved from http://www.nytimes.com/2010/10/31/technology/31ev.html?_r=0.

Oberoi, A. (n.d.) The history of online advertising. *AdPushup.* Retrieved from http://www.adpushup.com/blog/the-history-of-online-advertising/.

Pavlik, J. V. (2008). *Media in the digital age.* New York: Columbia University Press.

McGonigal, J. (2011). *Reality is broken: Why games make us better and how they can change the world.* New York: Penguin Press.

Moriarty, S., Mitchell, N., & Wells, W. (2015). *Advertising & IMC: Principles and practice (10ᵗʰ ed.).* Upper Saddle River, NJ: Pearson.

Nielsen, S. E., Smith, J. H., & Tosca, S. P. (2008). *Understanding video games: The essential introduction.* New York: Routledge.

Pew Research Center (n.d.). Social networking fact sheet. Retrieved from http://www.pewinternet.org/fact-sheets/social-networking-fact-sheet/.

Prensky, M. (2001). Digital natives, digital immigrants. *On the Horizon, 9*(5), 1–6.

Rogers, E. M. (2003). *Diffusion of Innovations* (5ᵗʰ ed.). New York: Free Press.

Rosso, M. A., McClelland, M. K., Jansen, B. J. and Fleming, S. (2009). Using Google AdWords in the MBA MIS course. *Journal of Information systems Education, 20*(1), 41–49.

Ryan, J. (2011). *Super Mario: How Nintendo conquered America.* New York: Penguin.

Sheff, D. (1999). *Game over: Press start to continue.* New York: Random House.

Smith, A. (2015, April 1). Chapter one: A portrait of smartphone ownership. *Pew Research Center.* Retrieved from http://www.pewinternet.org/2015/04/01/chapter-one-a-portrait-of-smartphone-ownership/.

Spangler, T. (2015, May 28). Netflix bandwidth usage climbs to nearly 37% of Internet traffic at peak hours. *Variety.* Retrieved from http://variety.com/2015/digital/news/netflix-bandwidth-usage-internet-traffic-1201507187/.

Subramanian, A. M., Chai, K., & Mu, S. (2011). Capability reconfiguration of incumbent firms:

Nintendo in the video game industry. *Technovation, 31*(5–6), 228–239.

Suler, J. (2004). The online disinhibition effect. *Cyberpsychology & Behavior, 7*(3), 321–326.

Turkle, S. (2011). *Alone together: Why we expect more from technology and less from each other.* New York: Basic Books.

Turkle, S. (1995). *Life on the screen: Identity in the age of the Internet.* New York: Simon & Schuster.

U.S. Census Bureau. (2014, November 13). Nearly 8 in 10 Americans have access to high-speed Internet. [Press Release]. Retrieved from http://www.census.gov/newsroom/press-releases/2014/cb14-202.html.

Vaughan-Nichols, S. J. (2013, April 22). Happy birthday, Mosaic: 20 years of the graphical web browser. *ZDNet.com.* Retrieved from http://www.zdnet.com/article/happy-birthday-mosaic-20-years-of-the-graphical-web-browser/.

Wang, Y.-H. (2011). Teenage girls' views and practices of 'sexy' self-portraits on a Taiwanese social networking site. *Interactions: Studies In Communication & Culture, 2*(3), 209–224.

Warner, C. (2009). *Media Selling: Television, Print, Internet, Radio.* Malden, MA: Blackwell Publishing.

Wyatt, E. & Cohen, N. (2014, February 23). Comcast and Netflix reach deal on service. *The New York Times.* Retrieved from http://www.nytimes.com/2014/02/24/business/media/comcast-and-netflix-reach-a-streaming-agreement.html?_r=0.

Xie, J. (2013, March 1). Technology in schools still subject to digital, income divides. *PBS.org.* Retrieved from http://www.pbs.org/mediashift/2013/03/technology-in-schools-still-subject-to-digital-income-divides060/.

Zickhur, K. & Smith, A. (2012). Digital differences, *Pew Research Center.* Retrieved from http://www.pewinternet.org/files/old-media/Files/Reports/2012/PIP_Digital_differences_041312.pdf.

CHAPTER 9

Journalism: Practice, Technology, and Change

Jared Schroeder

Journalism is both a distinctive method of communication and an essential cog in the functional machinery of a democratic society. The news media, at its best, is an institution tasked with the role of communicating factual information to members of democratic society so they are capable of making informed, self-governing decisions (Kovach & Rosenstiel, 2014). This is a role that, ideally, differs from persuasive forms of communication, such as public relations and advertising. It is also a role that journalism has grown into over time, beginning with lowly printers with ink-stained hands during the colonial period and, ultimately, evolving into a field that has established and accepted processes and standards that those who practice journalism follow.

A journalist's first goal is to inform, and his or her "client" is the public. Such a role in society places journalism in a unique position, one that was not settled over night. The development of journalism has been defined by two powerful influences: an evolution of processes and practices geared toward informing the public and unyielding technological innovation regarding the tools utilized by its practitioners to communicate information to audiences. This chapter examines journalism's development with these characteristics in mind. American journalism has evolved, step-for-step, with the nation's development. From underground newspapers that heralded the first inklings of fight for independence against the British in the late eighteenth century to the latest live Twitter or Instagram-based coverage of a presidential candidate's speech, journalism has continued to evolve.

The Colonial Press: News Media Without Journalism

Journalism and **mass communication** are not synonymous. This is especially true in the twenty-first century, as any individual, using social media, can communicate messages to massive audiences (Castells, 2009). Journalism today carries with it a certain set of standards, such as an emphasis on accuracy, efforts toward **objectivity**, and a goal, from the start of the journalistic process, to inform individuals in society (Kovach & Rosenstiel, 2014; Singer, 2011). If you consider your expectations of the news media, it is likely you, possibly without having thought it through, carry similar assumptions of journalism. When journalists fail to meet societal expectations, which other forms of communication are not held to, people cry foul. Yet, initially, from the invention of the printing press by Johannes Gutenberg in the 1440s until well into the twentieth century, these standards as well as the term "mass communication" did not exist. Printers, whose vocations were operating cumbersome, hand-operated printing machines, published newspapers. Few, if any, characteristics of journalism as we know of it were present during this period. Interviewing, accuracy, and objectivity, for example, were not in the picture during the first half-century of the nation's history.

The early American press was primarily a partisan press, though some of the newspapers were commercial ventures (Schudson, 1978). Journalism historian Michael Schudson explained that partisan newspapers were financed by "political parties, factions of parties, or candidates for office who dictated editorial policy and sometimes wrote editorials personally" (p. 15). Such newspapers bear almost no resemblance to today's news media efforts. First, information was difficult to come by and traveled very slowly. Most newspapers were weekly and contained only about four pages, with much of the content simply being lifted from older newspapers that found their way to the printer's office. Second, the newspapers were expensive, six cents an issue (the average daily wage at the time was well below a dollar a day), and they were delivered in the mail via subscription. Finally, circulations at these newspapers averaged about 2,200. Small-circulations, less-than-up-to-date news, expensive rates, and substantial control by political parties did not stop early American citizens from reading the news. Media historian Paul Starr (2004) wrote that "the responsible citizen was informed and kept up with the times. Self-government, in other words, generated greater demand for information, particularly for news and newspapers" (p. 64). The partisan nature of newspapers also started a tradition of toleration, though not always gracefully, for attacks on the nation's leaders in the media as parties used their newspapers' power to harm their political opponents, whether information was true or not. Thomas Jefferson, for example, admonished James Madison to use sympathetic newspapers to attack their foe, Alexander Hamilton. After leaving office, John Adams lamented the harshness of the partisan press (Freeman, 2001).

All the News That's Fit to Print

The characteristics of journalism, as we know it today, started to take shape in the nineteenth century. The progress, however, emerged from the wreckage of the sensationalistic and wild **yellow-journalism** era that dominated the end of the nineteenth century. During the yellow-journalism period, publishers, most famously William Randolph Hearst and Joseph Pulitzer, battled for readers' attention and circulation numbers by emphasizing crime, scandal, and sex. Most famously, Hearst sent an illustrator for his *New York Journal* to Cuba in 1897 to cover the colony's uprising against Spain. Hearst used the *Journal* to advocate for American involvement in the conflict by sensationalizing what was happening in Cuba. When the illustrator arrived, he wired Hearst, "There will be no war. Wish to return" (Schudson, 1978, pp. 61–62). Hearst, famously, responded, "You furnish the pictures and I'll furnish the war" (p. 62). Soon after, the U.S.S. Maine exploded near Havana, ultimately drawing the United States into war with Spain. Some contend the newspaper war between Pulitzer and Hearst ultimately helped to instigate the actual war (Baran, 2008).

Two key technological innovations led to the development of yellow journalism, and, ultimately, the push-back from the period to actual journalistic standards as we know of them today: The economic shift to the **penny press** and the invention of the telegraph. Remember, early newspapers were expensive for average people and delivered as a subscription. This meant only the wealthy could afford to have news. In the 1830s, Benjamin Day introduced a new economic model when he dropped the price of the newspaper to a penny. He did so by taking advantage of new, steam-powered presses and by shifting the revenue stream primarily from subscriptions to advertising income. Suddenly, the news became affordable to ordinary people. At the same time, newspapers audiences were growing as the nation's population grew from just above 11 million in 1825 to more than 17 million in 1840 (Historical Statistics, 1975). Thus, newspaper audiences were growing, especially in urban centers such as New York and Day's *New York Sun* and its penny-press model brought the news to them. Soon, other publishers shifted their model and the number of newspapers increased substantially. *The Sun* sold 15,000 papers a day in 1834, and other major metropolitan papers around the country saw similar increases. The penny-press model not only increased circulations but also, as a result, effectively ended the dominance of political parties over newspaper content. Journalism could stand, economically, on its own, an important step in the development of journalism as a distinctive form of communication. For the first time, journalism was not beholden to political parties for its financial well-being (Cook, 2005). Schudson (1978) concluded that "until the 1830s, a newspaper provided a service to political parties and men of commerce; with the penny press a newspaper sold a product to a general readership and sold the readership of advertisers" (p. 25).

The shift, combined with the invention of the telegraph, led to growth in publishers hiring and paying correspondents. Newspapers started to do original reporting on foreign and domestic matters. If you think about the goal of this chapter, to discuss how journalism developed into a distinctive form of communication, the step to having an actual class of people who identify themselves as reporters, rather than press operators who manually operated presses and politicians who submitted editorials to trumpet their ideas, is a fairly major one. For this reason, this era represents the beginnings of modern journalism. When a group of people in society is devoted to a specific craft, in this case journalism, certain processes and practices develop that separate members of the group from those who are not. Communication theorist James Carey (1965) explained that during this period, "the journalist became a reporter, a broker of symbols who mediated between audiences and institutions" (p. 32).

Another key shift in the original germination of journalism as a field with distinctive processes and practices, only mentioned in passing so far, was development of the telegraph. Consider how life-changing a development networked communication has been during the past few decades. The telegraph was the first "network." Before the telegraph was invented, news could only travel as fast as it could physically be carried. An explosion in San Francisco would have to be carried, likely by horse, across the county to New York. This process could take weeks, assuming horse or rider did not meet their demise somewhere along the way. With the invention of the telegraph, information could be communicated across the country instantaneously. Suddenly, timeliness became a factor with news. In 1794, it took more than 20 days to get news from Charleston, South Carolina, to New York. By 1841, the lag was about six days (Starr, 2004). The telegraph sped the pace of news reporting, as newspapers now competed to have the most up-to-date information. It also allowed for the development of **wire services**, mainly the Associated Press, which formed in 1847 when five New York daily newspapers started to exchange news with each other (The AP's History, n.d.). The telegraph and the formation of wire services not only extended the breadth of coverage journalists could offer but the nature of the technology also led to the creation of common journalistic style. Sending a telegraph was an arduous, time-intensive process. Mid-nineteenth-century connections were not terribly reliable. For these reasons, editors began to demand that reporters, put the most important news first (Harrower, 2007). This practice eventually became known as the **inverted pyramid** format. The innovation effectively restructured the way journalism was done, as reporters across the country started to use a uniform structure. Reporters also started to use "bylines," meaning for the first time journalists' names were affixed to the tops of their stories. More than 150 years later, the inverted pyramid remains a primary story format used by journalists. Furthermore, the central questions that a journalist should seek to answer—who, what, where, when, why, and how—started to become a part of the news gathering process (Schudson, 1978). Beyond story structure, the development of wire services also meant that reporters started to standardize spelling, word uses, and other style concerns.

Clearly, developments during the nineteenth century were crucial to journalism's march toward being a distinctive form of communication. The only problem was that in many ways, journalism became worse before it became better. As noted earlier in the chapter, the boom in circulation led to cut-throat competition among newspaper publishers. Soon, stories were being sensationalized and newspaper publishers were poaching the top reporters from each other's papers. This era of yellow journalism incorporated use of all of the developing aspects of journalism that occurred during the nineteenth century, only other practices we expect of journalists had not developed or were not being used. Journalists were telling *stories*, as Schudson (1978) contended, rather than communicating information with the goal of *informing* the public. This began to shift when Adolph Ochs purchased the lowly *New York Times* in 1896. To separate his newspaper from all of the other competing dailies in New York, he decided to try the novel approach of printing accurate, objective information only, no sensationalized stories that were partially true. During a time when Hearst and Pulitzer had massive circulations as a result of their sensational stories, Ochs declared that the Times would publish "all the news that's fit to print," a motto that is still published on the *Times* front page every day (Ochs Obituary, 1935). The Times' focus on accurate, objective information seemed to catch on. About 50 years after Ochs purchased the newspaper, it had 700 newsroom employees and had become among the top news outlets in the United States (Diamond, 1995). Meanwhile, Pulitzer's *New York World* ceased publication in 1931 and Heart's *New York Journal* folded in the mid-1960s.

Beyond Newspapers

So far, the story of journalism has been the story of newspapers. The narrative begins to broaden in the twentieth century. Radio, photojournalism, and television news evolved in the twentieth century, forever changing the way people understood the world around them. The reporting that emanated from all of these emerging forms of media, however, was based on the processes and practices that had taken hold in journalism during pervious time periods. By the twentieth century, journalism was becoming a distinctive career field that required training. As early as the 1860s, universities started teaching journalism courses (Folkerts, 2014). The University of Missouri offered the first journalism degree in 1908, and by 1920, nearly a dozen other universities had followed. Such a shift from apprenticeships to organized curricula helped to standardize processes and practices across the country.

Radio news

As practice of journalism advanced, the technologies utilized to communicate news to audiences started to rapidly expand. Guglielmo Marconi started experimenting with sending wireless telegraph signals in the 1890s. Marconi succeeded in sending telegraph messages, without a line, across greater and greater distances (Baran, 2008). Reginald Fessenden built upon those advances and, in 1906, was the first to broadcast words and music. After World War I, technology had advanced to the point that it was affordable for families to begin purchasing large, furniture-like radio units for the home. KDKA in Pittsburgh was the first commercial radio station to broadcast, famously delivering the outcome of the 1920 presidential election over the airwaves. By the mid-1920s, radio stations were popping up in most areas of the country and Americans had spent more than $200 million on radios (Craig, 2000). Technological and economic conditions limited the capability of early radio to act as a dominating source of news. Equipment remained too large and bulky to be easily transported to news events and recording and editing technologies made it difficult to capture sound to later share as part of a story. Instead, radio was dominated by live, in-studio shows such as "The Lone Ranger" and "Little Orphan Annie."

For these reasons, Herm Morrison's coverage of the Hindenburg disaster marked a turning point in radio as a tool for broadcasting news. In 1937, Morrison, reporting for WLS Chicago, an NBC radio station, was in New Jersey to broadcast live during the arrival of the Hindenburg blimp. His account was taped and broadcast the next day, but it was not edited (Miller, 2003). Morrison described what he was seeing when the well-known blimp burst into flames. The craft crashed to the ground in flames, all while Morrison tried to relay what he was seeing to his audience. Morrison struggled to contain his emotions. In doing so, he amplified the powerful ability of radio to convey vocalized emotion and the sounds of events to an audience. In all of history, a person who was not present at an event had never been able to *hear* what had happened. Just more than four years later, another advantage of radio news was highlighted—the ability of radio to break into programming and immediately report breaking news. When Japan attacked Pearl Harbor on December 7, 1941, Americans learned of the attack when major radio networks reported the news as it reached them. Newspapers remained on the 24-hour news cycle, but radio could convey story developments has they happened. The next day, millions of Americans stood by their radio sets as they listened to President Franklin Roosevelt declare before a joint session of Congress that December 7, 1941, would be a date that would "live in infamy" ("Day of Infamy," 1941).

Radio news, along with radio in general, enjoyed its golden age during this period, before television arrived in the years that followed World War II. Journalists such as Edward R. Murrow put the war in Europe and the Pacific into the living rooms of American households. Murrow famously broadcast from London as the Nazi's bombed the city. Such a use of the powerful new form of media changed the way people understood what was happening in the world around them. As powerful as the written word can be, it cannot convey the emotion that comes from an air raid siren as people flea for their lives in one of the world's most prominent cities.

Photojournalism

Much like radio, photojournalism had its beginnings in the nineteenth century, but required more advances in technology to begin to develop into a discernable career field with specific practices and processes. Louis-Jacque-Mande Daguerre and William Henry Fox Talbott contributed massive advancements in how images were captured and developed during the mid-1800s (Craig, 1999). As the Civil War started, most print publications ran illustrations rather than photographs. Even while Matthew Brady and other photographers brought images of the war back to the nation's major cities, the technology was not in place to reproduce the images in print materials. Civil War photographs also failed to capture actual fighting. The photographs, however, helped people to *see* for the first time, rather than only read about, the massive scale of death and injury (Craig, 1999). The emergence of a class of photographers who adhered to traditional journalistic concepts happened during the same period that journalism more broadly started to become more standardized. As discussed earlier, ideas such as objectivity and accuracy and the use of interviewing sources emerged during the end of the nineteenth and continued to develop in the first part of the twentieth century (Griffin, 1999). The role of photojournalists who helped to bring images of World War I to the breakfast tables and recliners of American homes helped to cement photography as a key form of journalism. By the start of the war in 1914, photography equipment had become more mobile and less complex, which allowed journalists "to take a range of photographs which could show the spontaneous and the unexpected" (Carmichael, 1989, p. 7).

By the start of World War II, photography was firmly established as a tool for communicating information to news audiences. The war was heavily photographed by press-affiliated photographers, as well as those who were employed by the armed forces (Griffin, 1999). Photojournalists captured what would become iconic images of the D-Day invasion, the lifting of the American flag by Marines on Iwo Jima, and soldiers' triumphant returns home. The end of the war drew many who developed photography skills during the conflict into photojournalism. In the years that followed the war, news magazines and newspapers started to hire full-time photographers, and press photographers started to institutionalize their own set of professional guidelines (Griffin, 1999).

Television news

Radio news' time of greatest popularity was short—television made sure of that. When President Roosevelt famously declared war with Japan, stating December 7, 1941, would "live in infamy," the largest radio audience in history listened (Harrower, 2007; "Day of Infamy," 1941). Certainly, radio news ruled that day, but radio's golden era was already slipping away. Once again, television, yet another new technology, started evolving at the end of the nineteenth century, gained steam in the 1920s and made its big debut at the World's Fair in 1939 (Baran, 2008). By that time, CBS and NBC had started daily television newscasts. About 1,000 television sets per day were being purchased and brought into American living rooms by the end of World War II. Unlike radio, however, television did not have to break ground as the first non-print form of news media. Early television journalism combined the news reporting processes that were already forming in radio news and the popular newsreels that appeared in movie theaters.

Newsreels started to appear before movies in the 1930s. It might be difficult to imagine now, but the combination of audio and moving images in the form of newsreels represented a major step in how individuals in society receive news and information. For the first time, individuals in New York or Dallas or Chicago could receive film accounts of major events, such as the Hindenburg disaster or Pearl Harbor. They could *see* and *hear* the events (Hedgepeth Williams, 2002). The growth of newsreels heralded the coming of television as a dominant form of media. For Americans to not only read about what happened at Pearl Harbor but also see the burning ships, broken planes, and flattened buildings, changed the way they experienced the reality of the attack.

While television ownership increased substantially after World War II, television news did not find its defining moment until November 22, 1963, when President John F. Kennedy was assassinated in Dallas. Certainly, other landmark moments occurred before the Kennedy assassination, such as Edward R. Murrow's decision to stand up to Sen. Eugene McCarthy on his news show "See it Now" in 1954 and the first televised presidential debate between Kennedy and Richard Nixon in 1960, but coverage of the Kennedy assassination changed the way Americans consumed news (Zelizer, 1992). Television networks broke into their programming to deliver the news and more than 95% of all homes with televisions stayed tuned for the hours of unbroken coverage (Harrower, 2007). Americans watched as Walter Cronkite composed himself and carefully read a piece of paper that was handed to him as he reported on the events: "From Dallas, Texas, the flash—apparently official—President Kennedy died at 1:00 p.m. Central standard time, 2 p.m. Eastern standard time, some 38 minutes ago" (Morales, 2003). Only days after the assassination, Americans saw Jack Ruby shoot and kill assassination suspect Lee Harvey Oswald on live television. It was during this period that Americans adopted television news as a credible source of information. Coverage of the Apollo 11 moon landing in 1969 and the Watergate scandal in 1972 only further cemented the role of television news in the lives of Americans.

Perhaps the final noteworthy advance in the history of television news was the creation of CNN in 1980 and the addition of CNN Headline News a year later. The shift from daily broadcast news at certain times during the day to a 24-hour news format influenced the scope of news coverage and accessibility because it became essentially on demand in a repeating loop (Gilboa, 2005). Much as with broadcast radio and television news, CNN's innovation did not immediately draw audiences—it took a catalyst or major event to cause people to adopt cable news as a part of their information diets. The start of the Gulf War drew viewers to cable news in ways similar to what occurred with the Kennedy assassination and broadcast television news. CNN's news-only format allowed audience members to tune in and get updates at their convenience. CNN was also the only network to continuously cover the American air attack on Baghdad. The eventual rise of CNN as a viable source for news led to the establishment of Fox News and MSNBC in 1996.

Freedom and Regulation

Change has been a key theme within this chapter. The history of journalism is defined by a continuous march of innovations, developing practices and processes within the craft, and turning-point moments that ultimately led to shifts in how individuals receive news. This chapter has yet to mention, however, one key factor in the story of journalism—the decision by the nation's founders and related interpretations of the **First Amendment** of the Constitution by the Supreme Court to protect freedom of expression and to strike down most efforts by the government to limit the flow of ideas in a democratic society. The First Amendment, ratified in 1791, states that "Congress shall make no law . . . abridging the freedom of speech, or of the press" (Bill of Rights, 1791). While the promise of freedom of expression belongs to everyone, such protections have been particularly important to journalists, who have traditionally occupied the role of information providers to citizens so they can make decisions in a democratic society.

The First Amendment, and its promise of freedom of expression, was the product of Enlightenment-era thinking. The nation's founders were children of the **Enlightenment era**, which spanned from the seventeenth to the eighteenth century in Europe. Enlightenment thinkers, among other beliefs, assumed that individuals were rational and able to make sense of the world around them and that truth was universal and objective (Gade, 2011; Seibert, 1956). This assumption of rationality and the ability of individuals to make sense of the world around them made it crucial that information and ideas be freely exchanged within society. One of the key turning points in freedom of expression in the United States came in 1919, when Justice Oliver Wendell Holmes introduced the **marketplace of ideas theory** of the First Amendment (*Abrams v. United States*, 1919). In a case in which a group of socialists were charged for communicating anti-government messages that sought to create labor strikes and hinder the military during World War I, the Supreme Court ruled that the First Amendment did not protect speech that threatened the government. While this precedent was later overturned, Justice Holmes, in a famous dissent, contended that the only way for truth to be found was through an open marketplace of ideas. He wrote, "when men have realized that time has upset many fighting faiths, they may come to believe even more than they believe the very foundations of their own conduct that the ultimate good desired is better reached by free trade in ideas—that the best test of truth is the power of the thought to get itself accepted in the competition of the market" (p. 630). Justice Holmes's words have remained, nearly 100 years later, as one of the dominant conceptualizations of how freedom of expression should be understood in society.

In other key rulings that allowed journalism develop and fulfill its role in society without government limitations, the Supreme Court ruled that the First Amendment does not allow for the government to exercise **prior restraint** over what journalists write. Essentially, the government cannot censor the press. That decision arose in a 1931 case, *Near v. Minnesota* and was more famously reinforced in *New York Times v. United States* in 1971. In the 1971 case, more famously known as the Pentagon Papers case, a former high-level analyst gave the *New York Times* a highly classified government document that detailed the United States' role in the Vietnam conflict. When the *New York Times* published the first articles using the documents, the Nixon administration sought and received a temporary injunction, making it illegal for the newspaper to print more information using the classified documents (*New York Times v. United States,* 1971). While the *New York Times* fought the injunction in the Courts, the *Washington Post* acquired a copy of the documents and started to report on the major findings. The Nixon administration sought and received an injunction halting the *Washington Post* from printing stories using the documents. To the Nixon administration's great surprise, and frustration, the classified documents found their way to major newspaper to major newspaper as the government sought to halt publication of the revelations, many of which showed the United States government was lying to Americans about what was happening in Vietnam (Ellsberg, 2002). Ultimately, the *New York Times'* case reached the Supreme Court, and the justices firmly struck down the government's restrictions on what the *New York Times* could publish. Justice Hugo Black wrote, "Every moment's continuance of the injunctions against these newspapers amounts to a flagrant, indefensible, and continuing violation of the First Amendment" (*New York Times v. United States,* 1971, pp. 714–715). Justice Black continued, "for the first time in the 182 years since the founding of the Republic, the federal courts are asked to hold that the First Amendment does not mean what it says" (p. 715). The Pentagon Papers case marks an important chapter in American history because it showed that the government cannot use its power to censor journalists from reporting information they have obtained.

Another important moment for journalists came several years earlier, in 1964, when the *New York Times* was drawn into a **defamation** lawsuit after L.B. Sullivan, a city commissioner in Montgomery, Alabama, contended that an advertisement in the newspaper contained falsities and damaged his reputation (*New York Times v. Sullivan,* 1964). The advertisement, notice it was not a news story, included minor factual errors. The case is important to the history of journalism because when the Supreme Court ruled in favor of the *New York Times*, it made it difficult for government officials and, in a later ruling, celebrities, to win cases against those who reported information about them. A ruling in favor of Sullivan would have meant that media outlets would have to greatly limit their reporting for fear of facing massive financial damages as a result of defamation cases. Justice Brennan, in writing the Court's opinion, concluded "we consider this case against the background of a profound national commitment to the principle that debate on public issues should be uninhibited, robust, and wide-open, and that it may well include vehement, caustic, and sometimes unpleasantly sharp attacks on government and public officials" (*New York Times v. Sullivan*, 1964, p. 721).

While the Supreme Court has consistently understood the First Amendment as protecting the government from limiting freedom of expression, journalists have not always succeeded in claims that sought to expand those rights. The Supreme Court has ruled that journalists do not, for example, have a right to refuse to testify before a grand jury or to respond to allow the government to search the newsroom (*Branzburg v. Hayes*, 1972; *Zurcher v. Stanford Daily*, 1978). This certainly does not mean that journalists do not fight such orders, and most states have laws that provide journalists some protection from being forced to testify (Shield Laws, n.d.).

While the courts have made substantially more rulings regarding freedom of expression, enough to absolutely bore you into a coma, the goal in this chapter is to emphasize that the history of journalism, how it has developed and how it has exercised its role of informing individuals in a democratic society, has been shaped by a general interpretation of the First Amendment as protecting journalists, and others, from government restriction regarding the information they seek to communicate.

Bringing It Together

The story of journalism's development in the United States is dominated by innovation in technologies, the growth of journalism as distinctive practice with specific skills and processes, and catalyzing events that helped to shift journalists and audiences toward uses of new media and the practices that go with them. Along this development, the First Amendment's promise of freedom of speech and of the press helped to protect journalism's growth.

The story of journalism's development is not complete. The emergence of networked technologies during the past few decades have only worked to reinforce the themes surrounding journalism's story that are discussed earlier. The pace of news has sped up as audiences expect minute-by-minute updates. The economic model for many news outlets has eroded as new online tools and audience members have shifted to other information sources. In short, journalism is in a process of adaptation now, just as it was at other key times in its history. From the printing press to the telegraph, to the penny press, to broadcast radio, to more mobile photography equipment, to film recording, to television sets, to cable news, and to online news and social media, the story of journalism's history is defined by technological change and the adaptation of central, longstanding processes and practices, such as objectivity and accuracy, that developed as journalists went from lowly press owners who produced newspapers that were largely funded by political parties to today's mobile journalists, who produce audio, video, photography, and text as they communicate information to citizens in a democratic society.

References

Abrams v. United States, 250 U.S. 616 (1919).

AP's History. (n.d.). The Associated Press. Retrieved from http://www.ap.org/company/history/ap-history. Accessed 27 August 2015.

Bill of Rights. (1791). Charters of freedom: National archives. Retrieved from http://www.archives.gov/exhibits/charters/bill_of_rights_transcript.html. Accessed 28 Augusts 2015.

Baran, S. J. (2008). *Introduction to mass communication: Media literacy and culture.* New York: McGraw-Hill.

Branzburg v. Hayes, 408 U.S. 665 (1972).

Carey, J. (1965). The communication revolution and the professional communicator. *Sociological Review, 13*(S1), 23–38.

Carmichael, J. (1989). *First World War photographers.* New York: Routledge.

Castells, M. (2009). *Communication power.* New York: Oxford.

Cook, T. (2005). *Governing the news: The news media as a political institution.* Chicago: University of Chicago Press.

Craig, D. B. (2000). *Fireside politics: Radio and political culture in the United States, 1920–1940.* Baltimore, MD.: John Hopkins University Press.

Craig, R. L. (1999). The rise of the visual. In B. Brennen & H. Hardt (Eds.), *Picturing the past: Media, history, and photography* (pp. 35–59). Champaign, IL.: University of Illinois Press.

Day of Infamy. (1941). National Archives. Retrieved from http://www.archives.gov/global-pages/larger-image.html?i=/historical-docs/doc-content/images/day-of-infamy-speech-l.jpg&c=/historical-docs/doc-content/images/day-of-infamy-speech.caption.html. Accessed 20 August 2015.

Diamond, E. (1995). *Behind the Times: Inside the New York Times.* Chicago: University of Chicago Press.

Ellsberg, D. (2002). *Secrets: A memoir of Vietnam and the Pentagon Papers.* New York: Penguin Group.

Folkerts, J. (2014). History of journalism education. *Journalism & Mass Communication Monographs, 16*(4), 227–299.

Freeman, J. B. (2001). *Affairs of honor: National politics in the new republic.* New Haven, CT: Yale University Press.

Gade, P. J. (2011). Postmodernism, uncertainty, and journalism. In W. Lowrey & P. J. Gade, *Changing the news: The forces shaping journalism in uncertain times* (pp. 63–82). New York: Routledge.

Gilboa, E. (2005). The CNN effect: The search for a communication theory of international relations. *Political communication*, 22(1), 27–44.

Griffin, M. (1999). The great war photographs: Constructing myths of history and photojournalism. In B. Brennen & H. Hardt (Eds.), *Picturing the past: Media, history, and photography* (pp. 122–157). Champaign, IL: University of Illinois Press.

Harrower, T. (2007). *Inside reporting*. New York: McGraw-Hill.

Hedgepath Williams, J. (2002). The purposes of journalism. In W. D. Sloan & L. M. Parcell (Eds.), *American journalism: History, principles, practices* (pp. 3–13).

Historical Statistics. (1975). United States Census Bureau. Retrieved from https://www.census.gov/history/pdf/histstats-colonial-1970.pdf. Accessed 27 August 2015.

Kovach, B., & Rosenstiel, T. (2014). *The Elements of journalism: What newspeople should know and the public should expect.* New York: Three Rivers Press.

Miller, E. D. (2003). *Emergency broadcasting and 1930s American radio.* Philadelphia: Temple University Press.

Morales, T. (2003). Cronkite remembers JFK. *CBS News.* Retrieved from http://www.cbsnews.com/news/cronkite-remembers-jfk/.

New York Times v. Sullivan, 376 U.S. 254 (1964).

New York Times v. United States, 403 U.S. 713 (1971).

Ochs Obituary. (1935). The New York Times: On this Day. Retrieved from http://www.nytimes.com/learning/general/onthisday/bday/0312.html. Accessed 18 August 2015.

Schudson, M. (1978). *Discovering the news: A social history of newspapers.* New York: Basic Books.

Shield Laws (n.d.). Society of Professional Journalists. Retrieved from http://www.spj.org/shieldlaw.asp Accessed 28 August 2015.

Siebert, F. S. (1956). The libertarian theory. In F. S. Siebert, T. Peterson, & W. Schramm (Eds.), *Four theories of the press: The authoritarian, libertarian, social responsibility and soviet communist concepts of what the press should be and do* (pp. 39–72). Champaign, IL.: University of Illinois Press.

Singer, J. (2011). Journalism and digital technologies. In W. Lowrey & P. Gade (Eds.), *Changing the news: The forces shaping journalism in uncertain times* (pp. 213–229). New York: Routledge.

Starr, P. (2004). *The creation of the media: The political origins of modern communications.* New York: Basic Books.

Zelizer, B. (1992). *Covering the body: The Kennedy assassination, the media, and the shaping of collective memory.* Chicago: University of Chicago Press.

Zurcher v. Stanford Daily, 436 U.S. 547 (1978).

CHAPTER 10

Professionalism and Ethics in the Press

Ioana A. Coman

News Stories, or: Why Do We Even Need Journalists?

We live in a highly digitized, mediatized, and connected world. Most likely, you are constantly checking your Twitter, Snapchat, Facebook, and other social media accounts; favorite blogs; and Web sites (news outlets, news aggregators, or not news related) at least every hour (if not more often). In fact, a recently released Pew Research Center Survey (Perrin, 2015) showed that 90% of young adults (aged 18–29 years) fully use social media and that even among older Americans (65 years and older), the social media usage is more than tripled since 2010. Facebook remains the most popular social media site, followed by Pinterest, Instagram, LinkedIn, and lastly, Twitter (Duggan, 2015). For more and more Americans, Twitter and Facebook serve as a source of news, with 63% of Twitter users and 63% of Facebook users saying that "each platform serves as a source for news about events and issues outside the realm of friends and family" (Barthel et al., 2015).

Moreover, even if you are not actively going on these apps, your phone or tablet screen is constantly lighting up, bombarding you with notifications from all these sources. The access to information has never been easier (but easy does not mean simple).

Consider the following scenario: an event happens (it can be anything—a fire, a concert, a tornado hits, a terrorist attack). Traditionally (most likely, long before your time), you would find out about the event from traditional news outlets or sources (radio, print, TV). Maybe if you happened to have a family member or a friend involved in or witnessing the event, you would get a phone call from them, as the event happened, or immediately after it happened. But most people would find out about what happened, from the news. As Jared Schroeder (2015, p. 113) said in the previous chapter: "A journalist's first goal is to inform, and his or her "client" is the public. Such a role in society places journalism in a unique position, one that was not settled over night."

And this role might be becoming less clear. In his 1995 book *The Power of News*, Michael Schudson proposed the following exercise (Schudson, 1995, p. 1):

> Imagine a world, one easily conceivable today, where governments, businesses, lobbyists, candidates, churches, and social movements deliver information directly to citizens on home computers. Journalism is momentarily abolished. Citizens tap into any information source they want on computer networks. They also send their own information and their own commentary; they are as easily disseminators as recipients of news. (. . .) Each of us our own journalist. What would happen? (Schudson, 1995, p. 1).

His imaginary exercise is the reality in which we all live today. Nowadays, with the emergence of the Internet, 4G (and most recently, LTE), smart phones, and all sorts of social media, chances are that people—not journalists—break the news first and maybe even keep everyone updated as things happen (see Hudson River Plane Crash—Reuters 2011). It is in this context, when we have so many non-journalistic sources sending out information, that I often hear people (of course, not the Journalism students ☺), say things like "Anyone can report the news" or "Anyone can be a journalist." So then the question arises: do we even need journalists? Well, again Schudson (1995, p. 2) already offered the answer:

> People would want ways to sort through the endless information available. What is most important? What is most relevant? What is most interesting? People would want help interpreting and explaining events. It is all very well to be able to call up at will the latest Supreme Court decisions, but who among us is competent to identify the key paragraphs and put them in context? A demand would arise not only for indexers and abstracters but for interpreters, reporters and editors. (. . .) Journalism—of some sort—would be reinvented. A professional press corps would reappear. (. . .) It is hard to picture the contemporary world, even in the face of a technology that makes each of us potentially equal senders and receivers of information, without a specialized institution of journalism (Schudson, 1995, p. 2).

And as we can all see, *journalism is still alive, kicking and constantly reinventing itself*! So maybe then the question should not be if we still need journalists, but rather *why* we still need journalists:

> But why? Why do people feel a need for journalism? Why do people long to hear the news—not just gossip, not just information about people and places they know, not just a record of mysteries and marvels worldwide, not just practical bits of advice and useful notices, but a composite, shared, ordered, and edited product? (Schudson, 1995, p. 2).

The answer is simple: *because people need not just information but meanings.* And journalism, as a profession, and mass media, as a system, offer

1. <u>Selected</u> information (following certain criteria jointly shared by the publics and journalists),
2. <u>Organized</u> in unanimously predictable forms (genres, formats, types of mass media products),
3. <u>Communicated</u> in an accessible language (clear, referential, neutral, balanced, etc.)
4. And loaded with a certain <u>meaning</u> (derived from the journalists' information selection, organization, and processing; from the journalistic writing; from explicit elements of interpreting the facts—fragments in hard and feature stories; or from specific genres like editorials, debates, and cartoons).

The people who are Tweeting, Snapchatting, and so on and who witnessed or were involved in the event (let's call them non-journalists) simply offer chaotically raw bits of information. On the other hand, through their news stories, the journalists take the bits and pieces of raw information (obtained from different sources), they verify them, and then they organize them in logical, easy to follow format. The **news stories** offer context to and meaning of the event.

It is essential to understand that the information coming from non-journalistic sources can many times be fake, contradictory, opinionated, or meant to persuade people to buy certain things or do certain things. On the other hand, *journalists are bound by law, by ethics, and by professionalism to report accurate information, to the best of their abilities.* Journalistic professionalism should be a guarantee of information correctness, or **accuracy.** Moreover, journalists perform a selection of information, in order to not destabilize or confuse people with nonessential information. So what are the criteria used to order this informational chaos and offer reliable news stories?

Newsworthiness: Key Factors

As we saw previously, journalists comb through almost infinite information when producing their news story. Journalists have to decide what events to cover, what sets of information are important enough to make a news story, or in other words, what is

newsworthy. Several basic factors are used to determine whether a story is newsworthy (they are presented in different variations, in any journalism textbook—Stovall, 2015; Kanigel, 2012; The Missouri Group, 2014, etc.):

Timeliness: Has the event just happened? Is it new? Nowadays, this question is a challenging one, as in the 24/7 news cycle that we live in, new news becomes old news very fast. However, new aspects of a story emerge and need to be explained, so even if the event itself becomes "old news," the consequences, context, causes, or any new information will still be timely.

Proximity: Has the event happened close to "home?" A story on the Green Bay Packers (a football team from Green Bay, WI) might not be newsworthy to someone in Europe. But other information can be newsworthy for people who might not be in close geographical proximity of the event but might really care about the Packers. In this globalized, highly connected digital world, you also have to understand that proximity might not only be geographical but also issue based. Readers all over-the-world read *The New York Times'* web news stories.

Conflict: Does the story contain arguments, fights, and/or disagreements? Most news stories contain opposing views, and rivalry, be it in sports stories (two football teams fighting to win the game), politics stories (two political candidates fighting for the same position), or crime stories (police versus criminals).

Prominence: News stories have to be (and mostly are) about people. But the newsworthiness degree increases when the event or story involves someone well-known and important.

Human Interest: People and their issues, sufferance, and happiness are sometimes more interesting to read about than abstract numbers or data. How does a story affect an individual person or family?

Impact/Consequence: Does the event or story have some impact or effect on the reader's life? Anything that affects us (health care, weather, economy) is newsworthy.

Usefulness: Does the story have elements that would help the readers avoid trouble, make better decision, and improve their life quality? Examples include stories on how to choose a college or how to pay down credit card debt.

<u>Novelty:</u> Is the story about something that happens outside the routine of daily life? The unusual, bizarre, and strange are newsworthy. The famous example is: dog bites man is not news, but when man bites dog (unusual) is certainly news.

Journalists and editors have to decide what is newsworthy enough be covered as news and what is newsworthy enough to be covered for more than a day, or in more than one news story. However, these factors of newsworthiness are not to be taken in an abstract and absolute matter. As media scholar Pamela Shoemaker (2006) argued, news and newsworthiness are not synonyms. While news can be considered "a primitive term, one whose existence is not questioned," newsworthiness "is a cognitive construct, a mental judgment" (Shoemaker, 2006, p. 105). As a journalist deciding what makes your news story newsworthy, you have to understand your audience. These newsworthiness factors should always be put in the context of your audience: Is this subject useful or/and timely for my specific audience?

If you do not understand and know your audience, you will fail. What seemed newsworthy to you (maybe because all other media reported on a peculiar story, and you want to jump in the bandwagon) might turn out to be perceived as non-news or irrelevant for your audience. Recently, Miley Cyrus brought a homeless man to accept her 2014 VMA Award in order to raise awareness for homeless youth; later, it turned out that he had a warrant for his arrest for violating his probation in Oregon (Stampler, 2014). The VMA awards took place on August 24, and initially the news concentrated just on Miley's PR stunt. Two days later, a multitude of news outlets reported on the newly discovered information about the homeless man's warrant for arrest. Among them was ABC News, who posted a headline about the arrest warrant and a link to their story on Facebook. A series of negative replies to the post followed, as readers made remarks disparaging the network's focus on the story and suggesting it was better left up to tabloid gossip than major news outlets. ABC News' audience did not seem to perceive that news story as newsworthy. This happens almost every day. As a fun exercise, try to look at the stories different media outlets (CNN, ABC News, your local newspaper, etc.) post on social media and their Web site and the connected comments from the audiences. How many times and at what stories do the commenters complain about a news story not being newsworthy for them?

Journalistic Professionalism in Today's Media Landscape

As we saw at the beginning of this chapter, we still need journalists—perhaps now more than ever. It is *journalists' education, training, and core principles to which they adhere that differentiate the professional journalists from non-journalists* (citizen journalists, bloggers, etc.). As Kovach and Rosentiel (2014, p. X) argued, the core elements of journalism (journalists' professionalism) are still very much essential today:

> As the contours of the digital revolution have grown clearer, we have grown even more confident that not only do the elements of journalism endure—but in an age where anyone may produce and distribute news, they matter even more.

Good reporters, through their news stories, help people to "know the facts and the context of events, to understand how they should react to that information, and to work on compromises and solutions that make their communities better" (Kovach & Rosentiel, 2014, p. X–XI).

Take a look at Kovach and Rosentiel's (2014, p. 9) 10 Principles of Journalism, represented in Figure 1. They hold the key for understanding what journalism professionalism means.

1. Journalism's first obligation is to the truth
2. Its first loyalty is to the citizens
3. Its essence is a discipline of verification
4. Its practitioners must maintain an independence from those they cover
5. It must serve as a monitor of power
6. It must provide a forum for public criticism and compromise
7. It must strive to make the significant interesting and relevant
8. It must present the news in a way that is comprehensive and proportional
9. Its practitioners have an obligation to exercise their personal conscience
10. Citizens have rights and responsibilities when it comes to the news as well – even more so as they become producers and editors themselves

Figure 1: A visualization of Kovach and Rosentiel's (2014, p. 9) 10 Principles of Journalism

Sourcing, Fact Checking, and Accuracy

As media scholar Jane Singer (2015) argued, in a media environment where anyone can be a publisher, journalistic norms are essential in allowing journalists to distinguish themselves from non-journalists. Independence, verification, and accountability remain core notions of journalism professionalism that set them apart and help maintain their credibility.

Schudson (2011, p. XV) highlighted the fact that journalists today operate in a complex world of information management, a world full of **parajournalists** (such as PR firms, political spin doctors, governmental, corporate, and nonprofit institutions). Furthermore, "news as something produced by working people every day is primarily the result of the interaction between journalists and parajournalists, including especially what journalists themselves call **sources**" (Schudson, 2011, pp. XV–XVI). *Journalists depend on sources* (documents, people, etc.). Every good **news story** has at least three or four different sources.

Information selection takes place depending on the value, prestige, and credibility of sources. Journalists need to decide the sources' reliability, and to do so, they usually look for certain characteristics. According to French media scholar Jean Charron (1991, p. 115), journalists invoke six criteria when evaluating source reliability: (1) productivity (the source's ability to produce interesting and quality information in enough and constant quantities); (2) credibility (journalists' trust in the reliability of received materials); (3) social visibility (the source's position within the societal hierarchy); (4) source authority (experience and competence of the source as compared to other possible sources); (5) social and geographical proximity (how reachable the source is for the journalist); and (6) flexibility (the source's power to adapt to the journalistic work procedures, language, and professional code).

Dealing with facts, being able to offer only verified information in their news stories is what differentiates journalists from non-journalists (Hermida, 2015). This process of verification became even more important in a world where misinformation or disinformation spreads at the click of a share or retweet. News stories need to be accurate. That's what your audiences expect.

"One-man bands"

Reporters are now expected to write, shoot video, record audio, update online content, and be active on social media. The aforementioned journalistic norms of professionalism and ethics (which will be explained next) are becoming more important and more challenging to keep up to, as journalists have to do more now with fewer resources. Add to that constant scrutiny from the public:

> Accuracy, of course, is a hallmark of the best journalism. But perfection has always been elusive. Nobody's perfect, after all, so mistakes will be made. In the digital age, accuracy is an even rockier road. Transparency and

interactivity mean errors will be highlighted in very public ways. Immediacy means the time spent verifying information has diminished, so the chances for error have increased (Briggs, 2016, p. 128).

Wolfgang and Coman (2015) looked at how the audience understands its own role in the journalism process and its engagement in news-mediated public discourse. They analyzed *The New York Times'* comments posted on the online news stories about the Newtown shooting. They found that commenters felt that it was their mission to debate the issue and come up with solutions. Commenters criticized, praised, and had direct demands from the general media as well as from specifically the outlet they were engaging with (*The New York Times*). In a sense, it can be argued that commenters became the watchdogs of media. And they were fierce and many times unforgiving. As Wolfgang and Coman found, "their comments conveyed the idea that they were owed by the media in general, and especially by the journalists of the publications where they were commenting, accurate, reliable and complete information" (Wolfgang & Coman, 2015). Maybe, as Singer (2015) and Hermida (2015) argued, it is time to add transparency to the list of values of journalism professionalism and to open up journalistic processes to the outside.

Journalistic Ethics

Bias and neutrality

Journalists should always try to be unbiased and objective. But the truth is, no human being can be 100% objective. Each of us might perceive the same event, or issue differently, depending on our background (cultural, geographical, experiences, family, etc.). Moreover, journalists have to decide what the focus of the story should be (the **angle**), what sources to use (what sources will not make it in the story), how long to cover a story, and so on. All these decisions in a sense lead to a certain degree of **bias**. However, that is not an excuse and should not lead to opinionated news writing. Instead, as a journalist, you should focus on writing a fair news story (presenting all sides), writing a well-sourced and documented (accurate) news story. To achieve neutrality when writing the news story, you

1. Should not insert your opinion in the story (the third-person point of view helps)
2. Should always attribute the information presented in the story (attribute your sources)
3. Should keep your language neutral (avoid embellished wording).

Media ethics and ethical concerns

In their day-to-day reporting process, journalists are faced with ethical decisions. Briggs' thoughts on what journalists should ask from their online audience in terms of ethics, might as well apply to what journalists themselves should do to be ethical:

> "A news organization should look to its terms and conditions on its Web site and see what it is expecting or requiring from the audience that is now contributing content. Be real. Be nice. Don't lie. Don't take credit for something that is not yours. Basic rules like that. You know, the stuff my kids learned in kindergarten" (Briggs, 2016, p. 122).

The following are the ethical concerns most connected to journalism (they are presented in any journalism textbook—Stovall, 2015; Kanigel, 2012; The Missouri Group, 2014, etc.):

1. Deception. When (at any time) is it ethical and ok to use deception? Investigative journalists (think undercover journalists) sometimes hide who they are in order to get the story. One thing is for certain, journalists should never deceive their publics through their news stories.
2. Invasion of Privacy. As a journalist, you write about people. When a crime happens, you most likely will have to interview the victims, their families, and the possible perpetrator(s). Often, children are involved. What was private information becomes public through your news story (names, feelings, and so on). Often times, journalists justify invading privacy by using the idea that the public has a right to know. But just how much should this right to know extend? Would the public's right to know justify releasing a murder victim's name, or photo? What public good could come from invading a family's privacy and releasing their or their children information? How do you decide what information is important? These are difficult questions to answer. To illustrate this dilemma, let us look at a recent example from Knoxville, Tennessee, where an 8-year-old girl was killed. The *Knoxville News Sentinel* (the local newspaper) ran a story naming the 11-year-old boy accused of killing the little girl. Was that ethical? Was that necessary enough for the public's right to know, to justify invading the boy and his family's privacy? Here is what the newspaper posted on Facebook in order to explain the decision:

> The decision to name the 11-year-old suspect was not easy. It came after intense discussion among editors weighing many factors. But the decision was the newspaper's. Officials in the judicial system abide by strict laws governing the release of such information.

> You can read Jack McElroy's (Knoxville News Sentinel's Editor) full column here: http://www.knoxnews.com/opinion/columnists/jack-mcelroy-why-is-news-sentinel-naming-an-11yearold-suspect_72305790.

3. <u>Conflicts of Interest.</u> As a journalist, you need to try to remain as objective as possible. In this sense, conflicts of interest can arise when journalists (1) can benefit from presenting the story in a certain way (i.e., writing a positive story on a company in which you own stocks, or on a company that sent you gifts, and free merchandise/services) and 2) are friends (or enemies) with the subject of their news story, or the sources of their news stories.

4. <u>Fabrication of stories and **Plagiarism**.</u> In their quest for the best story, some journalists have unfortunately exaggerated or outright falsified stories and information. In the 1990s, Stephen Glass was a rising star in journalism until it was discovered that some of his articles for *The New Republic* and other magazines were partially or completely fabricated (Somayia, 2015). Recently, he made the news again, as he repaid Harper's Magazine $10,000 for his discredited work (Somayia, 2015).

Another famous example is *The New York Times'* reporter Jayson Blair (check out the movie about him—A Fragile Trust: Plagiarism, Power, and Jayson Blair at the New York Times, released in 2014). In 2003, it was discovered that Blair fabricated details in his stories and plagiarized others. Even more recently, *NBC Nightly News* anchor Brian Williams was suspended in February 2015 without pay for six months because he misrepresented events occurring while he was covering the Iraq War in 2003.

When it comes to fabrication and plagiarism, there is no ethical defense! These two are offenses that go against the most sacred principles of journalism. Remember, journalism's first obligation is to the truth! (Kovach & Rosentiel, 2014, p. 9). A good place to start to find out more about journalistic ethics is the Society of Professional Journalists (SPJ) and its Code of Ethics (http://www.spj.org/ethicscode.asp). When in doubt about ethical dilemmas, take Briggs' advice: "*Most ethical dilemmas can be solved through transparency. If everyone knows what you're doing and why you're doing it, there is a very low risk of impropriety*" (Briggs, 2016, p. 123).

Final Thoughts

This chapter was meant to serve as an introduction to the journalism profession. It also largely dealt with the challenges journalists face. But, as Freedman said in his book, *Letters to a Young Journalist* (2011, p. 18): "I'm not trying to scare you off. I hope you find the challenges inspiring." Despite its challenges, being a journalist has its rewards. The world still needs great journalists: "Human beings will keep wanting to know what's news. They'll keep wanting to have a lucid explanation, a smart analysis, of the events around them" (Freedman, 2011, p. 175).

If you are contemplating journalism and want a short and entertaining way to find out more about how and why journalists do what they do, you should play Poynter's "Be a Reporter" Game (it only takes 15 minutes). You can find it at https://www.newsu.org/courses/be-reporter-game.

And for when you do decide to become a journalist, I, like Freedman, dare you:

"Come on, then. I'll grab my pen and notebook. You get your gear. There's some great story out there to cover. And when we're done, we'll go for a coffee or a drink and gripe about our editors and talk about how we have the greatest job in the world" (Freedman, 2011, p. 175).

References

Barthel, M.; Shearer, E.; Gottfried, J. & Mitchell, A. (July, 2015). *The evolving role of news on Twitter and Facebook.* Pew Research Center. Retrieved from http://www.journalism.org/2015/07/14/the-evolving-role-of-news-on-twitter-and-facebook/.

Briggs, M. (2016, p. 128) *Journalism next. A practical guide to digital reporting and publishing* (3rd ed.). Thousands Oaks, CA: Sage. CQ Press.

Charron, J. (1991). Les médias, les sources et la production de l'information. In Charon, J., Lemieux, J., Sauvageau, F. (Eds.) *Les journalistes, les médias et leurs source.* Québec: Gaetan Morin Editeur.

Duggan, M. (August, 2015). "Mobile messaging and social media—2015". Pew Research Center. Retrieved from http://www.pewinternet.org/2015/08/19/mobile-messaging-and-social-media-2015.

Freedman, S. G. (2011). *Letters to a young journalist.* Philadelphia, PA: Basic Books, A member of the Perseus Books Group.

Hermida, A. (2015). Nothing but the truth: Redrafting the journalistic boundary of verification (p. 37–50) in *Boundaries of journalism: Professionalism, practices and participation (shaping inquiry in culture, communication and media studies)*, Matt Carlson & Seth C. Lewis (Eds.). New York: Routledge.

Kovach, B. & Rosenstiel, T. (2014). *The elements of Journalism. What newspeople should know and the public should expect.* New York: Three Rivers Press.

Perrin, A. (October 8, 2015). *Social networking usage: 2005–2015.* Pew Research Center. Retrieved from http://www.pewinternet.org/2015/10/08/2015/Social-Networking-Usage-2005-2015/. Accessed 10 October, 2015.

Reuters (2011). *Factbox: News that broke on Twitter.* Reuters.com. Retrieved from http://www.reuters.com/article/2011/07/08/us-twitter-factbox-idUSTRE76700F20110708.

Schudson, M. (1995). *The power of news.* Cambridge: Harvard University Press.

Schudson, M. (2011). *The Sociology of News* (2nd ed.). NY: W.W. Norton & Company, Inc.

Shoemaker, P. J. (2006). News and newsworthiness: A commentary. *Communications: The European Journal Of Communication Research, 31*(1), 105–111.

Singer, J. (2015). Out of Bounds: Professional norms as boundary makers (p. 21–36). In Matt Carlson & Seth C. Lewis (Eds.). *Boundaries of journalism: Professionalism, practices and participation (shaping inquiry in culture, communication and media studies)*, New York: Routledge.

Somayia, R. (Oct. 16, 2015). Stephen Glass repays Harper's $10,000 for his discredited work. *The New York Times.* Retrieved from http://www.nytimes.com/2015/10/17/business/media/stephen-glass-repays-harpers-10000-for-his-discredited-work.html.

Stampler, L. 2014. Time. *The homeless man Miley Cyrus brought to the VMAs turned himself in to police.* Retrieved from http://time.com/3221239/miley-cyrus-vma-police/.

Stovall, J. G. (2015). *Writing for the mass media* (9th ed.). Boston: Pearson.

The Missouri Group; Brooks, B.S.; Kennedy, G.; Moen, D.R. & Ranly, D. (2014). *News reporting and writing* (11th ed.). Boston: Bedford/St. Martin's.

Kanigel, R. (2012). *The student newspaper survival guide* (2nd ed.). Oxford, UK: Wiley-Blackwell.

Wolfgang, J. D. & Coman, I. (May, 2015). *New Media, New Phenomena: An analysis of online commenters' perceptions of media and commenter performance.* Presented at the ICA 2015 Annual Conference, San Juan, Puerto Rico.

CHAPTER 11

What is Public Relations?

Danny Shipka

Public Relations (or PR) is one of the most exciting yet misunderstood aspects of mass communications. Just the mere mention of it to hardened journalists unleashes a tirade of negativity with words like "manipulation," "propaganda," "spin," and even "lying" being thrown about in order to cast the profession into doubt. One look at popular culture doesn't help much either as we've seen *Scandal*'s Olivia Pope and *Sex and the City*'s Samantha Jones lie, blackmail or use sex as tools for getting what they want and accomplishing their goals. The fact is nothing could be farther from the truth. PR is not only a noble profession with a strong ethical base but one that is essential for every thriving business and organization.

Think about every successful business venture, every successful fundraising campaign for a nonprofit, or Beyoncé and Miley Cyrus. Between them may have a good product, noble cause, or even talent but without a proper PR campaign to reach the public each of them would languish in obscurity. Used correctly and ethically, PR can be an invaluable tool to any organization which is why it is important to understand what exactly PR is and the positive tactics and strategies that will keep you and your business successful.

When prospective students tell me that they want to go into PR or Strategic Communications, I always ask them "Why?" After I get a blank stare for about 5 seconds the response is usually something along the lines of "Because I'm good with people, I like people." Well, in the words of my former mentor at the University of Florida, Kathleen Kelly, ". . . so do cannibals." This means most people don't fully understand what PR actually is. They just know it looks like a glamorous and fun job. I tell them they're right, it can be glamorous and fun but mostly it's hard work that if practiced correctly can lead to great personal and professional success. If it's done unethically though, it can cause irreparable damage.

The good news is this, if you can understand and master the concepts of PR and perform your duties ethically, there's a job for you in whatever field you're interested in. If you want to go into sports, there's a team or organization waiting for you, entertainment, politics, medicine, law, even if you have a love for something obscure like chess or horseshoes there is an organization out there that needs good quality PR to help further their success. No other profession allows so much autonomy and allows you to practice in any field that you want. So let's take a look at PR, what it is, where it came from, and learn some tools to practice it successfully.

What is PR?

Recently, I sat in a freshman orientation seminar to talk to prospective students about careers in mass communications. A student pleasantly asked what the difference was between journalism and PR. Before I could answer, one of my colleagues from journalism, known for his negative opinion of PR, barked out, "You want to know the difference between the two? If you want to find out the truth, pick Journalism. If you want to manipulate and lie about the truth, pick PR." Of course I didn't agree, but I wasn't surprised. One of the reasons perhaps for so much criticism about PR is that no one can really define it (Moss & DeSanto, 2014, p. 17). Ask a group of 10 students what PR is and you're likely to get 10 different answers. Some will say it's event planning (not wrong), some will say it's fundraising (also not wrong), and most will give the standard answer of "it's about working with the public." It's a tough question. Even PR professionals in the field disagree on a basic definition that contributes to the general confusion about the field. So let's settle with this simple definition:

> **Public Relations** is the management function that establishes and maintains (via public relations, advertising and marketing) mutually beneficial relationships between an organization and the publics on whom its success or failure depends. (Cutlip, Center, Broom, 2000)

There's a lot of information in this definition but the most important words are "**mutually beneficial relationships.**" They represent the core of what PR is. Think about it. Aren't the best relationships based on the idea of giving what you can to someone and getting back what you need? Aren't you more apt to trust someone you've spent considerable time with? Do you sometimes give up things because its causing your relationship suffer? In a good relationship, the answer to those questions should be yes. The best relationships are never easy, they take time and sometimes pain to become successful. So remember, PR is not about the bottom line or a quick fix, it's about the continuous long haul of relationship building and maintenance. It's the give and take with the public and practicing good stewardship (more about that later) that will lead to success in the end.

Imagine doing PR for a new company, say a bank or a nonprofit organization that saves cats, moving into a brand new city. How would you integrate your company with the local audience? How do you reach out to them to get them through the doors, to think and talk highly of your company and, most importantly, how do keep them coming back? That's what PR does. Effective PR is the bridge between an organization and the public. It's a relationship that, like personal relationships, has to be taken care of with honesty and hard work. If you put the time and positive energy into a relationship, the outcome is more often than not, positive. If, on the other hand, you lie and manipulate your way through one, you're most likely to get dumped. There have been many organizations as well as celebrities and professional athletes have been unceremoniously dumped by their publics for not dealing honestly with them or engaging in behavior that didn't align with the people supporting them. Being "good with people" is alright but knowing how to effectively manage relationships is the key to success in the field.

The purpose of PR is to motivate, modify, or maintain attitudes, behavior, and information levels of targeted publics—internal as well as external meaning you, as the PR practitioner, are in charge of pretty much everything the public thinks about your organization or personality. Notice how I didn't use the word manipulation. Remember, the goal is to keep your publics supporting you over the long haul. If you start lying or misrepresenting yourselves to them, you're not going to last. Your job is to get people to think positively about your client, to change negative perceptions into positive ones, and to keep the public informed about what's going on in your organization. For example, let's say your client was Beyoncé. What would be your role as her PR agent? She's popular, is talented, and has endured very little personal scandal. You think you have it easy, right? Well think again. Keeping any artist #1 for long periods of time is nearly impossible: people get bored, audiences age out, newer artists have more appeal, etc. Most artists have a shelf life of 5 years or so. Some (Madonna, Sinatra, Elvis, Streisand, and a few others) have careers that span decades but they are exceptions to the rule. Your job here would be to try and develop new fan bases, keep happy the old ones, and combat any negativity that will crop up via snarky fans and media outlets that work against you. If your client is Justin Bieber, your job would be different as you would spend a lot of your time combating negative bias both by the press and online. See, every artist would have different needs even though they did the same things.

The most important thing to remember about PR is that it is audience based. That means your publics are your number one priority. ***Publics*** are communities of people at large (whether or not organized as groups) that have a direct or indirect association with an organization: customers, employees, investors, media, students, etc. (Business Dictionary, 2015). Your number one concern at all times is your audience/public.

In PR, publics are targeted. *Targeted publics* are those publics who specifically are gone after because that particular group may be more responsive to your organizational mission. For example, you'd not target a medical marijuana campaign to boys 10–18, no matter how much they'd like it, but you would look for those people with medical issues who would be supportive.

A public/audience can be either internal or external. *Internal audiences* are those people or groups who work within an organization. Why would you devote valuable time and resources to those people working within your organization? There's an easy answer to that. Sometimes a company is so big (think Apple) with many offices both regional and global; it requires a strong PR presence to inform people what's going on as well as create an environment in which employees feel like a valuable part of the organization. Even small- and mid-sized companies practice internal PR as a good way to keep the relationship between management and staff flowing smoothly. *External audiences* are those publics who reside outside of the office. They can be small groups (your local Cub Scouts) or large demographics (women, ages 18–45). Recognizing and maintaining a good relationship with both sets of publics is essential for continued success.

Other elements essential to understanding PR, according to Wilcox et al. (2011) include the following:

- PR is deliberate. The function of PR should never be unintentional. It should be a focused effort to influence, gain understanding, provide information, and obtain information (p. 6)
- PR is planned. PR never happens in a vacuum or on the spot. It should be carefully planned out at all times. Even in times of crisis, plans should have effectively been worked and reworked to handle every possible scenario and outcome.
- PR is performance based. Basically, this means how you do your job is how you will be judged on it. Remember, everything you do in PR is under scrutiny by the public. Screw up and you not only fail professionally, you fail publically. Do a credible job and you will earn the trust and goodwill of the public.
- PR is about public interest. This should be a no brainer but it's important to reiterate PR is not just about your company's bottom line. It's about the public's needs and interest. The work that you do should in some way be socially responsible and mutually beneficial, there are those words again, to both you and the public. If you can tap in to public sentiment and develop trust, your bottom line should take care of itself.
- PR is a management function. Gone are the days when PR people were relegated to the basement and only called upon to produce press releases to the media. Today's 24/7 news environment mixed with the explosive popularity of social media has kicked practitioners upstairs to the CEO's office. PR should and must be a part of the *dominant coalition*, meaning it should directly report and be a part of all discussions going on at the executive level. Can you imagine a college president sitting in a boardroom with his staff arbitrarily deciding to raise tuition 10% without a PR expert

there or implementing a no social media rule at their college? Yes, that's right, it would be a nightmare. That's why it's important to have a PR professional in all major decisions. It's worth remembering that their job is not to tell the executives what to do but to simply point out how their decisions are going to affect their publics.

The Four Models of PR

No, this isn't a new show on TLC (shhh don't tell them or they'll probably try to create one), but as detailed by Grunig and Hunt (1984), these are four ways in which to approach and practice PR. Each model represents the history and growth of the profession. Some of these models work better than others, (you won't be surprised which one I think is most effective) but all are still being practiced today.

The first model developed and still widely practiced is **Press Agentry/Publicity** model. Think about a movie trailer for the last Lindsey Lohan or Adam Sandler film that tried to persuade you it was an amazing movie, a new magazine launch, the "drop" of a new Adele album or preseason of any sporting teams season. What do they all have in common? They are good examples of using "hype" to create interest in an event or organization. If this sounds similar to using propaganda to relate your message, you would be correct. In fact, the definitions of the two words are similar. The derogatory meaning of propaganda as defined by the Oxford dictionary relates to "information, especially of a biased or misleading nature, used to promote or publicize a particular political cause or point of view" (2015). The idea behind Press Agentry is similar, get the word out and generate interest.

Press Agentry utilizes one-way communication techniques. That means the message is sent with no opportunity for feedback. An advertisement, a speech, and a pre-recorded television program are all good examples of one-way communication techniques. The model was developed by carnival barkers and circus owners like P.T. Barnum who used every trick in the book to entice the audience to see their show. They promise the audience maximum thrills (come see the two-headed man!) while often delivering minimum outcomes (the two-headed man is a guy with a fake head glued on his shoulder). That's the thing with Press Agentry, it doesn't have to be honest—it only has to get public buy-in. Donald Trump is probably the best example in today's society of someone who's mastered the art of Press Agentry. Listen to any speech he's given. They are great examples of someone who is a shameless promoter of a product, in this case himself and his business interests. Exciting, with a perfect pitch delivery, Trump will often present his views that, while entertaining, are devoid of particulars or facts. A very accurate representation of Press Agentry.

As you've probably guessed, I'm not a big fan of the Press Agentry model for executing effective PR techniques because the model makes it easy to engage in dishonest practices. The second model of PR rectifies that. The **Public Information** model arose out of the need for corporations to deal with the growing press. By the end of the industrial age, early 1900s, corporations were under increasing pressure to be more transparent about their policies. Practitioners like Ivy Lee believed that companies that developed good policies would reap the benefit of good public opinion and created a model in organizations and nonprofits could effectively communicate their goals and values.

Like the Press Agentry model, Public Information is a one-way communication tool. It's not designed to offer feedback, only inform. The major difference between the two is that public information is accurate, honest information without embellishment or drama. It doesn't employ the theatrical techniques of publicity. Think of the e-mails you receive from your university on a daily basis. Is their purpose to excite you, tempt you like publicity does? No, not really. They only seek to inform you what is going on. By providing you with this information they may perhaps persuade you to invest time, money, or expertise in their message.

We've looked at 2 one-way communication models each of which are practiced to some degree today. For PR to be truly effective, it must use a two-way communication model. A two-way communication model is one where feedback is asked for and received. The first two-way PR model was **two-way asymmetrical** and arose in the mid-1920s when advertising was becoming big business. How do you know what people want? That's easy—ask them! Practitioners of the time, like Edward Bernays, discovered that if you asked the public what thought you could find better ways to persuade them. Two-way asymmetrical isn't "equal" communication meaning one party, usually the one doing the investigation, has a higher authority and is in control of situation. For example,

Doctor: "What's wrong?"
You: "My knee hurts"
Doctor: "Show me where"
(You show them)
Doctor: "It's not serious, take two aspirin and call me tomorrow."

See how that works? It's definitely two-way communication. The point is that one has all the power. Here it is the doctor, who can make a diagnosis based on the feedback. Once the diagnosis has been made, no further relationship is required. In PR, this model is important because it gives you a greater understanding of your publics but fails as a long-term relationship building model (Grunig, 1992, p. 298).

One last example, every semester I ask my class what model they think the class is and every semester they get it wrong. Since I encourage feedback, respect what the students are saying and try to be all-round good guy, they naturally assume that the class is two-way symmetrical. Wrong, it's asymmetrical. Think about it, even though I welcome feedback, the power resides with me. My students may all want "A"s or not want homework, etc. but in the end, I make the decision based on my own evaluation. The relationship is not equal.

We've talked about three model of PR, all of which are still practiced to some degree in every campaign. What's missing from each of them is the mechanism in which to facilitate long-term relationships. The **two-way symmetrical** model is the ideal in this respect. It promotes a mutual understanding between organizations and their publics. Developed in the 1950s when companies began to realize that establishing and maintaining long-term relationships were essential to success (and widely practiced today). Two-way symmetrical works effectively because it uses a continuous feedback loop. Meaning the dialogue between organizations and publics never ends.

Think of every good relationship you've ever been in. What made it so good? Was it because you had your needs met? Was it because you were able to contribute something to it? The answer is probably both. We're apt to stay in relationships when we feel we are being listened to and in turn have a say in them. Good relationships depend heavily on positive communication between the parties and the two-way symmetrical model is the best way to achieve that.

What PR Isn't

We've spent some time talking about what PR is, it's important to tell you what it isn't. Let's start with the obvious thing it's not—journalism. Though good writing is essential to both, there are some distinct differences between the two fields. The first is objectivity. Journalists are supposed to be objective. Though "news" programs like Fox News stretch the credibility of that statement of late, journalists work under the coda that their reporting is free from bias. The PR professional, on the other hand, is biased. I don't want to say totally biased because if their organization is not behaving ethically, it is my hope that PR professional would be honest about it. They do have a client in which they're representing and, therefore, have a particular viewpoint. Another difference is audiences. As I mentioned earlier, PR is about targeted audiences. The goal is to find those audiences who can enhance or need whatever you're advocating. In journalism, there usually is no targeted audience. The goal is simply to present the story to everyone (Wilcox et al., 2000, p. 13). Finally, journalistic output is relegated to print or digital media in a mass media venue like newspapers, television, or Web site delivery. PR may utilize those media outlets but equal attention is paid to face-to-face communication, events, and small group discussions.

Since the advent of PR, the relationship between the two professions has been uneasy at best, downright acrimonious at worst. Why? Personally, I never understood the degree to which journalists hate the PR profession until it was explained to me by someone who worked in both areas. She said the problem is that journalist have a job to do, to uncover the truth, and they often see the PR person as standing in their way to get to it. Journalists want to talk to those in charge but they instead get the PR person who is clearly don't trust to give forthright answers. I suppose that makes sense, but it shouldn't mean that two professions can't forge a truce. Since its goal of PR to facilitate relationships, I'm going to put the responsibility of developing positive working relationships with journalists on them (don't worry, they can handle it). Having good relationships with journalists is essential as the press can often have a large impact, positively or negatively, on public perception. Here are a few tips that can help.

1. Get to know the journalist. Check out their writing, know their beat. Understand what they do and how they do it.
2. Don't bother them with information or events that aren't newsworthy: Journalists are busy folks. Calling or flooding their e-mails trying to promote an event or gain press coverage for things that aren't in the general public's welfare gets old quickly. Only contact them when you've really got something you know will be of interest. They'll appreciate it and take you more seriously the next time you call.
3. When a reporter asks for information, provide it. This seems like a no-brainer but you'd be surprised how many organizations make the mistake of trying to hide, delay, and cover up things to reporters. This just makes them more determined to find a story and makes your job more difficult. If the material they are looking for will somehow have a negative impact on your organization, so be it. You should, as a good PR practitioner, already know how to take care of it.
4. Don't ever attempt to bribe a journalist. Look, journalists aren't dumb, they know when they are being schmoozed, so providing them with food, gifts, and incentives to try and garner positive press will only irritate them. Treat them with respect and provide things to them that you make available to everyone else.
5. Understand they have a job to do. It's important that PR professional understand that journalists have responsibility to their news organization and are not carrying out personal vendettas against them. The two professions don't have to work at cross purposes. They just have to develop a mutual understanding.

Marketing and PR share some similarities. The American Marketing Association (AMA) defines marketing as "the activity, set of institutions, and processes for creating, communicating, delivering, and exchanging offerings that have value for customers, clients, partners, and society at large" (you can read the full definition at https://www .ama.org/AboutAMA/Pages/Definition-of-Marketing.asp). The goal of any good marketer is to research and target those publics who may have a vested interest in what a company offers, a goal which is similar to PR. Marketing though is more centered on the product and not the message. It's not about cultivating long-term relationships, only short-term ones that lead to purchasing of a product. Think of marketing as the quick hit and PR as the slow burn.

PR and advertising have a complicated but symbiotic relationship. Bovee defined advertising as "non-personal communication of information usually paid for and usually persuasive in nature about products, services or ideas by identified sponsors through the various media" (1991, p. 7). So both PR and advertising use persuasion as means of influence public opinion but one major difference is advertising is a one-way communication function that uses the mass media, like journalism, to sell its products, like marketing. This means that advertising is not concerned with feedback or in the development of relationships. It's more a tool to inform publics about a particular product or event. A good PR professional will recognize the importance of advertising within any campaign, as it gives visual representation to persuade the public to buy into your message. PR and advertising are becoming so intertwined that companies, agencies, and universities are combining the two disciplines, along with some marketing techniques, into new departments under the name Strategic Communications. This evolving style of communications is designed to help build and facilitate better relationships with the public.

I Want a Job: Careers in PR

Okay, here's the part you care about. You want to know, "Are there a lot of jobs in PR and can I get one?" The first answer is a most definite "yes". There are all kinds of PR-related jobs in all kinds of different areas including but not limited to

- Employee relations
- Community relations
- Investor relations
- Media relations
- Government relations
- Public affairs
- Consumer relations
- International relations
- Crisis communication
- Risk communication
- Health communication
- Litigation public relations
- University relations
- Sport and entertainment.

And that's just a sample of what you can get into. As I mentioned before, EVERY single business, nonprofit, and/or legitimate organizations requires good PR to keep it successful. Finding out in life what interests you may be difficult. Once you know what they are though, finding a career in PR with that focus will be relatively easy.

The second part of the initial "how do I get a job?" question depends on you. "Being good with people" or planning successful events, while helpful, is simply not good enough to maintain a successful career in PR. You need skills that will allow you to communicate effectively, on paper, in person, or in the digital realm. The most important skills are

1. Writing: Yes, I said writing. There is no more important skill to being a successful PR practitioner than being a good writer. I know, your face just fell and you were tempted to say what Heidi Montag said on the premiere episode MTV's *The Hills* (2006) when she said to the PR director of the company she was interviewing

with "I don't want to do THAT part, I want to do the people part." Being a good writer is imperative—learn the rules, learn AP style, (more groaning), and learn how to spell. If you don't . . . well, has anyone heard from Ms. Montag lately? No, I thought not.

2. Be an **environmental scanner**: I'm often stunned at how uninterested students are in the world around them. It's essential for PR practitioners to know what's going on in the world politically, economically, and socially. You never know where the next idea, trend, issue is going to rise up. You should be reading and listening to people on a daily basis.

3. Be a team player: PR is not for those who love to work solo. It often involves working within a larger group and delegating large portions of the job to others. Learn the basics of group dynamics and keep smiling.

4. Use your logic: It's important to keep your cool not only because things may, and frequently do, go wrong but because it's important to be able identify issues and trends that may affect your organization.

5. Tone down the "bubble": Ask anyone to describe a PR professional and more likely than not, will describe a loud, overtly confident person who promises the moon and delivers nothing. PR professionals have worked hard to change the perception of the business. Future practitioners should take it upon themselves to up hold the ethics and values of the profession to high regard. No one takes a bubble-head seriously. It's okay to act personably, in fact you should. Just don't overdo it.

Putting It All Together

Here is a simple example of how PR works, practically from a case perspective. It utilizes the R.O.P.E.S. process which, if applied to any situation, will guide the practitioner through the campaign or issue. R.O.P.E.S. stands for

Research
Objectives
Programming
Evaluation
Stewardship

The process is followed in order and always successful at achieving a productive outcome. Let's try it with this example:

You're a part of a major league baseball team that is moving to a mid-market city (600,000 pop.) The city does not have professional sports team but one minor league soccer team. It's the start of the season and it looks like it'll be a .500 year. How do you get near full capacity crowds to support the team in the first year and how do you keep them coming back?

How do you solve this? First, I'd be excited by the opportunity. You have a chance to make a huge, positive difference in the community. Second, I'd ask what the budget is. Seriously! All the good intentions in the world will do you no good if you can't afford it. Let's for sake of the argument say the budget is healthy. We then move on to R.O.P.E.S.

Research: The first thing you do, ALWAYS, is conduct research. Not conducting research would be like driving without gas. You won't get anywhere. If you skimp on this section your campaign will be doomed. Good research takes time, so do it right. It should be conducted thoroughly using a variety of quantitative and qualitative methods. The important thing here would be to try and gauge public opinion. I would conduct focus groups and interviews (qualitative) with not only citizens but with business leaders and politicians. I would also conduct a large survey (quantitative) to people in the city and state to ascertain what things they're interested in as well as their fears, concerns, etc. I would also look very closely at other cities and teams and see how their efforts fared.

Objectives: After the research has been conducted and vetted, it's time to set some reasonable objectives. Objectives should always be quantifiable, meaning that there should be a number goal you wish to attain as well as time frame. Notice how I also said reasonable. For this case, I would never say I'm going to improve attendance by 75% every week because it's simply unattainable. You're judged by meeting your objectives, so set them realistically. Here I would say we say based on the research, some good objectives would be to see the stadium filled to 70% capacity on 13 different occasions and a 30% rise in attendance by returning fans by the end of the season (Oct. 1).

Programming: All right, we've set the objectives based on the research. Now get to work achieving them. Event planners of the world, unite! How do achieve the goals you just set with the idea of cultivating a relationship (meaning you want them to come back)? How about a branding campaign to introduce the players and management to the public? Have them appear at events, teach little leaguers how to play better ball. Why not invite the little leaguers to the games? Remember your program must be compatible with your organizational mission. For example, you wouldn't have a program that showcased a rival team. Be creative but be smart.

Evaluation: This is the how are we/did we do phase. Remember we set up the objectives early, here is where we see if they are being met. For this case, I would look at attendance records as well as doing some surveys to gauge public opinion. If the goals are being met, we move on to the Stewardship phase. If they aren't, then it's back to the research phase all over to see if you missed something or if more research is required.

Stewardship: Congratulations, you've made it to the most important phase in process! It's the phase, ironically, that is least talked about among practitioners and scholars alike. The definition of stewardship is the responsible overseeing and protection of something considered worth caring for and preserving (dictionary.com, 2015).

By now you should have it ingrained in head that PR is singularly about establishing and maintaining relationships. Stewardship is how we keep a relationship going. What's the hardest part of any personal relationship? It's the day-to-day maintenance and upkeep. Meeting someone new is easy and fun. Keeping it easy and fun after 20 years takes work. In our example, what ways can you keep fans coming back year after year regardless of victories? Frequent visitor perks, special events, mailers that invited feedback, occasional surveys, etc. are a good start.

PR and the Future

PR is undergoing a radical transformation in the new digital age. With the rise of social media and the 24/7 news cycle, the profession has had to adapt to the publics' need for instantaneous information presented in an exciting, visual way. They seem to have adapted well as PR has evolved into an essential component to any organization or business. The new strategic approach, combining PR with some of the functions of advertising and marketing, will ensure that the profession will only grow stronger.

References

Bovée, C. L., & Arens, W. F. (1989). Contemporary advertising. Homewood, Ill: Irwin.

Business Dictionary online (2015). Retrieved from http://www.businessdictionary .com/definition/publics.html#ixzz3qGDeLJb3.

Cutlip, S.M., Center, A.H., & Broom, G.M. (2000) Effective Public Relations (8th Edition). Upper Saddle River, NJ: Prentice Hall.

Grunig, L. (1992). Activism: How it limits the effectiveness of organizations and how excellent public relations departments respond. In J. E. Grunig (Ed.), *Excellence in Public Relations and Communication Management*. Hillsdale, NJ: Lawrence Erlbaum.

Grunig, J. E., & Hunt, T. (1984) Managing Public Relations. New York: Holt, Rinehart and Winston

Moss, D., & DeSanto, B. (2014). *Public Relations, A Managerial Perspective*. New York: Sage Press.

Stewardship [Def. 2] (n.d.) In *Dictionary.com*. Retrieved from http://dictionary.reference .com/browse/stewardship?s=t.

Wilcox, D. L, Cameron, G. T. Ault, P. H., Agee, W. K. (2000) *Public Relations Strategies and Tactics*. New York: Allyn & Bacon

Wilcox, D. L, Cameron, G., Reber, B., & Shin, J. (2011). *Think Public Relations*. Pearson Education.

CHAPTER 12

Public Relations: Theory and Crisis

Amanda K. Kehrberg

Public relations (PR) is a very young profession, but it is an even younger field of scholarship. If we imagine journalism as an enigmatic Gray Lady, peeking out from behind stacks of worn tomes and emptied red pens, then PR is comparatively still a bright-eyed intern, picking up morning lattes and checking Instagram for new trends (a kind of **environmental scanning**, right?). It's true; PR has only been developing its own theory for about the past 35 years. In this time, it has already made great strides in defining the goals, strategies, and concepts important to PR research—and essential to improving outcomes for practitioners. And like the field of communication more broadly, PR has stood on the shoulders of the great fields that preceded it, drawing inspiration from the work of social psychology (Sigmund Freud was, after all, the uncle to PR founding father Edward Bernays), sociology, and even (more recently) computer science.

Theoretical Approaches to Public Relations

"Theory" can seem like an uninviting and abstract term, but the truth is that we all rely upon theories in our day-to-day lives, even if we do not use the word itself. Have you ever heard of a man named Sir Isaac Newton whose head was in the way of a falling apple? Then you are familiar with the theory of gravity—and chances are, even if its origin story is exaggerated, it affects where you might lay your picnic blanket under a ripened apple tree. If you work in a PR agency, you may find a corner of the office with a stack of books bearing names of important theories: Maybe they were donated by the crisis expert after she finished graduate school; maybe they are intended for the company book club but keep getting preempted by a popular vote in favor of chic graphic novels on "working smart." But whether your colleagues crack the pages of these books once a month or once a year, you can be sure that theory informs every strategy and tactic. If they value diversity in the workplace, they are actually following a tenet of excellence theory (Grunig et al., 2006). If they segment an organization's publics to better understand how to construct messages for each group, they are following the situational theory of publics (Grunig, 1978, 1989). In PR, theory is like the grandfather of what you might know as **best practices**. It is through developing and testing theory that researchers have established the principles of effective and ethical PR that become the best practices of working professionals.

From Functional to Cocreational

The first thing to understand about PR theory is that it has undergone a significant paradigmatic shift in recent years, from a **functional** to a **cocreational** perspective (Botan & Taylor, 2004). The traditional functional perspective in PR views publics as *useful* in achieving the organization's goals. The emphasis is placed on what is good for the organization or what it hopes to achieve, and interactions with publics are undertaken only for the functions they serve. Reading about this perspective, you can probably see how PR has often had a reputation—however unwarranted—for unethical behavior. Would you put your trust in an organization that only hoped to use you for its own benefit?

In contrast, the cocreational perspective views publics as an important part of a mutually beneficial relationship that must be founded on listening as well as talking. As opposed to the one-way communication of the functional perspective—in which the organization sends out messages to publics, but does not receive them—the cocreational perspective places value on open, welcoming, two-way communication to achieve mutual goals. The organization actively works with publics to cocreate meaning, fostering trust, and growing relationships in the long term. The cocreational perspective is understandably considered the best path for practicing ethical PR.

One way to understand this shift is through the context of technological change. The shift from functional to cocreational parallels one from a model of mass communication, in which mass media transmitted messages one way to broad publics with few choices, to Jenkins (2006) calls convergence culture. In the era of media convergence, technology is defined by interactivity and user choice and control: For organizations and publics, this opens up new avenues of two-way, and even real-time, interactive communication. Not only do organizations have new ways to speak to their publics, but more importantly, publics have new ways to talk back to organizations. New interactive social media also offers publics powerful ways to organize and disseminate information; notably, the cocreational perspective also incorporates the PR strategies and tactics of these increasingly empowered activists and activist groups.

Excellence Theory

If Helen of Troy was the face that launched a thousand ships, then excellence theory is the theory that launched a scholarly field, providing researchers with a paradigm and professionals with a roadmap to successful practice. Has there ever been a theory so aptly named? The title captures what all theory sets out to do: improve our understanding of the world, and help us make our practice not just good, but *excellent*.

Excellence theory is a **normative** theory; this means that it proposes an ideal model of PR practice. A PR professor once demonstrated the meaning of normative by handing out sad-looking, wilting fruits and vegetables. In pairs, students described what each item would taste, feel, and look like if it were an ideal version of itself: A normative banana would be bright yellow, with just the right balance between soft and firm. Just like with the banana, excellence theory lays out the criteria we can use to judge whether public relations practices are normative, or excellent.

Through an extensive study of more than 300 organizations, excellence theory establishes that "the value of public relations comes from the relationships that organizations develop and maintain with publics" (Grunig et al., 2006, p. 55). Excellence theory yielded important principles of excellent (ethical and effective) PR. Depending on who you ask, there are anywhere from 14 to 10 to 8 principles of excellent PR, but here they are summarized into six key takeaways:

1. **Empowerment**: PR is most effective for an organization when it is valued and supported by senior-level management. PR efforts should be led by a communication executive who has a seat at the table (in the conference room with the fanciest chairs, if you will) with other top-level executives.
2. **Diversity**: Organizations have diverse publics, and that diversity should be reflected within the organization among its PR practitioners.
3. **Activism**: Activism is not something to fear; rather, organizations should embrace activism as a key part of a mutually beneficial conversation with their publics. Activism highlights opportunities for the organization to adapt and better understand the needs of their stakeholders, which will in turn help them to strengthen long-term relationships.
4. **Symmetrical Communication**: Excellent PR practice is founded on the model of two-way symmetrical communication. Two-way symmetrical communication is an ongoing dialogue between an organization and its publics, through which each has a voice and a stake in reaching mutually beneficial goals.

5. **Participatory Culture**: Excellent PR, from an internal perspective, are built through an organizational culture that values open, free participation rather than rigid hierarchy. Each PR practitioner should feel that he/she has a voice within the organization; this results in very high levels of employment satisfaction within excellent organizations.
6. **Research**: Building mutually beneficial relationships and open dialogues with publics depends upon effective use of research, including environmental scanning, issues management, and surveys of publics. PR practitioners must understand the issues that are important to publics, their perceptions of an organization, and what goals they perceive as served through communication with that organization, in order to build lasting relationships.

Excellence theory's paradigm of symmetrical communication proved a foundation on which years of PR theory to follow have been built, as you will see in the rest of the chapter. But it is also important to note that excellence theory has been critiqued for not fully incorporating the perspectives of other nations and cultures, for whom two-way symmetrical communication may not be the ideal model. Continuing research has begun to fill these gaps in expanding excellence theory into new, diverse contexts.

Contingency Theory

A contingency is essentially a possibility; it is something you can prepare for based on the chances of its occurring—like assuring that you are not in your car during a tornado watch—but you cannot know for certain whether it will happen. Have you heard the phrase "contingent on your response?" This means that a result will be affected by the actions of another party.

This is the foundation of contingency theory, which responds to excellence theory by arguing that organization–public communication is situational and contingent on a variety of factors (more than 80, actually, according to the research!). According to contingency theory, there is no single, consistent model of excellent PR. Rather, how an organization and public respond to each other, and the degree to which they are able to adapt to the other's goals, will be contingent on each situation.

Like excellence theory, contingency theory anticipates and embraces conflict as an inevitable aspect of organization–public relationships. When faced with a conflict, the organization and its publics may act in a multitude of ways along a communication continuum. On one side is **advocacy**, meaning that each works to serve its own goals; on the other side is **accommodation**, through which each side considers the other's interests as well as their own (Cancel et al., 1997). On one end of the spectrum, an organization or public advocates on its behalf alone; on the other end, it opens up possibilities for accommodating the other's perspective. According to contingency theory, there is no one, uniform spot on the continuum from which organizations should act; rather, how they respond to each new conflict will depend on dozens of variables (Cameron et al., 2001). These factors, or contingencies, include everything from the individual characteristics of the PR practitioner who manages the communications to the characteristics of the organization to the wings of a butterfly flapping in the Amazon (okay, not that last one, but you get the idea). The key takeaway here is that how an organization communicates with its publics is situational and depends upon many factors, including those the organization can control and those it cannot. How an organization and its publics respond to each conflict, through levels of accommodation and/or advocacy, is contingent upon these factors.

Relationship Management Theory

Emerging dialogue within PR scholarship about the defining function of PR solidified in the focus on the relationship as exemplified in relationship management theory. This theory is founded on the idea that PR is best defined by the management of the organization–public relationship. This relationship is defined as "the state which exists between an organization and its key publics, in which the actions of either can impact the economic, social, cultural or political well-being of the other" (Ledingham & Bruning, 1998, p. 62). Relationship management theory has been celebrated for several significant developments in PR conceptualization and practice (Ledingham, 2006):

1. Situating the *relationship* as the most important unit of analysis for PR scholarship—and the most important concept in PR practice.
2. Emphasizing the *management* function of PR and supporting the idea that PR managers should be involved in the executive-level decision-making in an organization.
3. Introducing research methods for measuring the success and strength of an organization–public relationship, and how it is affected by and affects other measures like public perceptions, attitudes, and beliefs.
4. Incorporating models of organization–public relationships that break down the key components of relationship quality.

According to relationship management theory, the quality of an organization–public relationship depends on factors like trust, transparency, accountability, credibility, history, and shared goals. These concepts probably look quite familiar; they are as self-evident in judging relational quality among friends and significant others, as they are for relationships between organizations and publics. Think about it: If your friend had a history of not showing up on time, how would your perception of her reliability affect your relationship? What about your friend who takes a long time to respond to text messages or phone calls? Or how does it affect your relationship with a friend if you do not show at least a few important interests? All of these factors can chance how you feel about someone, and the same is true for how you feel about an organization. A key point to remember here, too, is that relationships are dynamic— they change over time. If your friend who never showed up on time started making changes (accommodations, you could say!), eventually you would notice and respond by changing your attitudes and beliefs, and even your behaviors, toward that friend. This would likely strengthen your relationship in the long term.

Situational Theory of Publics (STP)

Think about a cause about which you care deeply: Would you consider yourself an activist for this cause? How do you demonstrate your activism—do you share informa- tion with friends, "Like" posts, or give money? Now think about a cause that you do not really care about; perhaps you were too free with your contact information when you saw the person in the adorable panda costume with the clipboard on your lunch break. Does your heart sink when you see your inbox filling up with requests for time, money, and other resources? Do you wish you only had the courage to say "no" to a talking panda?

By thinking about how you personally respond to various causes and issues, you can begin to understand how an organization or activist group might segment you through Grunig's (1978, 1989) situational theory of publics (STP). STP explains how publics can be segmented into different groups along an activism continuum, based on their level of involvement with a particular issue. Publics are categorized as latent, aware, and active. Latent publics are those who do not know that a problem exists; aware publics know it exists but have not yet taken action; and active publics have both recognized a problem and organized as a public to confront it. Active publics are thus more likely to communicate with an organization. Grunig's model takes a step further in predicting the variables that will transform publics from latent to aware to active: problem recognition, constraint recognition, and level of involvement. Problem rec- ognition is fairly easy to understand: Do you perceive that a problem exists? From there, level of involvement defines whether an issue is personal: Does the problem affect you directly? Finally, constraint recognition defines to what degree you feel you are capable of acting to remedy a problem: Do you feel like there are actions you can take? Do you feel that those actions would make a difference?

Constraint recognition is a very interesting variable in the context of today's so-called armchair slacktivism: If activist behavior is defined simply by joining a Face- book group or clicking the "Share" button, then constraints on your ability to act are as minimal as WiFi and finger strength. Does this mean that you do not have to have a strong level of personal involvement with an issue to act, since acting requires so little of you?

In summary, STP seeks to predict how publics are motivated to communicate in response to a perceived problem, and how organizations can understand publics' behavior better through segmentation. Originally, STP specifically looked at the communication behaviors of information seeking (Did you Google it?) and information processing and attending (Did you actually read the Google results?). Kim and Grunig (2011) updated STP with the addition of information sharing and information selecting as more active communication behaviors; they called this revised theory the situational theory of problem solving (STOPS). These additional tactics are very important in the information age—and particularly in the context of social media—when we have so many ways of filtering and sharing information with each other.

Dialogic Theory

Responding to the shift in PR theory to a relational perspective, and an increasing use of the word **dialogue** as a communication goal, dialogic theory (Kent & Taylor, 2002) lays out the principles of a dialogic approach to PR. As a reminder, the relational perspective of PR views communication efforts as tools to help manage mutually beneficial relationships between an organization and its publics. Among these communication tools is dialogue, which is itself both a process and a goal. According to Kent and Taylor (2002), "Dialogue rests on a willingness to 'continue the conversation'—not for the purposes of swaying the other with the strength of one's erudition, but as a means of understanding the other and reaching mutually satisfying positions" (p. 30). A dialogic approach to PR is arguably the most ethical approach to communicating with publics and also can offer great rewards for the organization; and yet, it involves great resources and risk, and may not be expedient in every situation.

What does that mean, exactly? Take a look at the principles of dialogic communication according to Kent and Taylor (2002):

1. **Mutuality:** In dialogic communication, organizations and publics must enter the conversation with an understanding that they are mutually linked. They are seeking not to serve only their self-interests but to find mutually beneficial ways to move forward in the relationship. Dialogic communication involves collaboration and the motivation to understand each other's perspectives.
2. **Propinquity:** Propinquity essentially means that those participating in dialogue are present, active, and engaged, both in the short term and the long term. This can be as simple as responding in a timely manner, or as complex as participating fully, with one's whole self, in the dialogic process.
3. **Empathy:** For dialogue to be successful, it must be characterized by support, communality, and acknowledgement of the value of each participant's contributions.
4. **Risk:** Dialogue is risky; one enters into dialogue without necessarily knowing which direction the conversation will take. This can leave each participant feeling vulnerable; and, in a sense, it should. Vulnerability "offers the possibility of growth" (p. 28).

5. **Commitment:** Commitment refers to the genuine, open, trustworthy, and authentic engagement of participants in dialogue. Only though shared commitment to the continuing conversation, organizations and publics can cocreate new, shared meaning.

This likely all sounds a little idealistic, like the list you made in middle school of your ideal future spouse's qualities (and you weren't wrong; Justin Timberlake is probably excellent at dialogue). This underscores an important point about dialogue theory: It is *not* easy. In spite of its emergence in an era in which we have access to the most sophisticated tools of interactive, immediate communication we have yet encountered, dialogic communication has proved an elusive goal. Research continues to show that organizations interacting with publics even through spaces with great potential, like social media, are not behaving dialogically (McAllister-Spooner, 2009). In light of these findings, Kent (2013) suggested that maybe existing social spaces are not fit for dialogue and that organizations must create new spaces and invite publics to engage with them there (probably not Snapchat).

Additional Approaches

There are several additional theoretical perspectives that are highly valuable in PR research, but that were not created specifically from within the PR field. The most important of these is easily rhetorical theory, discussed in detail earlier in our textbook. Critical theory—which looks at power relations in society—and cultural theory also have an important history within PR research. There are even emerging trends embracing the work of cultural studies scholars on fandom as a kind of active public. Conceptually, fans seem to be the ideal stakeholder—one whose emotional relationship and identification with an organization, media text, or figure is so strong that they rally to defend the organization (Grossberg, 1992). For example, one recent study found that college football fans employed situational crisis communication theory strategies in defending their team in a time of crisis (Brown & Billings, 2013).

Discussed below are two of the most important consistent and emerging theories in PR research: feminism and network theory.

Feminist Theory. In their early writings about the burgeoning field of PR, Edward Bernays and wife Doris Fleischman wrote that a woman was more capable of performing any of the jobs created by the new profession, with the primary barrier being convincing her colleagues and clients of that obvious fact (Henry, 1999). As of 2015, women hold approximately 70% of all practitioner positions, which is why PR has been sometimes dubbed a "pink-collar" profession; and yet women account for only 30% of senior-level managers (Shah, 2015). Firms like Edelman, which launched its Global Women's Executive Network (GWEN) program to help promote women leaders within the company, have made important steps in recent years to improve this stark imbalance; but there is still more to be done.

How do we account for this gender gap in leadership? One way is to draw on feminist theory, which explores how gender inequality is socially constructed and institutionally maintained. One of the topics feminist theory covers is how ideas about normative femininity confine women into certain social roles and expectations: For example, women are stereotypically expected to be more caring, nurturing, and communal, while men are praised for being aggressive, individualistic, and ambitious (Eagly & Carli, 2007). Since leadership has traditionally been described using masculine-coded qualities like strength and dominance, women are subject to both internal and external prejudices that make them feel unfit for executive-level positions. You can see how this divide plays out in PR, which is defined by both relationship-building and a management function: One of these is traditionally coded as feminine (relational), while the other is coded as masculine (management).

Feminist theory can also help inform practitioners as they make choices about how to best form and grow relationships with diverse publics, particularly with regard to women's issues. One important theory to develop out of feminist thought, for example, is **intersectionality theory** (Crenshaw, 1991). Intersectionality theory argues that a person's social identity categories are not independent but overlap and blur in important ways that help us to better understand each individual's experience and sense of self. What this means is that a person cannot be understood simply as a woman or as an African-American or as a mother but as the combination of all of these identities. This is especially important to understand when segmenting and crafting messages for publics: All women cannot be expected to feel the same way about an issue and should not be addressed as though "woman" is their only identity.

Lastly, speaking of Fleischman, you should know that she was an incomparable wit. As she writes in her 1955 book on being a wife, the "world's most successful propaganda campaign" was "convincing women that hunting (or selling cogwheels) is hard, noble and virile" (p. 4). Surely another successful campaign—unintentional though it may have been—was too often emphasizing the founding *fathers* in PR history and neglecting profoundly impactful figures like Fleischman.

Network Theory. Network theory allows researchers to graph and visualize the relationships among a community of *actors*. Here, the term "actor" does not signify an Anne Hathaway or a Kevin Spacey; it refers more broadly to a member of a network, whose connections with other members can give us information about the strength of relationships and how they affect the sharing of messages. The method of *doing* network theory research for PR scholars is called **social network analysis** (SNA). SNA allows researchers to map out and analyze the connections between actors in a network; these connections can be defined by things like "following" on Twitter or hyperlinking via blogs or being a member of an organization (Saffer, 2013). Because PR is focused on relationship building and maintenance, SNA has become an increasingly prized tool to help scholars and practitioners alike understand how they can grow their **social capital**. Social capital can be defined in many ways, but put simply, it is the value of one's social networks, the goodwill and trust built through relationships that may yield a kind of useful action (whether that is a job recommendation, a ride to the airport, or a "share" of an important post) (Sommerfeldt, 2013).

Network theory is a rapidly expanding field of research within PR, but one of the most important concepts to know is the importance of **weak ties**. Weak ties are people or organizations with whom we are very loosely connected; they are considered the biggest relational gain of online social networks (Granovetter, 1973). Think about the people with whom you are connected on sites like Twitter and LinkedIn: Are they 250 of your closest, best friends? Or are they a more expansive and varied collection of people you may have met at an event, friends of friends, colleagues whose Halloween parties you would rather avoid, and other people or groups that piqued your interest? All of these connections represent your very own social network, within which *you* are one of the actors. PR network research is most concerned with your *position* in the network and what that says about your level of power and influence: If you post a message, how far will it spread? Are you connected to only like-minded people, or are your connections diverse? The number and position of weak ties that you have—like that one friend's brother, who now works in PR at a major New York firm?—can greatly spread your influence, because weak ties reach other networks of people to whom you otherwise may not have access.

Think of it like this: Your strongest ties are your close friends and family; you probably spend a lot of time with them, share important information and thoughts, and agree on many topics (well, perhaps not with all family!). On a given day, your closest friends may also post the same kitten-snuggles-puppy video—and why not? You all cherish your shared love of unconventional animal love! But it is your weak ties from whom you will see posts that challenge your existing perspectives and offer entirely new information. This effect is all the more important in an era of information overload, in which we often use our social connections as filters for the ample information we have access to every day.

In summary, network theory allows PR researchers to visualize the position of an organization or activist within a larger network. This can help the organization better understand how to distribute information with the greatest impact and build further relationships to increase its influence and reach.

Crisis Management

Crisis is sexy. It is dynamic, dramatic, and involves split-second decision-making of the sort American culture often prizes (as in "flying by the seat of your pants"). It makes exciting movies, riveting television, and page-turning novels. It is no accident that some of the best known media representations of PR practitioners work in crisis. Just look at *Scandal*'s eminently skillful heroine, Olivia Pope (played by Kerry Washington). As a crisis manager in Washington, D.C., Pope tactfully manages an unending array of political, corporate, criminal, and personal crises (*including . . . her love life!*).

She does all of this in a metaphorical white hat and a nonmetaphorical tailored, and somehow spotless, off-white suit. She is the superhero any budding PR practitioner might dream of being—and for critics, she is also the master manipulator to be feared and regulated.

Crisis theory itself does not quite reach Olivia Pope levels of sexiness, but when it comes to PR theory on the whole, crisis theory is surely the cool kids' table in the lunchroom. Take a seat; but be cautious, there is risk involved.

Situational Crisis Communication Theory (SCCT)

Enter a beginning graduate class on PR, and you will likely find a line of students waiting to present their 5-min introduction to situational crisis communication theory (SCCT). Why is SCCT so popular? For PR practitioners and students who have not yet donned their scholar caps, SCCT has an approachable practicality. It maps out a list of steps and guidelines that you can follow linearly and has the added benefit of allowing the reader to imagine she *is* Olivia Pope.

Ready? You are a crisis manager facing a crisis that *demands* a response. Your organization cannot let this crisis go unacknowledged; it must respond. What is at stake? Both your organization's reputation and its relationships. First, you must assess the reputational threat faced in this particular crisis situation; SCCT is based on the understanding that each crisis type has a most effective response strategy (Coombs, 2006, 2010). To do this, (1) identify the crisis type and (2) identify whether the organization has a history of related crises. SCCT organizes crisis types into three crisis clusters:

1. **Victim Cluster:** In this crisis type, the organization is itself also a victim; thus, the reputational threat to the organization is *mild*. Examples include natural disasters.
2. **Accidental Cluster:** In this crisis type, the organization unintentionally caused the crisis, so the reputational threat to the organization is moderate. Examples include technical accidents and recalls.
3. **Preventable Cluster:** This crisis type is classified as a severe reputational threat, and you can surmise why: The organization knowingly caused the crisis by engaging in inappropriate, risky, or illegal behavior. Examples include management misconduct and misdeed.

Once you have identified the crisis type and reputational threat, you can move on to selecting the appropriate crisis response strategy. Crisis response strategies are **rhetorical**—they are acts of communication in response to a given **exigence**. According to SCCT, these response strategies include

1. **Denial Strategies:** Deny the existence of a crisis, or deny responsibility for the crisis.
2. **Diminishing Strategies:** Seek to minimize or diminish the crisis.

3. **Rebuilding Strategies:** Offer compensation or apology for the crisis.
4. **Reinforcing Strategies:** Engage in positive reinforcement of shared goals or values among an organization and its publics, such as thanking or celebrating stakeholders for their role in the organization's ongoing efforts.

The selection of the response strategy depends upon the level of reputational threat, but it also may be constrained by legal or financial liability; that is, an apology may not be the appropriate response in every instance, even when it seems to offer appropriate sympathy. SCCT includes guidelines for matching crisis type to response strategy: For example, preventable crises are best handled with the rebuild strategies, while rumors may be easily diffused with deny strategies. In every case, crisis managers should act ethically by offering *adjusting information* and *instruction information* to affected publics before turning their attention to the threat to the organization's reputation (Heath & Coombs, 2006). Adjustment/adjusting strategies help to support publics' psychological needs after a crisis, while instruction strategies help to support their physical needs.

Risk Management Theory

One argument for the existence of society is to effectively manage risk for everyone involved: Consider, for example, the role of policemen, firefighters, government regulations, and other institutions, laws, and policies that help to alleviate the fear of danger you might otherwise experience in your day-to-day life. There are ways you manage risk on your own, as well; you may wear a helmet when riding a bike, for example, or choose to not go rock climbing with your friend who swears a few YouTube videos have made him an expert.

For PR professionals, risk management and communication are important to maintaining strong relationships between an organization and its publics. Consider, for example, the current debate over the safety of fracking. A PR professional working for an energy company may seek to communicate with publics in local areas about how the company is managing the risk involved in the practice (wind power companies may also want to communicate about risk to local birds, but as publics, they are not very responsive to dialogue). Communication is successful when both parties feel safe and supported. *Support* here is the goal: Publics will support an organization when they feel that their needs and concerns are being adequately addressed—that their voices are being heard and valued (Heath & Coombs, 2006). Risk communication may involve tactics like posters or public service announcements urging people to avoid harmful behaviors or take preventive care measures, but it is most effective when it is an ongoing conversation rather than a one-way transmission (McComas, 2010; Palenchar, 2010). This is partially because of an important societal trend: the devaluation of the expert. In some ways, American society is founded on the questioning of the expert of monarchs and popes alike. But it is arguable that this devaluation of expertise has accelerated with the rise of the digital age, which allows increased access to both platforms of communication and formerly "expert" tools (think only of Photoshop and Instagram—aren't all your friends now professional photographers?).

According to risk management theory, risk communication is most effective and ethical in seeking to increase publics' knowledge and feeling of control over potential risks. Publics are more likely to tolerate risks when they believe that the benefits are greater than the potential negative consequences. Risk communicators seek to increase knowledge, engender a sense of control, and reduce uncertainty. Through these strategies, they seek to cultivate trust in and support of an organization—both, of course, aspects of a successful relationship.

Analytics and Measurement

Environmental scanning and issues management have arguably become increasingly easy in the information age, in which PR practitioners and the organizations they represent have seemingly constant access to the attitudes, beliefs, and perceptions of publics—at least as expressed openly in online environments. Yet wading through this onslaught of information, and reasoning how to best measure the key variables you want to know, can also be difficult. In PR firms across the world, there is an increasing need for a specialist in analytics—someone who can slog through the data endlessly streaming from each and every screen and find the meaning in it.

For example, analytics are especially important in measuring the effectiveness of social media engagement. Yet there has been debate through the years over which measure best indicates success: Initially, the number of followers, fans, or "Likes" was counted, lending organizations some sense that their messages were reaching receptive eyes. Facebook founder Mark Zuckerberg effectively overturned this idea and changed how PR measures its social media outcomes. What Zuckerberg knew, and scholars from social network experts to network science researchers have since supported, is that sharing was the true measure of success in the socially networked age (Shih, 2011). Sharing was both a goal and itself an outcome: When stakeholders shared information, it traveled throughout their networks, finding people the organization would never otherwise reach. This increased the organization's reach and influence exponentially and showed a level of active engagement (and identification) not otherwise represented in a simple number of Likes.

Overall, it is important to understand that theory is built on research. Understanding the concepts behind theories is important, but using those theories in PR practice involves measuring relevant variables and analyzing findings. You may not always see Olivia Pope doing this aspect of PR—but then again, that is what the rest of the team is there for!

Bringing It All Together

Even if you do not feel like a theory nerd just yet, hopefully, this chapter helped you to draw connections between the concepts and normative guidelines of theory and the real-world strategies and tactics of PR practice. The most important overall take-aways to understand are two key shifts in PR theory: (1) the shift from a functional to a cocreational perspective, meaning that PR practitioners and organizations should view publics as partners in dialogue and co-constructing meaning, and (2) the shift from a focus on communication to *relationships*, with communication tactics under-stood as a tool for building and maintaining mutually beneficial relationships between organizations and publics. In practice, not un-ironically in the ever-tweeting age of social media, where specialists disseminate new, "snackable" bites of content it seems every hour, what this trajectory really reveals is a renewed focus on *listening*. This is the aspect of dialogue and engagement that can be easiest to neglect: to take a step back, take a breath, and hear the voices seeking to reach out.

References

Botan, C., & Taylor, M. (2004). Public relations state of the field. *Journal of Communication, 54,* 645–661.

Brown, N. A., & Billings, A.C. (2013). Sports fans as crisis communicators on social media websites. *Public Relations Review, 39,* 74–81.

Cameron, G. T., Cropp, F., & Reber, B. H. (2001). Getting past platitudes: Factors limiting accommodation in public relations. *Journal of Communication Management, 5*(3), 242–261.

Cancel, A. E., Cameron, G. T., Sallot, L. M., & Mitrock, M. A. (1997). It depends: A contingency theory of accommodation in public relations. *Journal of Public Relations Research, 9,* 31–36.

Coombs, W. T. (2006). Crisis management: A communicative approach. In C. H. Botan & V. Hazelton (Eds.), *Public Relations Theory II* (pp. 171–198). New York/London: Routledge.

Coombs, W. T. (2010). Crisis communication: A developing field. In R. L. Heath (Ed.), *The SAGE Handbook of Public Relations* (pp. 477–488). Los Angeles: SAGE.

Crenshaw, K. (1991). Mapping the margins: Intersectionality, identity politics, and violence against women of color. *Stanford Law Review, 43*(6), 1241–1299.

Eagly, A. H., & Carli, L. L. (2007). *Through the Labyrinth: The Truth about How Women Become Leaders.* Boston: Harvard Business Review Press.

Fleischman, D. (1955). *A Wife is Many Women.* New York: Crown Publishers.

Granovetter, M. S. (1973). The strength of weak ties. *American Journal of Sociology, 78*(6), 1360–1380.

Grossberg, L. (1992). Is there a fan in the house? The affective sensibility of fandom. In L. A. Lewis (Ed.), *The Adoring Audience: Fan Culture and Popular Media* (pp. 50–68). London/New York: Routledge.

Grunig, J. E. (1978). Defining publics in public relations: The case of a suburban hospital. *Journalism Quarterly*, 109–124.

Grunig, J. E. (1989). Sierra club study shows who become activists. *Public Relations Review*, XV(3), 3–24.

Grunig, J. E., Grunig, L. A., & Dozier, D. M. (2006). The excellence theory. In C. H. Botan & V. Hazelton (Eds.), *Public Relations Theory II* (pp. 21–62). New York/London: Routledge.

Heath, R. L., & Coombs, W. T. (2006). *Today's Public Relations: An Introduction.* Thousand Oaks, CA: SAGE.

Henry, S. (1999). "There is nothing in this profession…that a woman cannot do": Doris E. Fleischman and the beginnings of public relations. *American Journalism*, *16*(2), 85–111.

Jenkins, H. (2006). *Convergence Culture: Where Old and New Media Collide.* New York/London: New York University Press.

Kent, M. L. (2013). Using social media dialogically: Public relations role in reviving democracy. *Public Relations Review, 39,* 337–345.

Kent, M. L., & Taylor, M. (2002). Toward a dialogic theory of public relations. *Public Relations Review, 28,* 21–37.

Kim, J., & Grunig, J. E. (2011). Problem solving and communicative action: A situational theory of problem solving. *Journal of Communication, 61,* 120–149.

Ledingham, J. A. (2006). Relationship management: A general theory of public relations. In C. H. Botan & V. Hazelton (Eds.), *Public Relations Theory II* (pp. 465–484). New York/London: Routledge.

Ledingham, J. A., & Bruning, S. D. (1998). Relationship management and public relations: Dimensions of an organization-public relationship. *Public Relations Review, 24,* 55–65.

McAllister-Spooner, S. M. (2009). Fulfilling the dialogic promise: A ten-year reflective survey on dialogic internet principles. *Public Relations Review, 35,* 320–322.

McComas, K. A. (2010). Community engagement and risk management. In R. L. Heath (Ed.), *The SAGE Handbook of Public Relations* (pp. 461–476). Los Angeles: SAGE.

Palenchar, M. J. (2010). Risk communication. In R. L. Heath (Ed.), *The SAGE Handbook of Public Relations* (pp. 447–460). Los Angeles: SAGE.

Saffer, A. J. (2013). Intermedia agenda building of the blogosphere: Public relations role in the network. Institute of Public Relations. Retrieved from http://instituteforpr.org.

Shah, A. (2015, April 16). Why aren't there more female CEOs in PR? *The Holmes Report.* Retrieved from http://www.holmesreport.com/long-reads/article/why-aren't-there-more-female-ceos-in-pr.

Shih, C. (2011). *The Facebook Era: Tapping Online Social Networks to Market, Sell, and Innovate.* Boston: Pearson Education.

Sommerfeldt, E. J. (2013). The civility of social capital: Public relations in the public sphere, civil society, and democracy. *Public Relations Review, 39,* 280–289.

Organizational Communication: Principles, Practices, and Leadership

Phillip G. Clampitt, Ph.D.

Employees, managers, and executives often cite communication as the number one problem in their organizations. The statistics about organizational communication are alarming, and the stories often frightening. First, let's look at the numbers:

- About 66% of *Harvard Business Review* readers believed that they "often suspect they're not coming across as intended"[1]
- Only 51% of employees are satisfied with the communication in their organizations[2]
- Only 26% of business executives believe that the company business strategy is "well communicated and understood"[3]

The stories behind the numbers should alarm almost any employee from the first-line worker to the CEO of a *Fortune 500* company. Consider the following:

- Lori LeDume (alias) strolled into her dream job interview staring at her mobile phone. She plopped into the chair directly in front of the interview team and continued typing a text messages. Click-click. Another text message chimed on her mobile. She responded. Click-click. Several minutes passed without a handshake or even a nod to the interviewers. The interviewing team members stared at each other in bemused silence when finally one interviewer asked the interviewee, "Are you ready yet?" LeDume's response: "Yeah, I am now." Lori was not offered a second interview.

- A team of bank employees at HSBC made a mock video of an ISIS execution as part of a "team building" day. The press got wind of it and the Internet went crazy with the images. The six employees were fired for their poor taste, failure to live up to HSBC's corporate values, and their "utter, utter idiocy."[4]
- In 2008, Dick Fuld, the CEO of Lehman Brothers, was one of Wall Street's longest-tenured and successful financial executives. That all changed with the subprime mortgage crisis that ultimately bankrupted his company and sent the world's economy into a tailspin. His company's communication structure, protocols, and practices heavily contributed to its eventual downfall. In particular, numerous Lehman Brothers' analysts prognosticated the eventual collapse of the subprime mortgage market and recognized the grave threat it posed to the company and its investors. Those voices were rarely heard, not even in the elevator. It's hard to warn a CEO during an elevator talk when the CEO has his own private elevator.[5]
- Unfortunately, these are not atypical incidents. Communication breakdowns occur on the individual, group, and organizational levels. Organizational communication students, practitioners, and scholars study the issues lurking behind statistics and stories like these. They seek to understand and respond to the unique challenges of effectively communicating in organizations.

Successful students of organizational communication master these challenges on three fundamental levels:

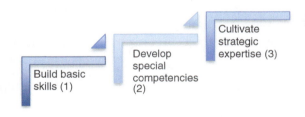

- Building basic communication skills
- Developing special competencies in key areas
- Cultivating strategic expertise.

In this chapter, we discuss each of these levels while discussing how they are interrelated. Thinking of each level as a stair step proves helpful. For example, decision downloading (Level 3) requires strategic expertise but you will need all the basic skills and competencies from Levels 1 and 2 to succeed.

Building Basic Communication Skills—Level 1

A number of basic communication skills are examined in this book, but we want to highlight four essential ones for organizational communication students: (1) speaking and listening, (2) written, (3) visual, and (4) research.

Speaking and Listening Communication Skills

Mastery of speaking and listening communication skills provides the most fundamental building block of organizational communication effectiveness. Why? Because so many people are talking and *not* listening. But that does *not* mean that they are talking about the right things, listening to the right messages, in the right way and at the right time! There is a time for a joke, for instance, but not during a discipline interview.

Employees, managers, and executives use their speaking and listening communication skills in a wide range of informal to formal situations, from a one-on-one chat in the hall to large group presentations in an auditorium. On the informal end of the continuum would be a chat in the elevator. It may seem like a natural, ho-hum type of event. It might be. But what if you are in the elevator with a busy executive who you have been trying to contact for weeks? Could this be your one opportunity to pitch an idea? In fact, that is why some organizational communication practitioners train people on making "elevator talks."

In the middle of the continuum are semi-formal types of oral communications such as task discussions with employees or regular team meetings. At the far end of the continuum are more formal types of public presentations. Typically, larger groups require more formal communication approaches and greater planning than casual encounters. However, if you have only one chance for a chat with the CEO, you better have the right elevator pitch!

Providing a thorough discussion of the oral communication skills required for effective interpersonal, small group, and formal presentations goes beyond the scope of the chapter. However, it is important to highlight three core sensibilities necessary in all speaking and listening situations:

- **Recognize that what your audience hears is far more important than what you say**. And you often don't know what they are hearing or how they might misinterpret your message. Just ask the bargain-hunting grandmother who unwittingly ended up in a strip club down the street from the shopping mall. Why? She read the marque that said, "Clothing 95% off."
- **The relationships implied by your words often exert more influence than your intended message**. People will often forget what you say but they rarely forget how you made them feel while saying it. Was it commanding? Was it belittling? Was it inspiring? Were you speaking as a colleague to colleague or as a drill sergeant to new recruit? These are the kinds of things people remember long after the words fade.
- **What you choose *not* to say is as important as what you choose to say**. Sometimes "silence is golden" because you can allow people to draw their own conclusions or save someone from embarrassment. On the other hand, "a word fitly spoken is like apples of gold in pictures of silver" because you can provide comfort, wisdom, or insight at just the right time. Both of these classic proverbs are important. Knowing when to invoke which one separates the mere "talkers" from the effective communicators.

Written Communication Skills

Many workplace communication problems occur because of written communication breakdowns. It could be an unheeded e-mail, a misunderstood memo, or misinterpreted social media post that set off negative shock waves in the company. Many of these problems could be avoided by following the advice of business writing professionals. A detailed examination of those skills goes beyond the scope of this chapter, but it is worth emphasizing the following basic principles:

- **Master the basics of spelling, grammar, and punctuation**. Misspellings, grammar mistakes, and punctuation errors inhibit understanding, which undermines your credibility and hinders your effectiveness. There's a potential added bonus—it might get you a date! After all, some online daters will only date those who know how to use proper grammar. A case in point: OkCupid dater, Jeff Cohen, quickly ditched a potential romantic interest after reading her message about a pending rendezvous point, "I will see you their."[6]
- **Write concisely**. Some bloviating bureaucrats meander from point to point, haphazardly making parenthetical comments, in a higgly-piggly fashion, obscuring their meaning in strange sounding phrases designed to impress the uninitiated even as their missives obscure accountabilities, blur meanings, and defy scrutiny while inhibiting further inquiry. The previous sentence contains over 40 words to make a simple point: the more the words are, the more likely you'll be misunderstood.
- **Highlight your organizational structure**. Most effective organizational communicators use bullet-pointed and numbered lists. Why? They usually expedite understanding, aid retention, and hasten action.

Visual Communication Skills

Susan Kare created the icons for the first Macintosh Apple computer. Today, many professionals regard her as a kind of Rembrandt in the icon-creation world. She noted, "Good icons work the way traffic signs do. (They) involve a type of poetic problem-solving in order to arrive at a design that can be understood universally and communicate a function at a glance."[7] Similar sensibilities guide effective organizational communicators. While there are many visual design principles worth noting, three important ones are highlighted below:

- **Graphics, photographs, or videos serve a documentary function**. A written endorsement of this book from the President of the United States provides a high level of support. But a picture with the president reading the book conveys even more. In fact, a colleague of mine wrote a book about communication that was briefly discussed and shown in a British sitcom. After the episode aired, sales of the book soared.

- **Images draw attention**. Typically, with a written text or a newsletter, the reader's eye initially zooms in on the image. That's why effective organizational communicators carefully test and select those images. And they don't clutter their written communications with too many images. Why? They want to direct attention to the most important issue, fact, or insight. Think of the image as the one headline that you want readers to see. Likewise, skilled organizational communicators know when to use diagrams or pie charts rather than photos or videos. They know the power of diagrams and pie charts to highlight relationships and core features of a process, initiative, or event.
- **Images usually convey emotional content better than written words**. Signaling the strength of your company can be done with numbers or text, but an image might convey the sentiment in an instant. Likewise, indicating the compassion of your business might be best communicated with an image of the CEO pictured with community leaders and children. In short, effective organizational communicators select the right images to convey the emotional connection your organization seeks to establish with shareholders, employees, and customers.

Research Skills

Effective organizational communicators understand and appreciate the fundamentals of research. This does not mean that they must become statistical wizards, survey gurus, or experimental design experts. Rather they know enough about gathering, analyzing, and evaluating information so they can exercise good judgment about *what* and *what not* to communicate with various stakeholders. To do this, they should master, at a minimum, the following basic research skills.

- **Know how to conduct an audience or stakeholder analysis**. Effective communicators know their receivers' preferences, biases, and "hot buttons." If you cannot identify answers to those questions, then you will diminish the likelihood of communicative success. Sounds simple. It's not. Why? Because organizations contain many different audiences with different perspectives. Learning how to categorize employees on various issues often proves challenging. For example, on health-care issues, the firm might realize that different age groups of employees have different concerns, so it might break down its audiences based on age or gender. On the other hand, in the same organization, if you're communicating about a new acquisition, it might make more sense to break down the audiences by department affiliation. (For more specifics, see www.drsowhat.com > guides > audience analysis.)
- **Learn how to gather and evaluate factual information**. Organizational communication practitioners spend a surprising amount of time acting like news reporters, trying to get to essence of the story. The reason is simple. They are expected to develop a working knowledge on a wide range of topics in a short amount of time. One week they may craft a plan for rolling out a new employee benefit package,

and the next week they may share highlights from a strategic planning retreat. This requires intellectual dexterity and energy, but it can be very exciting! Skilled practitioners soon learn that "job one" is separating rumors from realities and fears from facts. Tactically, this means that before crafting any communication, they develop a list of a specified number of facts and evaluate each one before proceeding. (For more specifics, see www.drsowhat.com > guides > 100 facts.)

- **Understand how to interpret and evaluate basic quantitative and qualitative data**. Organizational communication practitioners may not be *required* to generate research, but they will certainly be obligated to communicate it to various audiences. That's why they need some basic financial and social scientific literacy. Quantitative or numerical data can be deceptive, confusing, or illuminating. Effective organizational communicators know the difference. Likewise, qualitative data based in words or images can be enormously enlightening when properly handled. For example, a word cloud can highlight employee sentiments to open-ended survey questions about the corporate climate. The word cloud in the next illustration was generated from an employee survey question that asked, "What three words best describe your current feelings about your project?" A word cloud reveals the strength or the frequency that words are noted. Note the prominence of the word "disjointed" (along with related words such as "disorganized" and "unorganized"). This company not only decided to craft a response to the concern felt by many employees but also noted the more positive comments about excitement and confidence. In contrast, if the executive team had focused on a single unflattering statement made by one survey respondent, that would have received undue attention without the guidance of an organizational communication professional.

Developing Special Competencies—Level 2

At the very moment you are reading this sentence, millions of people are preparing, presenting, or listening to PowerPoint presentations. But how many of those presentations will really be effective? Far fewer. That's because many will bore viewers, some will dazzle without enlightening, and others will obscure important relationships between the bullet points.[8] Organizational communicators cannot avoid PowerPoint presentations (or "decks," as they are often called), but they can dodge these pitfalls. How? By adroitly synthesizing the Level 1 skills discussed above. For example, researching your audience helps you determine what content to emphasize. Likewise, skillfully using your speaking and listening skills should be the focal point, not the slides. As one critic put it, "a presentation, believe it or not, is the opening move of a conversation— not the entire conversation."[9] Of course, effective PowerPoint presentations require a thoughtful and an artful combination of your written and visual skills. For example, in most cases, short sentences are preferred to long ones.

Crafting a great PowerPoint presentation is one example of a Level 2 task. This requires not only a special competency associated with the particular task but also the thoughtful and artful use of verbal, written, visual, and research skills (Level 1 skills). There are numerous challenges of this sort, but we highlight below some of the more common ones you'll encounter as an organizational communication professional.

Onboarding New Employees

Organizational communicators are often tasked with crafting, presenting, and monitoring the **onboarding** of new employees. Typically, onboarding employees involves activities such as

- Escorting employees to HR briefings
- Showing employees how to do routine administrative tasks
- Giving employees a tour of the facilities.

Successful onboarding goes beyond these basics. That's where organizational communication professional can add extra value. By using and synthesizing their basic skills, they can

- Promote conversations between new employees and coworkers about working styles
- Discuss how new employees can maximize their contributions
- Orient new employees about the nuances of the working environment.

Activities like these significantly decrease turnover, thereby improving the profitability of the business.

On a tactical level, successful onboarding often includes discussing the organization's cultural norms by sharing stories about the organization's passions. Likewise asking each department to craft a "Top Ten" list of "things every new person should know about this team/group" often proves useful. This exercise often prompts inspiring and worthwhile conversations about how to be a successful team member. Some teams take the idea even further by asking the new employee to craft a "Personal Instruction Manual," which is basically a guide of how to best work with him or her. It is based on the premise that when you buy a new product you receive an operating manual of dos and don'ts; so why don't we do the same thing for new employees? So they have the new employee develop an instruction manual about themselves, highlighting life experiences and how they influence their working style. For example, one employee noted his experience as a college debater and how he likes to hear both sides of an argument before making up his mind. (For more specifics, see www.drsowhat.com > guides > instruction manuals.) Teams that share instruction manuals avoid many potential areas of conflict and misunderstanding.

Conducting Appraisal or Developmental Interviews

Most people don't like tests and being judged. Yet, that's how everybody improves and finds their niche in an organization. Effective performance appraisers bridge the gap between employees' motivations and anxieties. An **appraisal interview** is simply a structured discussion about the employee's performance on the job. The word "appraisal" may sound overly judgmental, so I prefer the word "developmental" because it emphasizes employee growth rather than evaluation. Regardless of the term, the purpose remains the same: you are evaluating employees' performance in order to help them make a greater contribution to the organization.

The appraiser's role can be uncomfortable because many people feel "Who am I to judge?" But that's exactly what good appraisers do; they make judgments based on relatively objective criteria. For example, "showing up to work on time" is a fairly objective criterion. A value-adding appraiser routinely makes this kind of judgment and cocreates an action plan with employees who fail to meet the standards.

Organizational communication practitioners can become part of this process in several ways. They may, of course, actually conduct developmental interviews. But they may also set up the process, educate employees about the performance appraisal system, and conduct training for managers on how to maximize the effectiveness of the interview. Doing so requires all the basic Level 1 skills as well as specialized knowledge about the hidden dangers and possibilities of this extremely important organizational event.

Updating Employees

Successfully updating employees seems like a rather ho-hum, easy to accomplish task. It's not. Too often, organizational communicators fall into the "spray-and-pray" trap. That is, they "spray" information through any available channel (usually e-mail) and "pray" that it is understood as intended.[10] The prayers are rarely answered for a host of reasons including

- Employees fail to read important e-mails because they got caught in a spam filter
- Employees ignore critical information because it is lost in a sea of other messages
- Employees misunderstand because they are discouraged from asking questions.

Effective organizational communicators know how to maneuver around these common potholes. They make sure that employees are provided with the timely information they need and want about their jobs and organizations.

This proves to be a tough task that requires mastery of Level 1 skills and also more specialized competencies in information management. The real challenge in the modern organization is *not too little* information, *but too much*. Consequently, expert organizational communicators know how to effectively filter information and channel it based on their audience analysis. They also know how to create value by writing executive summaries, indexing information, and selecting the right communication channels. For example, busy executives may only read the executive summary of a major report. If they want the details, they must easily find them in the report. Likewise, face-to-face works for some updates, while e-mail suffices for others.

Managing A Meeting

Most managers spend over half of their time in meetings. But that does not mean that their time is well spent. In fact, many complain about the numbers of meetings, their limited utility, and, sometimes, the sheer drudgery of the process. Yet, a good meeting can provide a number of different benefits including

- Enhanced knowledge-sharing between employees
- Improved decision-making as employees share perspectives
- Improved "buy-in" to a new initiative or the cultural values.

These benefits need to be balanced with the costs of holding a meeting. The primary cost for busy employees, managers, and executives is the time it takes to prepare and conduct the meeting. Few people think about the costs associated with creating consensus during a decision-making meeting or the price paid for collaborating with other employees on a project. Consensus development and coordination *done well* takes a great deal of employee time. Is it worth it? That depends on the nature of the task, organization, and competitive environment.

Skilled organizational communication practitioners master the management of these costs and benefits. In some cases, they might argue that it is "not worth it" to pay the coordination costs and decide to not hold the meeting. In other cases, they maximize the benefits and minimize the costs by

- Thinking carefully about who really needs to attend the meeting
- Developing action-oriented agendas
- Crafting meeting management rules designed to maximize benefits.

The prudent use of these meeting management principles rests on the Level 1 communication skills. For instance, conducting the proper research before the meeting can reduce the amount of time needed to inform team members while maximizing the time for coordinated decision-making. Bottom line: job applicants who can demonstrate that they can expedite meetings while improving their effectiveness will enhance their prospects.

Cultivating Collaborative Teams

As noted above, collaboration incurs significant organizational costs. However, collaboration can unleash innovative energy, fuel motivations, and inspire superior performance. How do you do this? Countless words have been written on the subject. Synthesizing and acting on those ideas often fall into the lap of organizational communication practitioners.

They soon learn that there are both structural and emotional elements to cultivating collaborative teams. The structural elements include crafting unifying goals, enlisting people with the right skill mix, and providing the right resources to do the job (e.g., time, material, and support staff).[11] Also, the team members must have good EQ's (emotional intelligence quotients).[12] In part, that means they know how to work well with others, avoid taking conflict personally, and put team goals above their own egos.[13]

A collaborative team's performance often makes the difference between success and failure in the marketplace. Bottom line: effective organizational communicators recognize this fact and use their skills to optimize the performance of collaborative teams.

Storytelling

Everyone knows a good story when they hear it. Yet, very few people know how to craft a really compelling one. That's one reason why many Hollywood producers are so successful. Skilled organizational communicators use stories to help their organizations achieve a wide array of objectives. In order to do so, they should strive to be as adept as Robert

McKee. Who is he? Mr. McKee is considered to be Hollywood's greatest teacher of the art of storytelling. His alumni have won over 60 Oscars and 200 Emmy awards.[14] He wrote that "A beautifully told story is a symphonic unity in which structure, setting, character, genre, and idea meld seamlessly. To find their harmony, the writer must study the elements of story as if they were instruments of an orchestra—first separately, then in concert."[15]

Living up to McKee's standards may be tough but mastering the basics of storytelling provides you with a communicative edge in the workplace. The basic structure of a good story contains the following elements:

- Exposition—Setting the stage with interesting characters and situational facts
- Conflict—Establishing some essential tension with another character or situation
- Climax—Creating heightened tension demanding resolution
- Denouement—Resolving the tension built up during the first three stages.

The beauty of this basic structure is that it can be used to craft a 30-second commercial or TV miniseries. The organizational communicator can use this simple structure to craft a newsletter, develop an elevator talk, present data, prepare an infographic, open a presentation, or stage a major organizational event.

Cultivating Strategic Expertise—Level 3

Cultivating strategic expertise requires a more macrolevel orientation than the skills discussed above. Consequentially, expert organizational communicators make wise trade-offs between a variety of competing organizational and communication goals. The **fundamental strategic principle** at this level is that *you can communicate almost anything but you can't communicate everything*. Therefore, you will have to make decisions about what to communicate and what *not* to communicate. Crafting effective strategies demands a mastery of Level 1 basic skills and many of the Level 2 competencies.

A **communication strategy** outlines the "macro-level communication choices we make based on organizational goals and judgments about others' reactions, which serves as a basis for action."[16] Macrolevel choices include issues and messages that reach across the entire organization. For example, activists have criticized PepsiCo for marketing so many products they deem as unhealthy. Crafting the right strategic message for employees, consumers, and activists was an organizational priority for the company. CEO, Indra Nooyi, brilliantly responded by dividing PepsiCo's product line into two major categories: those items "good for you" and those that are "fun for you."[17] This wonderful conceptual distinction preserves an important revenue stream (fun for you) while keeping critics at bay (good for you). Sounds simple, but it's not. It takes a great deal of thought about your audiences and requires action on the part of everyone in the organization to translate the strategic thought into action.

Discussing all the strategic communication issues organizations face would require an entire book. Below we discuss three of the more important ones.

Downloading Major Organizational Decisions

Some major organizational decisions are made by a very small group of employees that, for various reasons, cannot involve others in the decision-making process. These include mergers, labor contract terms, reorganizations, new acquisitions, crises, and creating ESOPs (Employee Stock Ownership Plans). Once the decision has been made it needs to be "downloaded" to employees, investors, and customers. In short, decision downloading occurs when executives or managers communicate to employees about decisions that were made without employee input.

Decision Downloading Protocol

- What is the decision?
- How was the decision made?
- Why was the decision made?
- What were the rejected alternatives to the announced decision?
- How does the decision fit into the mission or vision?
- How does the decision affect the organization (WIFO)?
- How does the decision affect employees (WIFM)?

Based on Clampitt, P. & Williams, M. (Winter 2007) "Decision Downloading." *MIT Sloan Management Review*, 48(2), 77–82.

Effectively communicating in such circumstances requires a strategic mindset, creative tactics, and first-rate execution gleaned from the Level 1 skills and Level 2 proficiencies discussed above. For instance, a great story in a written and/or oral format can help employees understand the decision-making process.

Researchers have found that answering the questions in the decision-making protocol highlighted in the sidebar will double the likelihood of employee buy-in.[18] A failure to communicate about any one of the items will diminish the likelihood of success. More specifically, all employees listen to two "radio stations" when major changes hit: WIFO (What's in It For the Organization) and WIFM (What's in It for Me). If the organization only broadcasts on the WIFO channel, employees will be less supportive of the change. But if they broadcast on both WIFO and WIFM channels, they improve the probability of buy-in—even if the WIFM channel must carry some negative news. Organizational communication experts help ensure that the downloading includes both elements, thereby increasing the likelihood the change will be successfully implemented.

Managing Cultural Issues

Organizations today face a host of ever-evolving societal concerns, like diversity issues, gender politics, and environmental matters. Organizational leaders are expected to not only grapple with these issues but also respond in ways that respect the desires of interest groups, government agencies, employees, investors, and other stakeholders.

Case in point: for years, various groups have expressed concern about the small number of women in the C-Suite, holding positions such as chief executive officer, chief financial officer, or chief information officer. Despite the notable, high-profile exceptions of Marissa Mayer (CEO of Yahoo), Indra Nooyi (CEO of PepsiCo), and Meg Whitman (CEO of Hewlett-Packard), the actual numbers tell a somewhat different story. In one study of 118 companies that included 30,000 respondents, women filled only 17% of the C-Suite jobs and 25% of the women surveyed believed their gender hampered their career progress.[19] But the issue is more complicated than what can be captured in one or two startling statistics. In the same study, the researchers found that as employees moved up their career ladders, men expressed a greater desire to attain the top job than women.[20] A complicated issue like this cannot be effectively resolved with some simple cosmetic organizational changes. Ditto for many other diversity and environmental issues. However, many organizational stakeholders demand some movement on these kinds of societal and cultural concerns.

Bottom line: Reconciling the complex tensions involved in these kinds of issues presents a major strategic challenge in the C-Suite. Strategically communicating about a complex issue intensifies the challenge. Yet organizational communication experts relish these Tough Mudder-like tests of their skills, motivations, and endurance. They soon learn to answer big picture questions such as

- What should be our core message with this issue?
- How should we deliver the message?
- When should we deliver the message?
- What channels should we use?
- Who should be the spokesperson on the issue?

Answering these questions requires a deep understanding of the key stakeholders (e.g., audiences), cultural context, and organizational imperatives. These are precisely the kind of strategic challenges organizational communication experts enthusiastically embrace.

Developing A Social Media Plan

Organizational communication experts possess exactly the kind of sensibilities needed to craft a great social media plan. They can make use of their skill-set to answer the following strategic social media questions:

- Coordinates—What should be our strategic goals? How are the goals connected?
- Content—What should we post on our social media sites?
- Channels—What social media channels should we use? Not use? (e.g., Facebook, LinkedIn, Twitter, and YouTube)

- Connections—How should our social media activities be connected to our other organizational activities? (e.g., marketing, recruiting, and educating employees)
- Corrections—How are we going to make the appropriate adjustments or corrections to our approach? What metrics should we use to trigger change?

Thoughtfully answering these questions and then knitting together the responses into a coherent strategy provides the key structural elements of a successful social media plan.

A great social media plan allows organizations to avoid major gaffes and harness social media's promise. For example, a good plan educates employees on what kind of content enhances the brand instead of damaging it. Of course, a great plan without employee commitment almost always fails. That's where the collaboration and consensus-building skills come into play. It's also where storytelling can exert considerable influence. For example, sharing stories about employees who were fired for social media pranks that undermine the organization's values might be just the kind of vivid reminder needed for some employees. Maybe it would have helped the six HSBC employees discussed at the beginning of the chapter.

Building A World-Class Communication System

Many organizational leaders give very little thought to the structural design of their communication system. They often rely on a haphazard patchwork of newsletters, e-mails, committee meetings, and special communication events. Typically, even less thought occurs around the proper role and coordination of the various channels used in the organization. Organizational communication experts study these structures, evaluate the level of effectiveness, and seek to optimize their utility.

Grasping the totality of an organization's communication system requires a special mindset that can envision the "big picture" while mastering the technical details of a particular channel. For example, it is important to know how employees use e-mail in tandem with other channels to accomplish their tasks. It is also important to know the technical possibilities and limits of the email system. Then, there are the strategic questions about what role various channels should play. For example, should e-mail be used to download major organizational decisions? In a word, no. Yet, some companies do so.

Organizational communication experts relish the opportunity to devise an approach for answering these kinds of structural questions. While it goes beyond the scope of this chapter to provide details on how organizational communication experts answer these questions, we can outline some general ideas:

- Inventorying—Collecting, listing, and understanding all the communication tools/channels used by the organization. What are the functions of each? Intended audiences?

- Assessing—Evaluating the effectiveness of the communication system. Are intended messages reaching the right people at the proper time with the desired effect?
- Strategizing—Conceptualizing the optimal mix of channels, messages, and feedback mechanisms. What does the organization need to do to better achieve its desired goals?
- Implementing—Building and training employees to use the optimal communication tools and structure. Are employees using the right communication channels/tools in the right way?

Organizational communication experts adroitly manage these major tasks. They do so by becoming skilled strategists while consistently drawing on their vast reservoir of Level 1 skills and Level 2 competencies.

Conclusion

The skills and sensibilities outlined in this chapter produce enduring value. For example, years ago, there was not one organizational communication expert who wrote or talked about social media. Today, the organizational communication expert who fails to discuss it would be guilty of malpractice. However, the timeless abilities to speak, listen, research, select visual images, tell stories, update employees, analyze audiences, and craft strategies (Levels 1, 2 and 3) perfectly positioned organization communication experts to quickly develop the special competencies (Level 2) necessary to adroitly manage social media challenges. The strategic mindset (Level 3) of the organizational communication experts sets them apart from mere tacticians. This mindset prepares them to deal with the emergent challenges that will surely pop up in the future. And that's why organizational communication experts will always be in great demand.

References

[1] *Harvard Business Review*, September 2015, p. 22.

[2] Clampitt, P. (2013). *Communicating for managerial effectiveness,* Los Angeles: Sage Publications, p. 7.

[3] Clampitt, P. (2013). *Communicating for managerial effectiveness,* Los Angeles: Sage Publications, p. 290.

[4] Gillman, O. & Spillett, R. (2015, July 6). Utter idiocy. *Daily Mail.* Retrieved from http://www.dailymail.co.uk/news/article-3151619/Six-HSBC-staff-sacked-filming-ISIS-style-mock-execution-team-building-day-karting-centre.html.

[5] Sorkin, A. (2009). *Too big to fail.* New York: Viking.

[6] Wells, G. (2015, October 2). What's really hot on dating sites? Proper grammar. *Wall Street Journal*, A1, 10.

[7] Pavlus, J. (2015, September 21). Masters of the small canvas. *Bloomberg Business Week*, 48–49, p. 48.

[8] Sebastian, K., Bresciani, S., & Eppler, M. (2015, September). Slip-sliding-away: A review of the literature on the constraining qualities of PowerPoint. *Business and Professional Communication Quarterly*, 78(3), 292–313.

[9] Schuman. R. (2014, March 7). Power Pointless: Digital slideshows are the scourge of higher education. *Slate*. Retrieved from http://www.slate.com/articles/life/education/2014/03?powerpoint_in_higher_education_is_ruining_teaching.html.

[10] Clampitt, P. (2013). *Communicating for managerial effectiveness*. Los Angeles: Sage Publications.

[11] Hansen, M. (2009). *Collaboration: How leaders avoid the traps, create unity and reap big results*. Boston: Harvard Business Press.

[12] Goleman, D., (1995). *Emotional Intelligence*. New York: Bantam Books.

[13] See http://psychcentral.com/lib/what-is-emotional-intelligence-eq/.

[14] See http://mckeestory.com for details.

[15] McKee, R. (1997). *Story: Substance, structure, style and the principles of screenwriting*. New York: Itbooks, p. 29.

[16] Clampitt, P. (2013). *Communicating for managerial effectiveness*. Los Angeles: Sage Publications, p. 297.

[17] Nooyi, I. (2015, September). How Indra Nooyi turned design thinking into strategy. *Harvard Business Review*, 93(9), 81–85, p. 85.

[18] Clampitt, P. & Williams, M. (Winter 2007). Decision downloading. *MIT Sloan Management Review*, 48(2), 77–82.

[19] Waller, N., & Lublin, J. (2015, September 30). What's holding women back. *Wall Street Journal*, R1–R2, p. R1.

[20] Waller, N., & Lublin, J. (2015, September 30). What's holding women back. *Wall Street Journal*, R1–R2, p. R1.

GLOSSARY

Accommodation—In contingency theory (a public relations theory), accommodation refers to one side of a continuum of engagement between organizations and publics in times of conflict; accommodation defines the behavior of an organization or public that seeks to understand the other side's position.

Accuracy—In journalism, getting the facts and everything presented in the news story right, reflecting reality.

Act—Part of Burke's dramatic pentad, it is what is actually unfolding over time in the context of communication.

Active listening—when an individual makes a concerted effort to step into the other person's shoes and suspend, at least temporarily, their own needs.

Active media—A category of theory suggesting the media are powerful and the audience is largely passive.

Active user—A category of theory suggesting users are critical and actively engaged in their media decisions.

Adaptors—Nonverbal behavior that satisfies a personal need or helps use adapt or respond to a situation.

Ad-block—Software programs installed at the browser level or elsewhere to keep advertising content from displaying on Web sites; it has been criticized for eliminating a source of revenue for said Web sites.

Advocacy—In contingency theory (a public relations theory), advocacy refers to one side of a continuum of engagement between organizations and publics in times of conflict; advocacy defines the behavior of an organization or public that acts only in its own self-interest.

Affect display—Facial expressions that communicate emotion.

Affiliates—Local stations who align with national networks to rebroadcast programming content.

Agency—Part of Burke's dramatic pentad, it is what facilitates the act in the communicative context.

Agent—Part of Burke's dramatic pentad, one of the individuals engaged in a communicative act.

Altruism—a sense of well-being toward others that transcends one's own needs (closely related with Dialogue).

AM broadcasting—A radio standard with lower-quality sound and a single channel of audio that can travel vast distances.

Angle—The focus of a journalistic story.

Appraisal interview—a structured discussion about an employee's performance on the job.

Appropriateness—Answers the question, "Did you manage the conflict in a way that was satisfactory to others?" One part of communication competence.

Aristotle—Greek scholar and philosopher (384–322 B.C.) who developed and taught the principles of rhetoric.

Arrangement—A canon of rhetoric concerned with how a speaker arranges and organizes invented elements.

Artifacts—Accessories or things we carry with us that tell others something about who we are—a form of nonverbal communication.

Attitude—A "sixth" part of Burke's pentad based on the underlying feelings of the agents participating in the act.

Audion vacuum tube—A device developed by Lee De Forest to detect and amplify radio signals and boost their range.

Banner ad—The classic form of online advertising, consisting of an image placed in the margins of a Web page that can be either static or animated; when clicked upon, the ad directs the user to a sponsor link.

Basic cable—Cable channels that do not require separate subscription or package fees.

Behavioral focus—Theoretical focus based on what people do, rather than the meaning behind the action.

Best Practices—In public relations (among other professions), best practices are the time-tested, widely accepted ways to do things right; the profession derives many of these best practices from theory and research.

Bias—Impartiality or lack of objectivity in news reporting; it can manifest in both obvious and unconscious ways.

Big three networks—The first three major broadcast networks (CBS, NBC, ABC) that operated without any major competition until the 1980s.

Biological determinism—a concept that states that biological factors that contribute to our physical appearance—such as hair, skin color, and sex organs—help decide our capabilities and future potential.

Broadband—A kind of Internet connection characterized by its "always-on" capability as well as its ability to transmit large amounts of data at higher speeds than dial-up.

Broadcast media—Media consisting of television, radio, and other media transmitted via the airwaves toward a mass audience.

Broadcasting—The spreading of information and entertainment content from one source across a large audience. Derived from an agricultural term.

Burke's Pentad—A five-part system developed by Kenneth Burke to identify the components of a communicative action.

CATV—Shorthand for cable television.

C-Suite—a common shorthand for an organization's executive team (e.g., chief executive officer, chief financial officer, and chief information officer).

Campaign—An advertising effort consisting of advertising across multiple platforms and advertising types, all brought together by common copy, advertising appeals, and content.

Canons—Parts of rhetoric, identified by Aristotle.

CAN-SPAM Act—Congressional legislation requiring online advertisers to mark their messages as marketing materials and also give consumers the option to "opt out" of receiving them.

Careful language—Language selected to avoid misunderstandings and misrepresentation.

Causality—A relationship between two variables suggesting that one causes the other.

Centrality—A measurement in social network theory of where an individual is located in a network.

Channel—The means through which a message is sent in the SMCR model.

Children's Online Privacy Protection Act (COPPA)—Congressional legislation placing specific guidelines on advertisers to ensure the privacy of users under the age of 13 years.

Chronemics—The study of how time is used in interpersonal interactions and cultures.

Clique—A small social group within a group, usually with an exclusive nature.

Cocreational—In public relations, this theoretical perspective embraces publics as cocreators of meaning; it champions open engagement between organizations and publics with the goal of fostering mutually beneficial, long-term relationships.

Communication accommodation theory—A theory that suggests people are more likely to adapt their language in order to gain social approval.

Communication competence—This stresses the dual importance of effectiveness and appropriateness in conflict communication.

Communication strategy—The macro-level communication choices we make about messages, channels, and feedback mechanisms based on the organization's goals and judgments about others' reactions; this, then serves as a basis for action.

Communications Act of 1934—Renamed and repurposed the Federal Radio Commission to the Federal Communications Commission; granted the FCC the ability to regulate other forms of mass communication and also enact policy requiring broadcasters to operate in the public interest.

Compassion and loving-kindness meditation—a contemplative practice to gain a greater appreciation in the form of altruism toward others.

Conflict—A discord or barrier that two interdependent people perceive and communicate to each other. The barriers often present a challenge to communication. Conflict is also a specific communication encounter or set of encounters that are performed, with informed or uninformed choice.

Conflict management—A broader term than conflict resolution that describes the real possibility that not everything will be resolved but simply "managed."

Conflict modes or **conflict styles**—Predispositions that an individual has to manage conflict in a given situation.

Conflict resolution—Any process of communication that is undertaken to help improve communication between individuals or groups and meet the needs of one or both parties.

Confounding variable—A variable other than the one you are looking for that may impact or change a dependent variable.

Connotative definitions—A personal or subjective meaning of a word.

Consolidation—A contemporary media trend in which media channels and outlets are increasingly owned by fewer and fewer companies.

Constitutive rules—Communication rules focused on definitions of words.

Constructive communication—Communication that helps strengthen and bring a relationship closer.

Contemplative inquiry—to balance the sharpening of our intellects with the systematic cultivation of our hearts.

Contemplative practices—A set of focus-oriented techniques that can help to quite the mind and allow a person to gain a greater awareness of their surroundings.

Content analysis—The quantification of textual analysis, based on counting recurring patterns, ideas, and symbols in a text.

Content creators—People who develop and post material for publication on online forms and outlets.

Context—In the SMCR model, the entire area and situation that surrounds communication—the environment.

Control objective of theory—Identify the dependent variables in a phenomenon to reach a desired or predictable outcome.

Convergence—A buzzword of the digital/information age, convergence refers to the coming together of old and new media, including the combining of media companies, the digitization of media content, and the technological convergence of multiple functions into one single device (like a smartphone).

Cookies—Small packets of data gathered by the Web sites you visit, intended to track your behavior and habits for marketing purposes.

Cord-cutters—People who have opted to receive their entertainment and information from online streaming services and HD over-the-air signals instead of paying for cable and satellite.

Correlation—A relationship between two variables that does not suggest one causes the other.

"CRAP" test—A test to determine the quality of an online information source based on its currency, reliability, authority, and purpose.

Critical theory—A branch of theory casting itself in opposition to powerful interests with the goal of opposing inequality and oppression.

Cultivation Theory—A theory, developed by George Gerbner, which suggests repeated and heavy exposure to television and other media shapes the worldview of the audience so that they think the real world is more closely aligned with what they see in the media.

Culture Industries—A critical theory suggesting powerful elites construct popular culture and hand it down to a passive audience that accepts a skewed version of reality on a constant loop of new diversions that keeps them from questioning this arrangement.

Cyber literacy—Our ability to critically analyze the value and truthfulness of online content.

David Sarnoff—The general manager of RCA who revolutionized radio as a business and popularized broadcast programming; while head of RCA, he bought out a great deal of radio patents.

Dayparts—Specific blocks of time during the broadcast day that carry different advertising costs.

Decision downloading—the process of communication about decisions to employees when they have not been involved in the decision-making process.

Deduction—A means of developing and testing theory where we start from an overarching observation or theory, develop a guess about how it might apply to a situation, and then make observations that prove or disprove a theory.

Defamation—The communication of untrue information that damages a person's reputation.

Deliberative rhetoric—A form of rhetoric in which rhetors debate and argue over matters of state or policy; more generally, it is rhetoric aimed at solving a problem or resolving a situation.

Delivery—A canon of rhetoric concerned with how style is used to make the audience feel a particular way.

Denotative definitions—The literal/dictionary meaning of a word.

Density—A measurement in social network theory of how many connections there are in a network.

Descriptive objective of theory—A theoretical objective based on labeling complex phenomena and assigning meaningful distinctions and symbols to its parts.

Destructive communication—Communication that damages a relationship.

Determinism—Ontological perspective that suggests human behavior is driven by forces beyond our control.

Developmental theory—School of interpersonal theory interested in how relationships between people are formed over time—manifests in the social penetration and turning points models.

Dialectic—The process of using arguments and discussions to resolve problems or inform others, as identified by Aristotle.

Dialogue—(In conflict resolution) Happens when people choose to view the situation or conflict through a new lens, through the lens of positive intent. (General) An exchange of communication between two people or sources, whether interpersonal or between organizations and publics.

Dial-up—A form of Internet connection carried along the same lines as telephone communication. They are ubiquitous but slower than other options.

Diffusion of innovation—Theory suggesting that there is a pattern to the adoption of new technologies and practices where the majority of people adopt them around the same time.

Digital divide—The gap between those who have access to technology and those who do not.

Digital media—Any sort of media transmitted primarily through digital means (computers, social media, etc.)

Digital natives—A term coined by Marc Prensky to describe students who have grown up with and fully understand the language of digital media.

Digital video recorders—Devices that allow users to digitally record TV programs with the purpose of being able to watch them later and skip past commercials.

Disinhibition—A feeling brought on by online anonymity and the lack of constraints present in online communication that causes us to act and communicate in ways we would not face to face; it can be either toxic or benign in nature.

Dominant coalition—*Being* a part of the top decision-making process of an organization or a company.

Doxa—In a critical approach to rhetoric, the underlying and often subconscious values in communication.

Dramatism—Kenneth Burke's theory that all of communication can be likened to a dramatic play.

Dynamic Nonverbal Communication—Nonverbal communication that changes over the course of an interaction—gestures, facial expressions, etc.

E-commerce—The conducting of business and retail sales online.

Edutainment—Games that use the trappings and logic of video games to reinforce educational lessons and facilitate learning among students.

Effectiveness—Answers the question, "Were you able to reach your goals in the conflict interaction?" One part of communication competence.

e-mail—The sending of electronic messages between online addresses.

Emblems—Nonverbal cues with specific and generally understood meanings for many people—hand signals, etc.

Enlightenment era—The Enlightenment era spanned from the seventeenth to the late eighteenth century in Europe. Enlightenment thinkers emphasized that people are rational and capable of making sense of their world. They also strongly believed in individualism. Many of the United States' founding fathers were adherents to Enlightenment-era thinking.

Environmental scanner—Someone who pays attention to the news, events, and public opinion of the world finding meaning and connections to their own environment.

Environmental scanning—This public relations practice refers to regular media monitoring (following the news and current events through multiple sources) to watch for important issues, events, and public opinion reports relevant to your organization.

Epideictic rhetoric—Rhetoric concerned with assigning praise or blame for an individual's actions.

Epistemological approach—Element of theory concerned with how we obtain and process knowledge.

Epistemic—A level of communication in a critical approach to rhetoric that is immediately manifest and obvious.

ESOP—Employee Stock Ownership Plan.

Ethnography—Qualitative method in which researchers embed themselves in a population and take careful notes about how it operates in order to obtain a deeper understanding of unfamiliar cultures.

Ethos—A rhetorical appeal based on the innate credibility and character of the speaker.

Exigence—Refers to an urgent situation that requires a rhetorical response, for example, a crisis for an organization is a kind of exigence. Faced with a crisis and its potential threat to an organization's reputation and relationships, the organization must respond through rhetoric (such as writing, or speech).

Experiments—A quantitative research method that seeks to discover how manipulation of an independent variable affects a dependent variable; conducted in a controlled environment to avoid confounding variables.

Explanatory objective of theory—An objective of theory based on understanding why something is happening or why it works.

External audiences—Those publics who reside outside of the office or organization.

Eye contact—Looking directly at someone when communicating with them.

Face—The identity we claim for ourselves in public situations.

Face negotiation theory—A prominent culture-based theory that explains conflict through a theoretical framework involving face and how it is negotiated in different cultures.

Facework—When people seek to uphold and/or respect another's face or, the opposite, insult or diminish another's face.

Fairness doctrine—An FCC policy that suggests broadcasters must both devote programming to controversial public issues and air opposing viewpoints on political issues.

Federal Communications Commission (FCC)—A government agency tasked with regulating stations and programming over the public airwaves as well as the Internet and other forms of mass communication.

Federal Radio Commission—An early governing body that oversaw the assignment of licenses to prospective private and commercial broadcasters.

Feedback—In the SMCR model, when the receiver responds to a sender and then becomes a sender themselves.

Feminism—A branch of critical theory suggesting society is driven by a patriarchal ideology that espouses a particular form of male-dominant gender roles harmful to men and women alike.

First Amendment—The first entry into the Bill of Rights, the First Amendment guarantees Americans freedom of speech, press, and religion, as well as the right to assemble and to petition the government to change a policy or policies.

FM broadcasting—A radio standard invented by Edwin Armstrong that offers two channels of audio and better sound quality than AM broadcasting.

Fragmentation—A contemporary media trend that suggests there are more media options than ever before, competing with each other and vying for the attention of smaller and more specialized audiences.

Free will—An ontological perspective that suggests people can communicate and choose in any way they see fit.

Focus groups—Qualitative research method consisting of in-depth conversations with a large group of 6–10 people run by a moderator with the purpose of getting in-depth and diverse perspectives and ideas.

Focused-attention meditation—The purpose of this practice is to train one's mind to concentrate on the present moment, while learning to return to one's breath. One kind of contemplative practice.

Forensic rhetoric—Rhetoric used to prove an individual's innocence or guilt by building a case.

Formats—A particular kind of music or programming broadcast by a radio station.

Functional—In public relations, this theoretical perspective puts the interests of the organization first, defining publics by how they can be used to help achieve the organization's goals.

Fundamental strategic communication principle—you can communicate about almost anything, but you can't communicate about everything.

Gamification—The application of game mechanics to real-world communication problems.

Griots—Individuals in African society who acted as orators to the public and spokespeople for the monarch.

Guglielmo Marconi—The Italian inventor and developer of wireless telegraphy; the man often considered to be the "father of radio."

Haptics—The study of touch in nonverbal communication.

Heurism—Means of evaluating theory based on its ability to encourage new thinking and inquiry.

High context cultures—Cultures that place more emphasis on nonverbal than verbal communication.

Human communication—The process of making sense out of the world around us and sharing that sense with others through verbal and nonverbal messages.

Hyperlinks—The lines of text that, when clicked upon, will direct you to other parts of the site or the Web.

Hypodermic needle theory—Suggests the media are powerful and affect all audiences equally and significantly; the audience is passive and cannot challenge the messages they receive, so messages can be explicitly tailored to get an audience to do what the media creator wants.

Hypothesis—A predictive statement of a relationship between variables at play in a phenomenon.

Iconoscope—A camera tube invented by Vladimir Zworykin that converted light rays into electrical signals.

Identity—A sense of oneself, comprising influences from biological, personal, and social factors, which change over time and which present itself differently depending upon motivations and influences.

Ideology—A recurring and ingrained pattern of belief that drives and guides communication and cultural interaction.

Illustrators—Nonverbal behaviors that accompany verbal messages to accent or complement them.

Impersonal communication—When someone communicates with another as if they are objects or they are simply there to fulfill some need without personal interaction.

In-depth interview—A qualitative research method in the form of a structured conversation with a respondent, aimed at exploring their involvement with and feeling toward a subject or phenomenon.

In-groups—A category of classifying people who come together around shared interests and/or experiences and who form a majority in a given setting.

Indecent content—Content that may be objectionable but is protected by the First Amendment.

Induction—A means of developing and testing theory where we start from smaller observations and then extrapolate them out to larger patterns and theories.

Internal audiences—Those people or groups that work within an organization that you are targeting for information.

Internet—The vast, global connections between computers, networks, and providers that allow for communication across digital channels.

Intersectionality theory—Refers to the idea that an individual cannot be defined by solely one marker of social identity—such as gender, race, or socioeconomic status—but that individuals must be understood through the combination of all of their overlapping, intersecting identities.

Innovators—Those who adopt technology immediately despite initial expenses, glitches, and other setbacks.

Interpersonal communication—A distinct transactional mode of communication involving two people for the purpose of creating, maintaining, and affecting relationship.

Intimate space—Zone of personal space reserved for very personal or intimate interactions.

Invention—A canon of rhetoric based on developing the content for communication—brainstorming, etc.

Inverted pyramid—Refers to a way to structure a news story that places the most important news at the beginning of the story. From there, the reporter organizes the information from most important to least important.

Issues management—An important public relations practice, issues management encompasses environmental scanning and research to identify potential problems relevant to the organization and act to remedy them before they fester into crises.

James Clerk Maxwell—Scottish physicist who first theorized the existence of electromagnetic waves that could be used to transmit signals through the air.

Jargon—A form of language specific to a given profession or group of people.

Kairos—A rhetorical concept based on the idea that there is a proper time and place for speaking.

Kinesics—A form of nonverbal communication study based on body movements, posture, and gestures.

Laggards—Those who adopt technologies at the last minute, when alternatives may no longer be available.

Large group communication—Communication between 8 and 15 people.

Least objectionable programming—Programs that are generally broad and inoffensive that large parts of the audience can agree on.

Lee De Forest—Inventor of the audion vacuum tube.

Linguistic Relativity—The idea that words have the power to create reality; the idea that we can only think of that we can assign names to.

Listening—Occurs when individual who is partaking in shared communication with another with the intent of understanding what the other is saying (rather than simply hearing the words).

Logos—A rhetorical appeal based on the use of reason and evidence to support one's perspective.

Low context cultures—Cultures that place more emphasis on verbal communication than nonverbal.

Malware—Unwanted and malicious programs installed on a user's computer without their consent by online advertisers or malicious sources.

Marketplace of ideas—A metaphor that likens the free exchange of ideas in a democratic society to a marketplace, where individuals examine products and select the best. The marketplace of ideas assumes that truth will always emerge when all ideas are freely exchanged. It is a rationale for the freedom of expression. Supreme Court Justice Oliver Wendell Holmes introduced the idea, which was strongly influenced by British philosopher John Milton.

Marxism—A branch of critical theory suggesting society is governed by a capitalist ideology that creates resource inequality and class struggles.

Mass communication—Refers to various forms of mediated communication in which a sender conveys information to large, often disconnected or anonymous audiences. Broadcast television and radio news are idea examples since stations send signals out to whoever can receive them.

Mass self-communication—The dissemination of self-generated, personalized content to mass audiences.

Media—The channels and platforms that convey ideas and information to audiences both small and large.

Media generations—Classifications of people based on the chronological context of the dominant technologies of the time (i.e., the "radio generation," the "television generation," etc.).

Media literacy—A collection of strategies and tactics aimed at helping users both critically receive and ethically create media.

Memory—A canon of rhetoric based on the ability of the speaker to recall information extemporaneously without notes, etc.

Message—In the SMCR model, the actual idea or concept being conveyed verbally or nonverbally that is encoded by the source and decoded by the receiver.

Miller test—A three-pronged test offered by the Supreme Court in the case *Miller v. California* that suggests media content must meet three criteria in order to be ruled obscene and therefore not protected by the First Amendment—the content must appeal to the prurient interest, must describe in an offensive way sexual conduct or excretory functions, and must lack serious literary or scientific value.

Mindfulness—Active and fluid information processing, sensitivity to context and multiple perspectives, and ability to draw novel distinctions.

Mindlessness—Communication that is "reactive, superficially processed, routine, rigid, and emotional" [as opposed to rational thinking].

Misrepresentation—Unintentional or intentional inaccuracy in terms of language on the part of the sender.

Misunderstandings—Unintentional or intentional inaccuracy in terms of language on the part of the receiver.

Monochronic—A culture that is very rigidly time oriented and prizes punctuality.

Monologue—When we treat each other as "objects," a sort of one-way conversation where we treat the other as a tool to get a particular task completed.

Morse code—A system of "dots and dashes" used to convey words via telegraph.

Muted group theory—A critical theory suggesting language is driven by a Western male experience, and those who do not fit in that group have their experience marginalized and "muted."

Mutuality—A measurement in social network theory based on the reciprocation of friendship and following in a network.

Mutually beneficial relationships—Those relationships where each member receives something of value.

Narrative database—A theory, introduced by Lev Manovich, which suggests that digital media is best conceived as the usage of a database interacted with through some form of interface that allows the user to create a narrative trajectory through the database.

Narrowcasting—The broadcasting of niche content to small, targeted audiences.

Negotiation—The bargaining process that we engage in to figure out a solution to a conflict.

Netnography—A qualitative research method in which a researcher embeds within an online community to learn how the communities behave, congregate, and interact.

Net neutrality—A policy that suggests Internet Service Providers should not be allowed to prioritize Internet traffic or limit speed and access to online content.

Neuro-plasticity—What this literally means is that we can train our brains through practice, even for compassion toward others.

Newsreels—Beginning in the 1930s, short films regarding news events were played in theaters before movies. Newsreels preceded television news as the first time audiences encountered news reports with moving images and sound.

News story—The end product that journalists have after they gather all the information, verify it, organize it in logical, easy to follow format that offers context and meaning to an event/situation.

Newsworthy/newsworthiness—What makes the event, information, happening important/relevant/interesting enough to become news, to be reported on.

Node—An individual in a social network.

Noise—Anything in the SMCR model that interferes with the message, either on the outside or the inside.

Nonverbal communication—Anything that helps interpret a message in terms of not what is said, but how it is said.

Normative—Essentially a synonym for "ideal," normative may refer to a theory or model aimed at representing best practices; it may also be used to describe socially constructed and culturally situated ideals for femininity and masculinity.

Objectivity—Much like the "scientific process" that researchers in the sciences follow, journalistic objectivity is an approach to gathering information that emphasizes gathering facts and verifying information, rather than reporting opinions and subjective content. In terms of theory, it is an epistemological perspective suggesting that there is a measurable truth outside of our perception that is true in all cases.

Obscene—Content that cannot be aired at any time and is not protected by the First Amendment.

Occam's razor—Philosophical perspective suggesting that when we are faced with two different and competing perspectives to explain a phenomenon, we should choose the simpler one.

Onboarding—The process of orienting new employees about the job and educating them about their new team, responsibilities, and the organizational culture.

One-man band—A new paradigm in reporting that suggests reporters should be able to shoot video, write copy, update online outlets, and perform multiple other functions on their own.

Ontological perspective—A theory's assumption about human nature.

Open-monitoring meditation—A technique that can help us get unstuck from our emotionally attachment to without much preoccupation. One kind of contemplative practice.

Out-groups—A category of classifying people who are excluded from the majority and are defined by shared traits that the "in-groups" believe to be negative.

Over the top service—A new form of content provider in which subscribers pay to get access to specialized video content exclusively from providers (such as major sports leagues and pay television channels) via online streaming without an intermediary TV provider.

Paradigm—All the options, choices, and forms available within a database.

Parajournalists—Individuals and organizations that use journalistic practices without being journalists themselves.

Parsimony—Means of evaluating theory based on how simple and straightforward the theory is.

Parts of speech—The three components of communication that make up Aristotle's prototypical model of communication (speaker, subject, and person addressed).

Pathos—A rhetorical appeal based on emotion, specifically putting people in a particular state of mind or feeling.

Paul Nipkow—The German inventor who developed the scanning disk.

Penny press—An era, beginning in the late 1830s, when newspapers took advantage of new steam-based press technology to shift their revenue from subscription income to advertising sales. The result was newspapers that cost a penny per edition.

Person addressed—In Aristotle's parts of speech, the recipient of the message.

Personal space—The zone of personal space used for interpersonal conversations.

Phenomenon—An event or happening studied by theory and research.

Philo Farnsworth—Inventor who transmitted the first electronic TV picture, considered the "father of television."

Plagiarism—Using anything taken from another person's writing/production and passing it as your own. Includes videos, parts of text, photos (even if you paraphrase, as long you do not attribute the information to its original source, it is considered plagiarism).

Political economy theory—A critical theory suggesting the experiences and stories in mass media are limited by and biased toward supporting the interest of powerful economic elites.

Pop-under ad—A less intrusive form of online advertising that will open up a new browser window underneath what the reader is currently reading.

Pop-up ad—An intrusive form of online advertising that will "pop up" a new browser window on top of what the user is currently reading.

Postmodernism—Epistemological perspective suggesting truth is socially constructed, subjective, and dependent on the observer.

Prior restraint—Government censorship that halts an idea before it can be expressed.

Propaganda—Communication, often from a government, that is aimed directly at emotions to make a biased case.

Podcasting—A form of broadcasting that uses digital media players and content aggregators like Apple's iTunes program to deliver narrowly targeted specialty programs on a subscription basis directly to listeners.

Polarization—The use of language that leaves little ground for nuance; the use of language that is either one way or the other.

Polychronic—A culture that sees time as more loose and fluid.

Power—A concept in relationships in which one individual may have particular advantages or control over another; the ability to get another person to do something that he or she would not otherwise have done. Power is relational because power is determined by the situation and people.

Predictive objective of theory—When theory attempts to make predictions about what will happen if certain variables in a phenomenon are altered.

Press agentry/publicity model—A one-way communication model designed to spread information regardless of accuracy. Often employs over sensational tactics to accomplish purpose.

Procedural rhetoric—The use of interactive models and simulations to make persuasive cases.

Public information model—A one-way communication model designed to inform the public in a truthful honest way. Initially used to convey a company's policies.

Public interest—A standard in broadcast policy that requires publicly licensed broadcasters to air programs that meet social needs.

Public radio—A radio format based on limited-interest programming such as classical music and in-depth news that is sponsored by corporate underwriting and listener contributions.

Public relations—The management function that establishes and maintains (via public relations, advertising, and marketing) mutually beneficial relationships between an organization and the publics on whom its success or failure depends.

Publics—Communities of people at large (whether or not organized as groups) who have a direct or indirect association with an organization: customers, employees, investors, media, students, etc.

Public space—Zone of interaction most often used by public speakers.

Purpose—Part of Burke's dramatic pentad, it is the reason why communication is happening.

Qualitative data—Data that is deeper and textual in nature, drawn from small samples that cannot be easily converted to numbers; used to focus on the reasons and motivations behind phenomena.

Quality of service—A form of control Internet Service Providers can use to maintain the integrity of their network.

Quantitative data—Data that is primarily numbers driven and can be analyzed in terms of trends and patterns.

Radio Act of 1927—Developed the Federal Radio Commission to oversee the licensing of private and professional broadcasters.

Ratings—A measurement of the total potential audience tuned into a particular station or watching a particular program.

Reality television—A lower-cost genre of television characterized by the combination of scripted and "documentary"-like content.

Reform objective of theory—An objective of theory based on identifying social inequalities or ills and working to change them.

Regulative rules—Communication rules that relate to the relationship or how words are used with different people.

Regulators—Nonverbal cues we use to send messages to others that we want to say something, that we are coming to the end of what we are saying or that we want things in the conversation to change.

Relational technologies—Technologies that allow us to maintain personal identities and identities.

Relationships—The ongoing connections we have with others.

Reliability—A measurement of the effectiveness of research based on its ability to consistently return the same results over time or between applications.

Receiver—In the SMCR model, the person or people who receive the audience, either intentionally or unintentionally.

Reginald Fessenden—A Canadian engineer who transmitted the first one-to-many wireless telephony message.

Relationship—In public relations theory and practice, the relationship has emerged as the primary unit of analysis and focus of research. The goal of effective and ethical public relations practice, and its varied communication tactics, is to build and strengthen long-term, mutually beneficial relationships between organizations and their publics.

Rhetoric—The process of using communication strategically to persuade others.

Rhetorical criticism—A procedural study of rhetoric that analyzes rhetorical artifacts and acts to determine their purpose and how rhetoric is used to attain that purpose.

Safe harbor—A time during the broadcast day that allows broadcasters more freedom in terms of content, language, and other programming elements.

Sample—A smaller, representative part of a larger population used in empirical research.

Sapir-Whorf Hypothesis—See **Linguistic Relativity**.

Satellite radio—A form of radio broadcast that uses satellites and repeaters to broadcast niche content to subscribers around the world without loss of signal or quality.

Scanning disk—A large metal disk developed by Paul Nipkow that allowed for the separating of images into electronically transmittable points of light.

Scene—Part of Burke's dramatic pentad, it is the context or setting in which communication occurs.

Scientific method—A means of scientific inquiry based on systemic and regimented approaches to observation and experimentation based on hypothesis.

Scope—A means of evaluating theory based on understanding the breadth of what the theory tries to explain or describe.

Screen name—A false name or "handle" used online to provide anonymity.

Seasons—Specific time periods in the year around which television audiences (and programs) are built—the fall tends to be the most popular for new programs and high audience ratings.

Self-determination—At the heart of mediation practice because mediators believe that successful solutions to conflicts should be determined by those deeply involved in that conflict (the two sides).

Social capital—Refers to the value earned through relationships within networks and other social structures; by cultivating goodwill and trust through social connections, an individual reaps the rewards through reciprocity.

Social construction—Social systems and expectations that shift and help define identities in terms of hierarchies, structures of power, society, and culture.

Social network analysis—Refers to an increasingly popular method of analyzing the structure of social connections and how information travels through this structure. SNA may be used to visualize the connections, for example, among all of one person's friends on Facebook.

Sources—People or records (documents online or printed—statistics, reports, news releases etc.) used by journalists to get information for their news stories.

Sourcing—The process of using people and records for the news story. All sources must be correctly attributed in the news story.

Pre-roll—A form of online advertising that plays skippable or unskippable video advertising before an online video.

Search marketing—A form of online advertising where advertisers bid against each other to have their Web sites associated with particular search terms.

Semiotics—The study of semantics and meaning.

Share—A measurement based on the percentage of the total audience *actually using* television or radio and tuned into a particular radio or TV station.

Signified—In semiotics, the meaning associated with a symbol.

Signifier—The visual form or shape to which a signified is assigned to create a symbol that has meaning.

Simulcast—The simultaneous broadcast of content across multiple channels—for example, radio broadcasters may rebroadcast their terrestrial signal as an online stream.

Slang—Lazy, blended speech.

Social cognitive theory—A theory, developed by Albert Bandura, which suggests that we are "socialized" into participating in culture by various socializing agents including our families, schools, and the media.

Social exchange theory—A theory suggesting that we make decisions in relationships based on the economic principles of maximizing our rewards and minimizing our costs.

Social media—Online services that allow users to connect with friends and family, such as Facebook and Twitter.

Social network analysis—Refers to an increasingly popular method of analyzing the structure of social connections and how information travels through this structure. SNA may be used to visualize the connections, for example, among all of one person's friends on Facebook.

Social network theory—A theory concerned with how relationships form between individuals and how those relationships influence the flow and spread of social capital.

Social penetration model—A model of developmental theory that suggests we must gradually go through "layers" to reach the core of an individual.

Small group communication—Communication between three and eight people.

Snackable—In public relations and marketing, refers to a quality of content shared on social media that can be easily and quickly enjoyed or absorbed. This bite-sized content—like fun quotes or a 6-s Vine—plays to the short attention spans of consumers in the digital age.

Social science—A branch of science focused on social issues like communication or politics rather than natural or technical phenomena.

Social space—Zone of personal space used for group interactions.

Source—In the SMCR model, the person and so on starting the communication or message through verbal or nonverbal means.

Spam—Unsolicited advertising messages sent via e-mail (and other channels).

Speaker—In Aristotle's parts of speech, the individual from whom communication originates.

Spokespeople—Individuals hired by a company to speak on behalf of their product or service; generally, they are likeable or credible in order to make an ethos appeal.

Spot—An individual broadcast advertisement.

Stages—In developmental theory, steps through which a relationship progresses.

Static nonverbal communication—Nonverbal communication that does not change over the course of an encounter—clothing, hair color, etc.

Stewardship—The responsible overseeing and protection of something considered worth caring for and preserving.

Streaming—A form of online content delivery where users can download a few packets of data at a time from a centralized source to listen to music and watch video.

Style—A canon of rhetoric concerned with how speech and communication are conveyed, rather than its content.

Subject—In Aristotle's parts of speech, the topic being discussed.

Survey—Quantitative research method consisting of an objective questionnaire distributed to a large sample of a population.

Symbol—The combination of a signifier and signified that conveys meaning.

Symbol system—An agreed-upon system of meaning that assigns particular signified meaning to particular symbols to create a shared language.

Syndicated programming—Programming that does not belong to a specific network and can be carried by any station wishing to pay for it. It can be either first-run original programming or rebroadcasts of programs that originally aired on other networks.

Syntagm—The narrative trajectory between options in a database developed through the use of an interface.

Targeted publics—Those publics who are specifically procured because that particular group may be more responsive to your organizational mission.

Territoriality—Study of how people and animals use space and objects to communicate occupancy or ownership of space.

Testability—Means of evaluating theory based on whether the theory can be investigated through empirical observation.

Theory—A set of ideas and relationships that describe or predict phenomena, developed through observation and testing.

Time-shifting—Watching television program at a later date than it was originally broadcast.

Top-level domain—The signifier on the end of a URL that indicates the nature of the organization that holds the URL—".edu" signifies an educational source, ".gov" signifies a governmental source, and so on.

Transactional communication model for diversity—a framework for communicating about difference that builds upon a rhetorical "exchange" among diverse identities that uses communication to represent a relationship among constituents where difference is strategically identified, expressed, and negotiated.

Transistors—Smaller, cheaper electronic devices that served a similar receiving and amplification purpose to the audion vacuum tube and served to make radios smaller and cheaper as well.

Turning points—An evolution of developmental theory suggesting relationship trajectories are characterized by specific points that mark changes in the nature of a relationship.

Two-way asymmetrical model—A two-way communication model where feedback is desired to make an educated decision. Often used in marketing and advertising.

Two-way symmetrical model—A two-way communication model that serves as a continuous loop of exchanging information to the benefit of all parties. The ideal model of public relations.

Uncertainty theory—A theory suggesting communication is built around managing uncertainty and ambiguity—among other axioms, it suggests that as the level of communication we have with someone goes up, our level of uncertainty goes down and we begin to like and trust that person more.

Unconditional positive regard—Is possibly the best strategy to take and is a state of mind where a person puts aside their own preconceived negative notions in order to listen.

Understanding—A goal of theory that allows us to demonstrate why something is happening without necessarily predicting it.

Underwriting—A form of donation-based advertising on public media; unlike traditional advertising, it cannot carry advertising slogan or calls to action.

Uniform Resource Locator (URL)—An online "address" used to navigate to Web content that identifies the source from which a page originates.

Uses and gratifications—A theory that suggests audiences use media to fit particular needs, such as surveillance, entertainment, and other needs.

Utility—Means of evaluating theory based on its practical value and usefulness.

Validity—The ability of a test to truly and accurately measure what it intends to measure.

Verbal communication—Communication built around using an agreed-upon symbol system to communicate with others (generally words or language).

Viral—A term in digital media when the audience relays the message well beyond the original reach intended by the sender of the message.

Vladimir Zworykin—Inventor of the iconoscope and part of RCA's legal battle with Philo Farnsworth.

Weak ties—Refers to a kind of loose social connection, like that of an acquaintance, friend of a friend, or colleague. Weak ties are said to be the greatest gain of online social networking, and they are understood to be powerful in that they provide paths to information we would otherwise not have access to.

Web analytics—A growing form of quantitative analysis using special code to track how long users stay on a page, where they come from, and many other data points.

Web browser—A program used to navigate the World Wide Web.

World Wide Web—The interface of graphics, text, hyperlinks, and site designs that allow us to navigate the Internet.

Yellow journalism—A period during the late eighteenth and early nineteenth centuries of intense competition and limited (often absent) journalistic values as publishers fought for readers with sensationalized stories, unnamed sources, and intense self-promotion.

WIFM—"What's in it for me?"—A question that should be answered during decision downloading.

WIFO—"What's in it for the organization?"—A question that should be answered during decision downloading.

Wire services—Organizations that provide news content to subscribers. The first wire services emerged after the invention of the telegraph made it possible for news outlets to share stories. The Associated Press is among the most well-known wire services.

Wireless telegraphy—The transmission of telegraph messages without wires through the air, developed by Guglielmo Marconi. A precursor to what would eventually become radio.

Wireless telephony—The transmission of sound and music through the air.